AMERICAN VISTAS
1607-1877

American Vistas
1607-1877

Third Edition

Edited by
LEONARD DINNERSTEIN
UNIVERSITY OF ARIZONA

and

KENNETH T. JACKSON
COLUMBIA UNIVERSITY

New York
OXFORD UNIVERSITY PRESS
1979

Library of Congress Cataloging in Publication Data

Dinnerstein, Leonard, comp.
  American vistas.

  Includes bibliographical references.
  CONTENTS: [1] 1607-1877.—[2] 1877 to the present.
  1. United States—History—Addresses, essays, lectures.
I. Jackson, Kenneth T., joint author. II. Title.
E178.6.D53   1979   973   78-17423
ISBN 0-19-502468-0 (Vol. I)
ISBN 0-19-502469-9 (Vol. II)

For
Marilyn and Philip Yablon
and
Kevan Parish Jackson

PREFACE TO THE THIRD EDITION

Once again we are gratified that reader enthusiasm for *American Vistas* dictated the publication of a new edition. As in the earlier volumes, we have endeavored to put together a group of significant historical essays that combine modern interpretations with eminently readable prose. We have also been guided by the principle of including articles that expand upon, or take off from, rather than merely repeating, points covered in most textbooks.

As in the past, the nature of our times has to some extent influenced our selection. Because instructors seem to be giving more attention to social history in their courses, we have enhanced our coverage of minorities, women, families, immigration, and population movements. At the same time we recognize that political and diplomatic topics are still an integral part of the introductory survey and have not slighted those areas.

When we prepared our second edition, students seemed particularly concerned with contemporary affairs. Our section in volume two of the second edition, therefore, reflected that attitude. Subsequent surveys, however, suggested that most history courses deal more with the past than the present and several individuals indicated that it would be more helpful for both instructors and students if we toned down the "relevance." As a result we have expanded earlier sections in the text to coincide with the teaching realities.

For the third edition we have been particularly fortunate in having a large number of serious critics who provided us with candid analyses of our previous selections. Their comments were so valuable that some essays which *we* had intended to drop were kept while others which *we* had liked were eliminated. Among those who provided cogent criticisms were Louis L. Athey, B. A. Barbato, S. Becker, William N. Bisehoff, Ronald G. Brown,

Charles Bryan, James Burran, Hoyt Canady, Loren B. Chan, Thomas V. DiBacco, Alan Edwards, W. J. Fraser, Jr., J. B. Freund, Lloyd J. Graybar, Gary J. Hunter, Helen F. James, Daniel P. Jordan, Albert S. Karr, Donald S. Lamka, Robert E. Levinson, Melvin E. Levison, Monroe H. Little, Donald MacKendrick, William E. Mahan, Jonathan Morse, Ronald A. Mulder, John Muldowny, J. W. Needle, Carol O'Connor, Robert Rodey, Robert D. Schulzinger, Jordan Schwarz, Donna J. Spindel, Roger Tate, William H. Woodward, Jr., and Eugene R. Wutke.

The secretaries in the University of Arizona History Department have greatly facilitated our work. Marilyn Bradian produced the manuscript with efficiency and dispatch; Dawn Polter and Dorothy Donnelly graciously provided a wide variety of other services. Joseph Coghlan of Oxford University Press made some astute observations concerning our selection of articles. As in the past, both editors would be grateful for individual comments and suggestions from readers. We also hope that articles included in this edition are as useful for classes as those that were selected for our earlier volumes.

L. D.
K. T. J.

August 1978

CONTENTS

I COLONIAL ORIGINS

I

The Man behind Columbus

EDWARD T. STONE

• Christopher Columbus, a weaver's son, was born in Genoa in 1451. He took to the sea as a boy and remained a mariner for the rest of his life. Although he was in Portugal in 1488 when Bartholomeu Días returned from his voyage around the southern tip of Africa with the sensational news that there was an eastern water route to the Indies, Columbus was convinced that a western route as well was feasible. When King John II of Portugal refused to finance an exploratory voyage, Columbus turned to the Spanish Court. He finally persuaded Queen Isabella to equip a tiny fleet, and he set out from the port of Palos in August 1492. A little more than two months later, on the morning of October 12, a lookout on the Pinta, one of his vessels, shouted: "Tierra! Tierra!" That discovery is generally regarded as the most important event in the history of Western civilization since the birth of Christ.

Columbus's reputation has not fared especially well in recent years. We now concede that he was a mediocre administrator and an impractical dreamer who never realized that he had found anything more than a new route to the Orient. We also believe that it was Leif Ericson, who reached the shores of Labrador about the year 1000, who was the first European to set foot in the New World—though there are other contenders for the honor, St. Brendon the Navigator and Madoc the Welshman among them.

The following article continues this tradition by suggesting that if Columbus had been left to his own devices his ships would never have sailed. According to its author, it was the Pinzón brothers, and especially Martín, who enlisted a crew and who got things moving. If only Martin Pinzón had lived a bit longer (Stone suggests), historians might have credited him with his critical role in the Columbus expedition.

As you approach the village of Palos de la Frontera, some fifty miles west of Seville in Spain's Andalusía, the squat little church of San Jorge looms in the foreground at the base of a rocky cliff that overlooks the tidal flats created by the mingling of the rivers Tinto and Odiel. The shallow estuary where the two rivers converge, known of old as the Saltés, is undistinguished scenically, an obscure corner of Spain virtually unknown to American tourists.

But a visitor mounting the steps to the plaza of the seven-hundred-year-old church from the road below soon becomes aware of a dusty marble plaque affixed to the crumbling brown façade of the sanctuary. Now chipped and broken, it is a sad remnant of a long-forgotten burst of civic pride. Chiseled on it are these words:

A LOS PINZONES
IMORTALES HIJOS DE ESTA VILLA
CODESCUBRIDORES CON COLON
DEL NUEVO MUNDO
3 AGOSTO 1910 EL PUEBLO DE PALOS

(to the Pinzóns: Immortal sons of this town, codiscoverers with Columbus of the New World; August 3, 1910; the community of Palos).

But didn't Columbus discover America all by himself? And who were the Pinzóns anyway? Good questions—and not one American in ten thousand probably knows the correct answers. Yet the role of the brothers Pinzón in the discovery of America, and particularly that of the eldest, their redoubtable leader, Martín Alonso Pinzón, can fairly be equated with that of Columbus himself.

Pinzón organized the expedition of 1492 after Columbus had failed to enlist a crew. Pinzón not only helped to finance the voyage but also advanced funds from his own pocket to the families of the sailors so they would not be in need during the absence of their breadwinners. One of the great sailors and navigators of his day, he contributed the maritime skill and knowledge necessary for the success of the expedition.

The *Pinta,* under Pinzón's command, invariably led the fleet, and it was her crew who first sighted land in the predawn hours of October 12. Pinzón was the discoverer of the island of Haiti, where the Span-

From *American Heritage* 27 (October 1976): 46–53. Copyright © 1976 by American Heritage Publishing Co., Inc. Reprinted by permission.

iards established their first New World colony, and he was the first European to strike gold in America.

Pinzón was, in fact, the de facto leader of the expedition, since the crews looked to him for direction rather than to Columbus, whom they mistrusted as a foreigner.

It is not difficult to assess the reasons for history's neglect of Martín Pinzón. He died obscurely in Palos within two weeks after the return of the fleet of discovery on March 15, 1493. (Only two ships returned; Columbus's flagship was wrecked on the north shore of Haiti on Christmas Eve.) Columbus and Pinzón quarreled bitterly in the West Indies, and only Columbus's own version of the voyage has survived in conventional histories of the Discovery. He was a prolific writer of journals and letters; even if he and Pinzón had not quarreled, his incessant portrayal of himself as the lone discoverer of the New World would have prevailed because there was no other version.

After the quarrel Columbus's complaints against his fellow argonauts were endless: the seamen of Palos were a bad lot, lawless and disobedient; the Pinzón brothers were greedy and insolent. The theme was picked up by two major contemporary historians, Father Bartolomé de Las Casas, an ardent admirer of Columbus, and Ferdinand Columbus, the illegitimate son of Christopher, who wrote a laudatory biography of his father. Subsequent histories of the Discovery were based almost exclusively on these three sources—Columbus himself, his son Ferdinand, and the partisan Las Casas.

But lying virtually forgotten for nearly three hundred years in the Archive of the Indies in Seville was a mass of unique historical data that revealed the great part Martín Pinzón played in the discovery of America. Preserved in the cramped handwriting of sixteenth-century court reporters are hundreds of thousands of words of sworn testimony about the first voyage that offer a considerably different view of the Enterprise of the Indies from that of the Columbus tradition.

Only gradually, in the last century and this, has this mine of historical evidence yielded its treasure through the work of successive Spanish scholars. Known as the *Pleitos de Colón* (litigation of Columbus), the transcripts of these extraordinary proceedings embody the eyewitness recollections of nearly a hundred residents of the *comarca*, or countryside, of the Tinto-Odiel, men who had been personally acquainted with both Pinzón and Columbus and who had witnessed or participated in the events in Palos immediately before the departure of the expedition of 1492 and after its return seven months later. At least five of the witnesses had been on the voyage.

The *Pleitos* were initiated by Diego Columbus, elder son of Christopher and the latter's successor as admiral of the Indies. Diego brought suit in 1508, two years after his father's death, to have restored to the Columbus family the titles and authority of viceroy and governor of the New World colonies, which King Ferdinand and Queen Isabella had revoked in 1499, deposing Columbus and appointing a new governor. Defending the case for the Crown, the *fiscal*, or royal attorney, chose to base his defense not on the grounds of Columbus's dubious record as governor but on the allegation that he was not the exclusive discoverer of America.

Testimony was presented in an attempt to prove that not only did Martín Pinzón organize and lead the expedition but that it was his idea in the first place. The latter claim, however, had so little evidence to support it that the Council of the Indies, before which the suit was tried, rejected it out of hand.

But the depositions relating to Pinzón's predominant part in organizing the fleet and his role as partner and collaborator in the Discovery were abundant and explicit and were never challenged or denied by the attorney, and witnesses for Diego. Indeed, at least one witness for the plaintiff, Juan Rodríguez de Mafra, a veteran pilot, volunteered in his sworn statement, made in 1515, that if it had not been for Pinzón, Columbus never could have enlisted a crew.

The proceedings dragged on for twenty-five years, with periodic hearings over wide intervals of time and in widely separated places. In the end Luis Colón, wastrel grandson of Columbus, was conceded a dukedom in lieu of the viceroyalty demanded in the suit. Meanwhile descendants of Martín Pinzón were granted a coat of arms by the emperor Charles V in belated recognition of Pinzón's contribution to the Discovery.

Thus but for the court records of the *Pleitos* the knowledge of Pinzón's great role would have vanished forever. Aside from those records the documentary history of the Pinzón family is scanty.

Traditionally 1441 is given as the year of Martín's birth in Palos. Nothing is known of his parents, but evidently the family had been settled in the Palos area for generations. Martín and his younger brothers, Vicente Yáñez and Francisco Martín, lived together in a large house on Calle de la Nuestra Señora de la Rábida, the main street of Palos. Presumably they had inherited the house together with a *finca*, or farm estate, located upriver near Moguer.

Over the years Pinzón built up a prosperous deep-sea shipping business in which his brothers participated. His ships—he owned as many as three at a time—ranged far into the Atlantic and Mediterranean, particularly in the Guinea trade down the West African coast.

Las Casas, whose father later accompanied Columbus on the second voyage in 1493, described the Pinzón brothers as "wealthy mariners and principal persons to whom nearly everyone in their town deferred." And Martín Pinzón, he went on, was the "chief and most wealthy and most honored, very courageous and well versed in matters of the sea."

But it is in abundant testimony presented in the *Pleitos* that the full measure of Pinzón's influence in his community is realized. Witness after witness, without a dissenting voice, told of the admiration and respect in which he was held by his fellow citizens as a sea captain and as a civic leader. And it was precisely Pinzón's influence in the Tinto-Odiel *comarca* that was to be decisive in the discovery of America.

The declaration of Francisco Medel, *regidor* (magistrate) of Huelva, made in Seville in 1535, is typical of many:

> The said Martín Alonso Pinzón was very knowledgeable in the art of navigation in all the seas and was a man than whom in all the kingdom there was no other more courageous in warfare nor more determined . . . for whatever he set his mind to, and at times he had one ship and at others two or three and this witness saw that he had them . . . and he had many honorable relatives and friends and superb equipment . . . to make the said discovery.

From the *Pleitos* we learn the name of Pinzón's wife, María Alvarez, but little else about her. She was probably the daughter of one of the deep-sea mariners of Palos who formed an elite fraternity in a town devoted to the sea. The men who sailed the swift caravels of Andalusía to the far ports of Europe and Africa considered themselves a cut above the humbler fishermen whose daily forays into salt water were confined to the immediate area.

The couple were probably married in 1469, when Pinzón was about twenty-eight. This may be inferred from the testimony of their eldest son, Arias Pérez Pinzón, who was forty-five years old when he testified in 1515.

The world in which Martín and María began their married life was not a tranquil one. Palos was a tough little frontier seaport in a turbulent land. Andalusía was the bloody battleground for the hatreds and ambitions of feudal nobles who maintained private armies and even fleets of war. Bands of robbers nested in strongholds in the mountains and made periodic forays on villages and towns, returning with impunity to their lairs. Also, along the Andalusían coast the towns were prey to raids by Moslem corsairs from North Africa. The area around Palos, situated at the head of the estuary of the Saltés, an open door to the ocean, was particularly vulnerable to forays.

According to tradition in Palos, Pinzón's two younger brothers continued to live with him on Calle de la Rábida after María moved in as a bride, and she kept house for all three. At the end of her first confinement she and Martín, atired in their Sabbath best and accompanied by two sponsors, carried their infant son to the baptismal font in the church of San Jorge, where a friar from the monastery of La Rábida solemnly christened him Arias Pérez Pinzón. In subsequent years came Juan Martín, Catalina, Diego Martín, Mayor, Leonor, and Francisco Martín.

Most of the children were reasonably healthy, but there was a distressing exception. One of the little girls—which one is not known—was subject to violent convulsions. Her malady was diagnosed as the dreaded *gota coral*—epilepsy in its most acute form. This melancholy ordeal in the married life of the Pinzóns is revealed in a curious document brought to light by the Spanish historian Navarrete. Couched in archaic Castilian legalese, it is a mandate issued by Ferdinand and Isabella on December 5, 1500, ordering the authorities of Palos to act on a petition by Arias Pérez Pinzón that his brothers be compelled to take their turns in caring for their epileptic sister in their respective homes.

Martín and María had been married five years when the wretched reign of Enrique IV, the last of the Trasámara dynasty, which had ruled Castile for a hundred years, ended with his death in Madrid in 1474. The throne was seized immediately by his young half sister Isabella and Prince Ferdinand of Aragon, whom she had secretly married five years before. Isabella had the support of a powerful faction of Castilian nobles who were profoundly disturbed by the moral degeneracy of Enrique's court.

Their accession precipitated a war with Portugal, whose king, Afonso V, claimed the Castilian throne on behalf of his niece, Juana. Afonso sent an invading army into Castile to enforce her claim, but it was routed by the forces of Ferdinand and Isabella in a battle on the Duero River in 1476.

Afonso did not attempt a second invasion, but the war continued at sea with singular ferocity. Martín Pinzón and his fellow seamen of Palos were in the forefront of the naval fighting that ranged up and down the Atlantic coast from Lisbon to Guinea in West Africa. In the *Pleitos* a number of witnesses testified to Pinzón's personal prowess. Commanding his own ship on privateering expeditions, he won the admiration of his contemporaries by his valor and daring.

"At the time of the war with Portugal, all the Portuguese feared him because each day he captured some of them," declared Gonzalo Martín of Huelva in his deposition in 1532. Fernando Iáñes Montiel, also of Huelva, said that "he knew very well the said Martín Alonso Pinzón and he was the most valorous man in all this land and with his ship he was feared by the Portuguese." Ferrán Yáñez described Pinzón as being "as courageous a man as there was in this land . . . and there was no Portuguese ship that dared face him."

Because of past irritations the fighting was especially bitter. The Spanish seamen resented the Portuguese claim to a monopoly of the African trade; the Portuguese were incensed by the Spaniards' incursions into what they considered their exclusive domain. The war finally ended with the Treaty of Alcáçovas in September 1479. Afonso gave up his claim to the Castilian throne; Ferdinand and Isabella recognized the exclusive right of the Portuguese to West African trade.

This last provision put a severe crimp in the economy of Palos. The shipowners and their crews henceforth had to depend largely on less lucrative trade with the Canaries and with Mediterranean and northern European ports.

So things went until one day in the winter of 1484–85 an indigent foreigner appeared at the gate of the monastery of La Rábida and begged for bread and water for his small son. It was a minor event that later was to have unimaginable consequences for Pinzón and for the whole world: the stranger was Christopher Columbus.

It was probably two or three years after this that María died and Pinzón took a second wife, Catalina Alonso, who was hated by her new stepchildren. There is no surviving record as such either of María's death or of the second marriage. But both events are implicit in two curious documents in the royal archives of Spain, both bearing the same date and marking another intervention by the Catholic sovereigns in the Pinzón family affairs.

They were discovered by the American scholar Alicia B. Gould y Quincy in the archive of Simancas. Both documents, signed by Ferdinand and Isabella, bear the date October 12, 1493, exactly one year after the discovery of America and six and a half months after the death of Pinzón. The first is a mandate to the authorities of Palos to take appropriate action on a petition by five of the Pinzón children—Arias Pérez, Juan Martín, Mayor, Catalina, and Leonor—to have their stepmother evicted from the family home. The second, directed to the woman herself, instructs her to comply with the wishes of the Pinzón heirs or show cause to the royal magistrates in Palos why she should not.

Thus when Pinzón first met Columbus some time in the latter half of 1491, the Pinzón household, with an epileptic daughter and with a second wife at swords' points with her stepchildren, was anything but happy.

Columbus had spent six bitter years, much of the time in dire poverty, trying to persuade the sovereigns to underwrite his expedition. They were mildly interested, but they were engaged in a costly war with the kingdom of Granada, the last stronghold of the Moors in Spain. Moreover, a commission appointed to examine Columbus's proposal, headed by the queen's most trusted adviser, Father Talavera, reported on it unfavorably. The queen informed Columbus he could not count on royal support.

Heartsick, Columbus returned to La Rábida, where, several years earlier, he had been too poor to care for his son and had left him in the care of the monks. He was determined to try his fortunes in France. But the guardian of the monastery, Father Juan Pérez, had become interested in the project and persuaded him to delay his departure until a new appeal could be made to the queen. Father Pérez at one time had been a *contador* (accountant) in the queen's household and had served as her confessor.

It is clear from testimony in the *Pleitos* that the new application to the queen was contingent on inducing Martín Pinzón to join the enterprise. The shrewd priest must have suspected that a weak point in Columbus's case was the lack of an experienced navigator and fleet organizer.

Unfortunately, at the moment Pinzón was on a voyage to Italy with a cargo of sardines. Once there, he and his twenty-one-year-old son, Arias Pérez, visited Rome and were taken on a tour of the library of Pope Innocent VIII. Their host is described as a "familiar" of the pope and an old acquaintance of Pinzón. He is not otherwise identified, but it is likely that he had once been a monk at La Rábida.

In the *Pleitos* the legal battery for the Crown made much of this visit of the Pinzóns to the Vatican in attempting to prove that Pinzón and not Columbus had initiated the voyage of discovery. Responding to Question XI in the interrogatory of October 15, 1515, Arias testified to the conversation he and his father had had with the papal servant, whom he described as a "great cosmographer."

"And there this witness and his said father were informed of these lands that awaited discovery," Arias continued. He further said that his father was so impressed by the evidence of undiscovered lands that he was determined to go in search of them himself.

There is a great deal of eyewitness testimony relating to the first meeting between Columbus and Pinzón on the latter's return from Italy. Typical was that of Hernando de Villareal, who said that he "knows that on arrival of the said Martín Alonso from Rome, the said Admiral [Columbus] reached an agreement with him and the said Admiral sent to court a friar of La Rábida and he made relation thereof to Their Highnesses. . . ."

The evidence in the *Pleitos* dovetails with the accounts of the renewed negotiations between Columbus and the sovereigns as related by Father Las Casas and Ferdinand Columbus in their respective histories. Father Pérez wrote to the queen from La Rábida. His letter was so effective that she replied within two weeks, summoning both Pérez and Columbus to the royal encampment of Santa Fe on the *vega*, or lowland, of Granada, where the Spanish armies were besieging the Alhambra. The queen sent 20,000 maravedis (about $140) to Columbus so he could shed his threadbare clothes and make a decent appearance at court.

The Alhambra surrendered on January 2, 1492. Three and a half months later the monarchs signed the Capitulations of Santa Fe, authorizing the voyage and making extraordinary grants of titles and perquisites to Columbus. By a stroke of their pens the erstwhile Knight of the Ragged Cape, as some of the courtiers had scoffingly dubbed Columbus in his years of travail, was transformed into the Very Magnificent Lord, Don Cristóbal Colón, Admiral of the Ocean Sea. Along with the Capitulations the sovereigns issued a directive to the town authorities of Palos to furnish and equip two caravels and to supply the necessary manpower for them.

Columbus returned in triumph to Palos, and the royal directives were read in the church plaza to a small knot of Palos officialdom. Unfortunately for Columbus, his new admiral's uniform and the decrees from the sovereigns did little for him in the jaundiced eyes of the local citizens. To them he was still the indigent foreigner without money or credit who was trying to force them to go on a desperate journey to God knew where.

To Alonso Pardo, town notary of Moguer, fell the task of seeking two caravels in accordance with the royal mandate. He managed to commandeer a couple of ships of dubious vintage whose owners were either unlucky or indifferent. Pardo, a witness years later in the Columbus family litigation, testified that "this witness saw that everyone scorned the said Christopher Columbus and believed he would die and everyone who went with him."

The hostile state of mind of the people of Palos is abundantly revealed in uncontroverted testimony presented in the *Pleitos*. Witness after witness, in interrogatories taken over a period of twenty years and in widely separated places, testified to the universal lack of confidence in Columbus when he tried to man and equip the fleet on his own.

"Everyone said the enterprise of the said Don Cristóbal was vain and they made a mockery of it," declared Martín Gonzalo Bisochero in the 1515 hearing in Moguer.

The villagers' hostility toward Columbus was even confirmed by witnesses sympathetic to Diego Columbus. One of them was Juan Rodríguez de Cabezudo, a Moguer farmer who had rented a donkey to Columbus when the latter went to court after his first interview with Pinzón. "Many persons made fun of the said Admiral," Cabezudo testified. "They . . . even reproached this witness for lending him a mule and publicly they scorned the enterprise."

Week after week the embargoed caravels swung idly at anchor in the Rio Tinto while Columbus strove in vain to enlist a crew. Apparently he must have given the sovereigns the idea that the villagers' stolid resistance portended a full-scale revolt. On June 20, nearly a month after the reading of the ordinance impounding the caravels, Their Highnesses sent a stern letter to the Palos authorities ordering Columbus's ships manned by any means necesary. And they sent an officer of the royal household named Juan de Peñalosa to see that the order was carried out. At the same time the *alcaide* (governor) of the castle was summarily ousted and replaced by the *corregidor* (royal magistrate), Juan de Cepeda, who armed it to repel any rebellion.

These drastic measures only hardened the passive resistance of the villagers. The boycott was complete.

The reader may well wonder whatever happened to the understanding Columbus had reached with Pinzón. The question has never been satisfactorily answered. There is only one reasonable conclusion: with the mandates of the sovereigns in hand, Columbus had decided he had no need for Pinzón's collaboration, no necessity to share the glory and profits of the expedition. Professor Manuel Sales Ferre of the University of Seville, who did extensive research in the transcripts of the *Pleitos*, believes the boycott was actively abetted by a resentful Pinzón, who used his powerful influence in the community to thwart Columbus at every turn. Thus the enterprise was caught in a riptide of contention between two stubborn wills—the one armed with the authority of the Crown, the other with Pinzón's moral authority in the *comarca*.

In the end Columbus had to go to Pinzón. Father Pérez was probably an active mediator in the impasse. Once Columbus had accepted the reality that all the king's horses and all the king's men couldn't put together a crew for him, there remained the task of winning Pinzón to a reconciliation. This probably was not as difficult as it might seem. Pinzón was now fifty years old, well past the life expectancy of those days. Undoubtedly he yearned for one more great adventure to crown his distinguished maritime career. Even more compelling, perhaps, was his longing to escape from his unhappy household.

It is not difficult to imagine the scene as the two protagonists faced each other, Columbus now conciliatory and expansive in his promises, Pinzón dour and still suspicious as he stated his conditions for undertaking the voyage. What were those conditions? No one knows for sure. If there was a written agreement, it has not survived. However, there was considerable testimony by witnesses in the *Pleitos* on this point.

The import of the sworn evidence is that the two partners agreed to share equally the rewards of the expedition. Obviously such an understanding could relate only to the material profits and not to grants of high office made to Columbus by the sovereigns.

The eldest of the Pinzón sons, Arias Pérez and Juan Martín, testified that Columbus had pledged half. So did Diego Hernández Colmenero, who after the voyage married Pinzón's daughter Catalina. Their testimony might be considered suspect because of their close relationship. On the other hand, unless one makes the gratuitous assumption that they were lying, who would be in a better position to know the facts than the immediate members of the Pinzón family?

However, there was strong corroboration from other witnesses. Alonso Gallego of Huelva said he heard Columbus tell Pinzón: "Señor Martín Alonso we will go on this voyage and if God grants that we discover land, I promise you . . . I will share with you as I would my own brother." Gallego added that he heard Columbus make that pledge "many times." Francisco Medel, *regidor* (alderman) of Huelva, testified that "Martín Alonso Pinzón said to this witness that Columbus agreed . . . to give him all that he asked for and wanted."

Father Las Casas, who was strongly partial to Columbus, nevertheless has left a fair assessment of the situation. "Christopher Columbus began his negotiation with Martín Alonso Pinzón," Las Casas wrote in the *Historia de las Indias*,

> begging that he come with him and bring along his brothers and relatives and friends and without doubt he made some promises because no one is moved except in his own interest. . . . We believe that Martín Alonso principally and his brothers aided Christopher Columbus greatly . . . because of their wealth and abundant credit, mainly Martín Alonso Pinzón who was very courageous and well experienced in seamanship . . .
> . . . And as Christopher Columbus had left the court in a very needy condition . . . it appears from accounts of expenses

made before a notary public in the said town of Palos that the
said Martín Alonso . . . himself advanced to Christopher Columbus a half million [maravedis], or he and his brothers . . .

With the decisive intervention of Pinzón, most of Columbus's difficulties vanished. Time was short if the expedition was to sail that
summer, and the energetic Pinzón went all out in organizing the voyage. He discarded the embargoed caravels and substituted two of his
own choice, the *Pinta* and the *Niña*. For a third vessel he and Columbus chartered a somewhat larger ship from the Bay of Biscay that happened to be in the Palos harbor with her owner, Juan de la Cosa of
Santona. Columbus chose her for his flagship. Although she has gone
down in history by the name *Santa María*, Columbus himself never referred to her by that name in his *Journal of the First Voyage*, invariably calling her *La Capitana*, or "the flagship."

With the ships in hand, Pinzón began the task of manning them.
His recruiting was little short of spectacular. He had a vast reservoir of
friends and relatives in the *comarca*, most of them seamen. When
word got out that the Pinzón brothers themselves would sail on the
voyage, many volunteers came to the recruiting table.

But Pinzón didn't leave it at that. He went up and down the little
main street and the waterfront of Palos, exhorting his fellow citizens
with all the fervor of a street evangelist. "Friends, you are in misery
here; go with us on this journey," he exclaimed to the men who gathered around him. "We will, with the aid of God, discover land in
which, according to report, we will find houses with roofs of gold and
everything of wealth and good adventure."

This lively eyewitness account of Pinzón's recruiting was given in a
deposition by Fernan Iáñes Montiel of Huelva. Alonso Gallego testified that Pinzón advanced money out of his own pocket to some of the
families of the sailors he induced to go on the voyage so they would not
be in need.

In the faint light of predawn on August 3, 1492, the little fleet glided
slowly down the Tinto toward the wide ocean and its rendezvous with
history. Columbus commanded the flagship, Martín Pinzón the *Pinta*,
and Vicente Pinzón the *Niña*, smallest of the three.

Twice during the outward crossing Pinzón again came to the rescue
of the expedition. As the voyage grew longer and longer a crisis oc-

curred on the flagship. A disgruntled and fearful crew openly threatened a mutiny.

Testimony concerning this episode is copious and explicit, much of it bearing an air of credibility. The consensus is that it was Martín Pinzón who silenced the grumblers and encouraged Columbus to continue the voyage. One of the most circumstantial of the many witnesses was Hernán Péres Mateos, a veteran pilot of Palos and a cousin of the Pinzóns, who said:

> . . . Having sailed many days and not discovered land those who came with the said Colón wanted to rebel . . . saying they would be lost and the said Colón told the said Martín Alonso what went on and asked what he should do and the said Martín Alonso Pinzón responded: "Señor, your grace should hang a half dozen or throw them into the sea and if you do not venture to do so I and my brothers will come alongside and do it for you, that the fleet which left with the mandate of such exalted princes should not return without good news."

Probably Pinzón bellowed his advice from the rail of his own ship in the hearing of everyone on the flagship. Whatever threat of mutiny may have existed promptly subsided. Mateos added that he had the story of the crisis from the Pinzóns themselves.

Perhaps even more important was the testimony of Francisco García Vallejos of Palos, who was a seaman on the *Pinta*.

"The said Admiral conferred with all the captains," Vallejos explained, "and with the said Martín Alonso Pinzón and said to them 'What shall we do?' (This was the sixth day of October of 92.) 'Captains, what shall we do since my people complain so bitterly to me? How does it appear to you that we should proceed?' And then said Vicente Yáñez [Pinzón]: 'We should keep on, Señor, for two thousand leagues and if by then we have not found what we have come to seek, we can turn back from there.' And then responded Martín Alonso Pinzón 'How, Señor? We have only just left and already your grace is fretting. Onward, Señor, that God may give us the victory in discovering land; never would God wish that we turn back so shamefully.' Then responded the said Admiral: 'Blessings on thee.' "

After the crisis had ended on the flagship and the *Pinta* had resumed her usual position far in advance of the other ships, Pinzón wondered if their due westerly course along the 28th parallel was the right one. Then, as sunset approached on October 6, there came a clear indication: birds.

They were land birds that foraged at sea by day and nested on shore at night, and they were flying over the caravel on what appeared to be a homing course—but not in the direction in which the ship was going. They were on the port side, headed southwesterly.

Pinzón reduced sail and waited for the flagship to catch up. As Columbus came alongside, Pinzón shouted his advice for a change of course toward the south. Columbus demurred and that night stubbornly adhered to his westerly course. But the next day he changed his mind and signaled a divergence toward the southwest. Columbus's journal entry for October 6 mentions Pinzón's advice and his rejection of it. The October 7 entry records the change of course, but characteristically it is now Columbus's own idea.

Pinzón's initiative in urging a change of course was confirmed by Seaman Vallejos of the *Pinta* in his testimony later in the *Pleitos*. Vallejos's version differs in minor detail from that of Columbus:

> He [the witness] knows and saw that [Pinzón] said on the said voyage: "It appears to me and my heart tells me that if we deviate toward the southwest we will find land sooner" and that then responded the said admiral don xtóbal colón "Be it so . . . that we shall do" and that immediately as suggested . . . they changed a quarter to the southwest . . .

Within five days after the change of course the fleet made its landfall on the tiny island of Guanahani in the outer Bahamas.

Had it continued due west along the 28th parallel, the voyage would have required many more days to reach the coast of what is now Florida. There is a good question whether the crews' patience would have endured that long.

Pinzón was mortally ill when the fleet returned to Palos on March 15, 1493. He was borne from his ship to the Pinzón family estate near Moguer, where he could rest in seclusion. But he wanted to spend his last days in the sacred precincts of the monastery of La Rábida among his friends the monks. Sorrowing relatives and friends bore him to the sanctuary of his wish, and there he died in the waning days of March.

2

The Puritans and Sex

EDMUND S. MORGAN

• In 1630, after an arduous Atlantic crossing aboard the
Arabella, John Winthrop and a small band of followers established the Massachusetts Bay Colony. In their "Holy
Commonwealth" the Puritans emphasized hard work, severe
discipline, and rigid self-examination and self-denial. Ministers had great political influence in the theocratic government, and profanation of the Sabbath day, blasphemy, fornication, drunkenness, and participation in games of chance
or theatrical performances were among their many penal
offenses. Even today the term "puritanical" suggests narrow-
mindedness and excessive strictness in matters of morals and
religion. Yet, as Daniel Boorstin and others have observed, the
Puritans were not simply an ascetic group of fanatics who
prohibited all earthly pleasures. Actually the severity of their
code of behavior has frequently been exaggerated. The Puritans were subject to normal human desires and weaknesses,
and they recognized that "the use of the marriage bed" is
"founded in Man's nature." Moreover, numerous cases of
fornication and adultery in the law courts of New England
belie the notion that all Puritans lived up to their rigid moral
ideology. In the following essay, Professor Edmund S. Morgan cites numerous examples of men and women, youths and
maids, whose natural urges recognized no legal limits. In
viewing their enforcement of laws and their judgments of
human frailty, we may find that the Puritans do not always
conform to their conventional stereotype as over-precise moralists.

Henry Adams once observed that Americans have "ostentatiously
ignored" sex. He could think of only two American writers who
touched upon the subject with any degree of boldness—Walt Whit-

From *New England Quarterly*, XV (1942), 591–607. Reprinted by
permission of the author and the publisher.

man and Bret Harte. Since the time when Adams made this pene-
trating observation, American writers have been making up for lost
time in a way that would make Bret Harte, if not Whitman, blush.
And yet there is still more truth than falsehood in Adams's statement.
Americans, by comparison with Europeans or Asiatics, are squeamish
when confronted with the facts of life. My purpose is not to account
for this squeamishness, but simply to point out that the Puritans, those
bogeymen of the modern intellectual, are not responsible for it.

At the outset, consider the Puritans' attitude toward marriage and
the role of sex in marriage. The popular assumption might be that
the Puritans frowned on marriage and tried to hush up the physical
aspect of it as much as possible, but listen to what they themselves
had to say. Samuel Willard, minister of the Old South Church in the
latter part of the seventeenth century and author of the most complete textbook of Puritan divinity, more than once expressed his horror at "that Popish conceit of the Excellency of Virginity." Another
minister, John Cotton, wrote that

> Women are Creatures without which there is no comfortable
> Living for man: it is true of them what is wont to be said of
> Governments, *That bad ones are better than none*: They are a
> sort of Blasphemers then who dispise and decry them, and call
> them *a necessary Evil*, for they are *a necessary Good*.

These sentiments did not arise from an interpretation of marriage as
a spiritual partnership, in which sexual intercourse was a minor or
incidental matter. Cotton gave his opinion of "Platonic love" when
he recalled the case of

> one who immediately upon marriage, without ever approaching
> the *Nuptial Bed*, indented with the *Bride*, that by mutual con-
> sent they might both live such a life, and according did seques-
> tring themselves according to the custom of those times, from
> the rest of mankind, and afterwards from one another too, in
> their retired Cells, giving themselves up to a Contemplative life;
> and this is recorded as an instance of no little or ordinary Ver-
> tue; but I must be pardoned in it, if I can account it no other

than an effort of blind zeal, for they are the dictates of a blind mind they follow therein, and not of that Holy Spirit, which saith *It is not good that man should be alone*.

Here is as healthy an attitude as one could hope to find anywhere. Cotton certainly cannot be accused of ignoring human nature. Nor was he an isolated example among the Puritans. Another minister stated plainly that "the Use of the Marriage Bed" is "founded in mans Nature," and that consequently any withdrawal from sexual intercourse upon the part of husband or wife "Denies all reliefe in Wedlock vnto Human necessity: and sends it for supply vnto Beastiality when God gives not the gift of Continency." In other words, sexual intercourse was a human necessity and marriage the only proper supply for it. These were the views of the New England clergy, the acknowledged leaders of the community, the most Puritanical of the Puritans. As proof that their congregations concurred with them, one may cite the case in which the members of the First Church of Boston expelled James Mattock because, among other offenses, "he denyed Coniugall fellowship vnto his wife for the space of 2 years together vpon pretense of taking Revenge upon himself for his abusing of her before marryage." So strongly did the Puritans insist upon the sexual character of marriage that one New Englander considered himself slandered when it was reported, "that he Brock his deceased wife's hart with Greife, that he would be absent from her 3 weeks together when he was at home, and wold never come nere her, and such· Like."

There was just one limitation which the Puritans placed upon sexual relations in marriage: sex must not interfere with religion. Man's chief end was to glorify God, and all earthly delights must promote that end, not hinder it. Love for a wife was carried too far when it led a man to neglect his God:

> . . . sometimes a man hath a good affection to Religion, but the love of his wife carries him away, a man may bee so transported to his wife, that hee dare not bee forward in Religion, lest hee displease his wife, and so the wife, lest shee displease her husband, and this is an inordinate love, when it exceeds measure.

Sexual pleasures, in this respect, were treated like other kinds of pleasure. On a day of fast, when all comforts were supposed to be

foregone in behalf of religious contemplation, not only were tasty
food and drink to be abandoned but sexual intercourse, too. On other
occasions, when food, drink, and recreation were allowable, sexual
intercourse was allowable too, though of course only between persons
who were married to each other. The Puritans were not ascetics; they
never wished to prevent the enjoyment of earthly delights. They merely
demanded that the pleasures of the flesh be subordinated to the greater
glory of God: husband and wife must not become "so transported
with affection, that they look at no higher end than marriage it self."
"Let such as have wives," said the ministers, "look at them not for
their own ends, but to be fitted for Gods service, and bring them
nearer to God."

Toward sexual intercourse outside marriage the Puritans were as
frankly hostile as they were favorable to it in marriage. They passed
laws to punish adultery with death, and fornication with whipping.
Yet they had no misconceptions as to the capacity of human beings
to obey such laws. Although the laws were commands of God, it was
only natural—since the fall of Adam—for human beings to break
them. Breaches must be punished lest the community suffer the wrath
of God, but no offense, sexual or otherwise, could be occasion for
surprise or for hushed tones of voice. How calmly the inhabitants of
seventeenth-century New England could contemplate rape or attempted rape is evident in the following testimony offered before the
Middlesex County Court of Massachusetts:

> The examination of Edward Wire taken the 7th of october
> and alsoe Zachery Johnson. who sayeth that Edward Wires mayd
> being sent into the towne about busenes meeting with a man
> that dogd hir from about Joseph Kettles house to goody marshes.
> She came into William Johnsones and desired Zachery Johnson
> to goe home with her for that the man dogd hir. accordingly he
> went with her and being then as far as Samuell Phips his house
> the man over tooke them. which man caled himselfe by the name
> of peter grant would have led the mayd but she oposed itt three
> times: and coming to Edward Wires house the said grant would
> have kist hir but she refused itt: wire being at prayer grant dragd
> the mayd between the said wiers and Nathanill frothinghams
> house. hee then flung the mayd downe in the streete and got
> atop hir; Johnson seeing it hee caled vppon the fellow to be sivill
> and not abuse the mayd then Edward wire came forth and ran
> to the said grant and took hold of him asking him what he did

to his mayd, the said grant asked whether she was his wife for
he did nothing to his wife: the said grant swearing he would
be the death of the said wire. when he came of the mayd; he
swore he would bring ten men to pul down his house and soe ran
away and they followed him as far as good[y] phipses house
where they mett with John Terry and George Chin with clubs in
there hands and soe they went away together. Zachy Johnson
going to Constable Heamans, and wire going home. there came
John Terry to his house to ask for beer and grant was in the
streete but afterward departed into the towne, both Johnson and
Wire both aferme that when grant was vppon the mayd she
cryed out severall times.

Deborah hadlocke being examined sayth that she mett with
the man that cals himselfe peeter grant about good prichards
that he dogd hir and followed hir to hir masters and there threw
hir downe and lay vppon hir but had not the use of hir body but
swore several othes that he would ly with hir and gett hir with
child before she got home.

Grant being present denys all saying he was drunk and did not
know what he did.

The Puritans became inured to sexual offenses, because there were
so many. The impression which one gets from reading the records of
seventeenth-century New England courts is that illicit sexual intercourse was fairly common. The testimony given in cases of fornication and adultery—by far the most numerous class of criminal cases in
the records—suggests that many of the early New Englanders possessed a high degree of virility and very few inhibitions. Besides the
case of Peter Grant, take the testimony of Elizabeth Knight about the
manner of Richard Nevars's advances toward her:

The last publique day of Thanksgiving (in the year 1674) in
the evening as I was milking Richard Nevars came to me, and
offered me abuse in putting his hand, under my coates, but I
turning aside with much adoe, saved my self, and when I was
settled to milking he agen took me by the shoulder and pulled
me backward almost. but I clapped one hand on the Ground and
held fast the Cows teatt with the other hand, and cryed out, and
then came to mee Jonathan Abbot one of my Masters Servants,
whome the said Never asked wherefore he came, the said Abbot
said to look after you, what you doe unto the Maid, but the said
Never bid Abbot goe about his businesse but I bade the lad to
stay.

One reason for the abundance of sexual offenses was the number of men in the colonies who were unable to gratify their sexual desires in marriage. Many of the first settlers had wives in England. They had come to the new world to make a fortune, expecting either to bring their families after them or to return to England with some of the riches of America. Although these men left their wives behind, they brought their sexual appetites with them; and in spite of laws which required them to return to their families, they continued to stay, and more continued to arrive, as indictments against them throughout the seventeenth century clearly indicate.

Servants formed another group of men, and of women too, who could not ordinarily find supply for human necessity within the bounds of marriage. Most servants lived in the homes of their masters and could not marry without their consent, a consent which was not likely to be given unless the prospective husband or wife also belonged to the master's household. This situation will be better understood if it is recalled that most servants at this time were engaged by contract for a stated period. They were, in the language of the time, "covenant servants," who had agreed to stay with their masters for a number of years in return for a specified recompense, such as transportation to New England or education in some trade (the latter, of course, were known more specifically as apprentices). Even hired servants who worked for wages were usually single, for as soon as a man had enough money to buy or build a house of his own and to get married, he would set up in farming or trade for himself. It must be emphasized, however, that anyone who was not in business for himself was necessarily a servant. The economic organization of seventeenth-century New England had no place for the independent proletarian workman with a family of his own. All production was carried on in the household by the master of the family and his servants, so that most men were either servants or masters of servants; and the former, of course, were more numerous than the latter. Probably most of the inhabitants of Puritan New England could remember a time when they had been servants.

Theoretically no servant had a right to a private life. His time, day or night, belonged to his master, and both religion and law required that he obey his master scrupulously. But neither religion nor law could restrain the sexual impulses of youth, and if those impulses could not

be expressed in marriage, they had to be given vent outside marriage.
Servants had little difficulty in finding the occasions. Though they
might be kept at work all day, it was easy enough to slip away at
night. Once out of the house, there were several ways of meeting with
a maid. The simplest way was to go to her bedchamber, if she was so
fortunate as to have a private one of her own. Thus Jock, Mr. Solomon
Phipps's Negro man, confessed in court

> that on the sixteenth day of May 1682, in the morning, betweene
> 12 and one of the clock, he did force open the back doores of the
> House of Laurence Hammond in Charlestowne, and came in to
> the House, and went up into the garret to Marie the Negro.
>
> He doth likewise acknowledge that one night the last week he
> forced into the House the same way, and went up to the Negro
> Woman Marie and that the like he hath done at severall other
> times before.

Joshua Fletcher took a more romantic way of visiting his lady:

> Joshua Fletcher . . . doth confesse and acknowledge that three
> severall nights, after bedtime, he went into Mr Fiskes Dwelling
> house at Chelmsford, at an open window by a ladder that he
> brought with him the said windo opening into a chamber, whose
> was the lodging place of Gresill Juell servant to mr. Fiske. and
> there he kept company with the said mayd. she sometimes having
> her cloathes on, and one time he found her in her bed.

Sometimes a maidservant might entertain callers in the parlor
while the family were sleeping upstairs. John Knight described what
was perhaps a common experience for masters. The crying of his child
awakened him in the middle of the night, and he called to his maid,
one Sarah Crouch, who was supposed to be sleeping with the child.
Receiving no answer, he arose and

> went downe the stayres, and at the stair foot, the latch of doore
> was pulled in. I called severall times and at the last said if shee
> would not open the dore, I would breake it open, and when she
> opened the doore shee was all undressed and Sarah Largin with
> her undressed, also the said Sarah went out of doores and
> Dropped some of her clothes as shee went out. I enquired of
> Sarah Crouch what men they were, which was with them. Shee
> made mee no answer for some space of time, but at last shee told
> me Peeter Brigs was with them, I asked her whether Thomas
> Jones was not there, but shee would give mee no answer.

In the temperate climate of New England it was not always necessary to seek out a maid at her home. Rachel Smith was seduced in an open field "about nine of the clock at night, being darke, neither moone nor starrs shineing." She was walking through the field when she met a man who

> asked her where shee lived, and what her name was and shee told him. and then shee asked his name, and he told her Saijing that he was old Good-man Shepards man. Also shee saith he gave her strong liquors, and told her that it was not the first time he had been with maydes after his master was in bed.

Sometimes, of course, it was not necessary for a servant to go outside his master's house in order to satisfy his sexual urges. Many cases of fornication are on record between servants living in the same house. Even where servants had no private bedroom, even where the whole family slept in a single room, it was not impossible to make love. In fact many love affairs must have had their consummation upon a bed in which other people were sleeping. Take for example the case of Sarah Lepingwell. When Sarah was brought into court for having an illegitimate child, she related that one night when her master's brother, Thomas Hawes, was visiting the family, she went to bed early. Later, after Hawes had gone to bed, he called to her to get him a pipe of tobacco. After refusing for some time,

> at the last I arose and did lite his pipe and cam and lay doune one my one bead and smoaked about half the pip and siting vp in my bead to giue him his pip my bead being a trundell bead at the sid of his bead he reached beyond the pip and Cauth me by the wrist and pulled me on the side of his bead but I biding him let me goe he bid me hold my peas the folks wold here me and if it be replyed come why did you not call out I Ansar I was posesed with fear of my mastar least my mastar shold think I did it only to bring a scandall on his brothar and thinking thay wold all beare witnes agaynst me but the thing is true that he did then begete me with child at that tim and the Child is Thomas Hauses and noe mans but his.

In his defense Hawes offered the testimony of another man who was sleeping "on the same side of the bed," but the jury nevertheless accepted Sarah's story.

The fact that Sarah was intimidated by her master's brother suggests
that maidservants may have been subject to sexual abuse by their masters. The records show that sometimes masters did take advantage of
their position to force unwanted attentions upon their female servants.
The case of Elizabeth Dickerman is a good example. She complained
to the Middlesex County Court,

> against her master John Harris senior for profiring abus to her
> by way of forsing her to be naught with him: . . . he has tould
> her that if she tould her dame: what cariag he did show to her
> shee had as good be hanged and shee replyed then shee would
> run away and he sayd run the way is befor you: . . . she says if
> she should liwe ther shee shall be in fear of her lif.

The court accepted Elizabeth's complaint and ordered her master to
be whipped twenty stripes.

So numerous did cases of fornication and adultery become in seventeenth-century New England that the problem of caring for the children of extra-marital unions was a serious one. The Puritans solved it,
but in such a way as to increase rather than decrease the temptation to
sin. In 1668 the General Court of Massachusetts ordered:

> that where any man is legally convicted to be the Father of a
> Bastard childe, he shall be at the care and charge to maintain
> and bring up the same, by such assistance of the Mother as na-
> ture requireth, and as the Court from time to time (according to
> circumstances) shall see meet to Order: and in case the Father of
> a Bastard, by confession or other manifest proof, upon trial of the
> case, do not appear to the Courts satisfaction, then the Man
> charged by the Woman to be the Father, shee holding constant
> in it, (especially being put upon the real discovery of the truth
> of it in the time of her Travail) shall be the reputed Father, and
> accordingly be liable to the charge of maintenance as aforesaid
> (though not to other punishment) notwithstanding his denial,
> unless the circumstances of the case and pleas be such, on the
> behalf of the man charged, as that the Court that have the cog-
> nizance thereon shall see reason to acquit him, and otherwise
> dispose of the Childe and education thereof.

As a result of this law a girl could give way to temptation without the
fear of having to care for an illegitimate child by herself. Furthermore,
she could, by a little simple lying, spare her lover the expense of sup-

porting the child. When Elizabeth Wells bore a child, less than a year
after this statute was passed, she laid it to James Tufts, her master's
son. Goodman Tufts affirmed that Andrew Robinson, servant to Goodman Dexter, was the real father, and he brought the following testimony as evidence:

> Wee Elizabeth Jefts aged 15 ears and Mary tufts aged 14 ears
> doe testyfie that their being one at our hous sumtime the last
> winter who sayed that thear was a new law made concerning
> bastards that If aney man wear aqused with a bastard and the
> woman which had aqused him did stand vnto it in her labor that
> he should bee the reputed father of it and should mayntaine it
> Elizabeth Wells hearing of the sayd law she sayed vnto vs that
> If shee should bee with Child shee would bee sure to lay it vn to
> won who was rich enough abell to mayntayne it wheather it wear
> his or no and shee farder sayed Elizabeth Jefts would not you doe
> so likewise If it weare your case and I sayed no by no means for
> right must tacke place: and the sayd Elizabeth wells sayed If it
> wear my Caus I think I should doe so.

A tragic unsigned letter that somehow found its way into the files of
the Middlesex County Court gives more direct evidence of the practice which Elizabeth Wells professed:

> der loue i remember my loue to you hoping your welfar and i
> hop to imbras the but now i rit to you to let you nowe that i am
> a child by you and i wil ether kil it or lay it to an other and you
> shal have no blame at al for I haue had many children and none
> have none of them. . . . [*i.e.*, none of their fathers is support-
> ing any of them.]

In face of the wholesale violation of the sexual codes to which all
these cases give testimony, the Puritans could not maintain the severe penalties which their laws provided. Although cases of adultery
occurred every year, the death penalty is not known to have been
applied more than three times. The usual punishment was a whipping
or a fine, or both, and perhaps a branding, combined with a symbolical
execution in the form of standing on the gallows for an hour with a
rope about the neck. Fornication met with a lighter whipping or a
lighter fine, while rape was treated in the same way as adultery. Though
the Puritans established a code of laws which demanded perfection—

which demanded, in other words, strict obedience to the will of God,
they nevertheless knew that frail human beings could never live up to
the code. When fornication, adultery, rape, or even buggery and sodomy appeared, they were not surprised, nor were they so severe with
the offenders as their codes of law would lead one to believe. Sodomy,
to be sure, they usually punished with death; but rape, adultery, and
fornication they regarded as pardonable human weaknesses, all the
more likely to appear in a religious community, where the normal
course of sin was stopped by wholesome laws. Governor Bradford, in
recounting the details of an epidemic of sexual misdemeanors in Plymouth, wrote resignedly:

> it may be in this case as it is with waters when their streames are
> stopped or damned up, when they gett passage they flow with
> more violence, and make more noys and disturbance, then when
> they are suffered to rune quietly in their owne chanels. So wick-
> ednes being here more stopped by strict laws, and the same more
> nerly looked unto, so as it cannot rune in a comone road of liberty
> as it would, and is inclined, it searches every wher, and at last
> breaks out wher it getts vente.

The estimate of human capacities here expressed led the Puritans
not only to deal leniently with sexual offenses but also to take every
precaution to prevent such offenses, rather than wait for the necessity
of punishment. One precaution was to see that children got married
as soon as possible. The wrong way to promote virtue, the Puritans
thought, was to "ensnare" children in vows of virginity, as the Catholics did. As a result of such vows, children, "not being able to con-
tain," would be guilty of "unnatural pollutions, and other filthy practices in secret: and too oft of horrid Murthers of the fruit of their
bodies," said Thomas Cobbett. The way to avoid fornication and per-
version was for parents to provide suitable husbands and wives for
their children:

> Lot was to blame that looked not out seasonably for some fit
> matches for his two daughters, which had formerly minded mar-
> riage (witness the contract between them and two men in *Sodom*,
> called therfore for his Sons in Law, which had married his
> daughters, Gen. 19. 14.) for they seeing no man like to come into
> them in a conjugall way . . . then they plotted that incestuous
> course, whereby their Father was so highly dishonoured. . . .

As marriage was the way to prevent fornication, successful marriage was the way to prevent adultery. The Puritans did not wait for adultery to appear; instead, they took every means possible to make husbands and wives live together and respect each other. If a husband deserted his wife and remained within the jurisdiction of a Puritan government, he was promptly sent back to her. Where the wife had been left in England, the offense did not always come to light until the wayward husband had committed fornication or bigamy, and of course there must have been many offenses which never came to light. But where both husband and wife lived in New England, neither had much chance of leaving the other without being returned by order of the county court at its next sitting. When John Smith of Medfield left his wife and went to live with Patience Rawlins, he was sent home poorer by ten pounds and richer by thirty stripes. Similarly Mary Drury, who deserted her husband on the pretense that he was impotent, failed to convince the court that he actually was so, and had to return to him as well as to pay a fine of five pounds. The wife of Phillip Pointing received lighter treatment: when the court thought that she had overstayed her leave in Boston, they simply ordered her "to depart the Towne and goe to Tanton to her husband." The courts, moreover, were not satisfied with mere cohabitation; they insisted that it be peaceful cohabitation. Husbands and wives were forbidden by law to strike one another, and the law was enforced on numerous occasions. But the courts did not stop there. Henry Flood was required to give bond for good behavior because he had abused his wife simply by "ill words calling her whore and cursing of her." The wife of Christopher Collins was presented for railing at her husband and calling him "Gurley gutted divill." Apparently in this case the court thought that Mistress Collins was right, for although the fact was proved by two witnesses, she was discharged. On another occasion the court favored the husband: Jacob Pudeator, fined for striking and kicking his wife, had the sentence moderated when the court was informed that she was a woman "of great provocation."

Wherever there was strong suspicion that an illicit relation might arise between two persons, the authorities removed the temptation by forbidding the two to come together. As early as November, 1630, the Court of Assistants of Massachusetts prohibited a Mr. Clark from "cohabitacion and frequent keepeing company with Mrs. Freeman, vnder

paine of such punishment as the Court shall thinke meete to inflict."
Mr. Clark and Mr. Freeman were both bound "in XX£ apeece that
Mr. Clearke shall make his personall appearance att the nexte Court
to be holden in March nexte, and in the meane tyme to carry himselfe
in good behaviour towards all people and espetially towards Mrs. Freeman, concerning whome there is stronge suspicion of incontinency."
Forty-five years later the Suffolk County Court took the same kind of
measure to protect the husbands of Dorchester from the temptations
offered by the daughter of Robert Spurr. Spurr was presented by the
grand jury

> for entertaining persons at his house at unseasonable times both
> by day and night to the greife of theire wives and Relations &c
> The Court having heard what was alleaged and testified against
> him do Sentence him to bee admonish't and to pay Fees of
> Court and charge him upon his perill not to entertain any mar-
> ried men to keepe company with his daughter especially James
> Minott and Joseph Belcher.

In like manner Walter Hickson was forbidden to keep company with
Mary Bedwell, "And if at any time hereafter hee bee taken in company of the saide Mary Bedwell without other company to bee forth-
with apprehended by the Constable and to be whip't with ten stripes."
Elizabeth Wheeler and Joanna Peirce were admonished "for theire
disorderly carriage in the house of Thomas Watts being married women
and founde sitting in other mens Laps with theire Armes about theire
Necks." How little confidence the Puritans had in human nature is
even more clearly displayed by another case, in which Edmond Mad-
dock and his wife were brought to court "to answere to all such matters
as shalbe objected against them concerning Haarkwoody and Ezekiell
Euerells being at their house at unseasonable tyme of the night and
her being up with them after her husband was gone to bed." Haarkwoody and Everell had been found "by the Constable Henry Bridg-
hame about tenn of the Clock at night sitting by the fyre at the house
of Edmond Maddocks with his wyfe a suspicious weoman her husband
being on sleepe [sic] on the bedd." A similar distrust of human ability
to resist temptation is evident in the following order of the Connecti-
cut Particular Court:

> James Hallett is to returne from the Correction house to his master Barclyt, who is to keepe him to hard labor, and course dyet during the pleasure of the Court provided that Barclet is first to remove his daughter from his family, before the sayd James enter therein.

These precautions, as we have already seen, did not eliminate fornication, adultery, or other sexual offenses, but they doubtless reduced the number from what it would otherwise have been.

In sum, the Puritan attitude toward sex, though directed by a belief in absolute, God-given moral values, never neglected human nature. The rules of conduct which the Puritans regarded as divinely ordained had been formulated for men, not for angels and not for beasts. God had created mankind in two sexes; He had ordained marriage as desirable for all, and sexual intercourse as essential to marriage. On the other hand, He had forbidden sexual intercourse outside of marriage. These were the moral principles which the Puritans sought to enforce in New England. But in their enforcement they took cognizance of human nature. They knew well enough that human beings since the fall of Adam were incapable of obeying perfectly the laws of God. Consequently, in the endeavor to enforce those laws they treated offenders with patience and understanding, and concentrated their efforts on prevention more than on punishment. The result was not a society in which most of us would care to live, for the methods of prevention often caused serious interference with personal liberty. It must nevertheless be admitted that in matters of sex the Puritans showed none of the blind zeal or narrow-minded bigotry which is too often supposed to have been characteristic of them. The more one learns about these people, the less do they appear to have resembled the sad and sour portraits which their modern critics have drawn of them.

3

The White Indians of Colonial America

JAMES AXTELL

• *Although the Indians encountered at Jamestown and at Plymouth and at a score of other sites along the East Coast were unlettered, unwashed, unclothed, and "uncivilized," the European settlers quickly discovered that they were also "of a tractable, free, and loving nature, without guile or treachery"—to quote a seventeenth-century eyewitness. These native peoples were especially open with their knowledge and experience. For example, after the first desperate winter at Plymouth, during which time half the Pilgrims died, the Indians gave the survivors food and taught them to grow corn under primitive conditions. The following November, after a bountiful harvest, the two groups jointly celebrated America's first Thanksgiving.*

Initially, many of the colonists believed that the Indians were descendants of the lost tribes of Israel, and the Europeans made honest, if somewhat misguided, efforts to Christianize them. But red-white relations deteriorated rapidly during the seventeenth century. Pressed by increasing numbers and eager to provide more space for their expanding society, the white settlers pushed farther and farther inland, thus forcing the Indians to battle for their very existence. As the struggle took on more violent dimensions—King Philip's War (1675–1676) was particularly bloody—myths of the worthlessness and brutality of the Indians had to be fabricated to justify the slaughter that ensued. Past experiences contradicting the image of the Indian as a savage tended to be forgotten.

The following article by James Axtell, which suggests that the simplicity, harmony, and cooperative spirit of Indian life had greater appeal to colonists than the benefits of "civilization" had to the Indians, should be read in the context of the suspicion, fear, and contempt which the white society was be-

> ginning to feel toward the Indian. We often think of the ap-
> peal of native culture as a recent phenomenon; yet those few
> European settlers who were intimately exposed to it often
> chose to remain "white Indians."

The English, like their French rivals, began their colonizing ventures
in North America with a sincere interest in converting the Indians to
Christianity and civilization. Nearly all the colonial charters granted by
the English monarchs in the seventeenth century assigned the wish to
extend the Christian Church and to redeem savage souls as a principal,
if not the principal, motive for colonization. This desire was grounded
in a set of complementary beliefs about "savagism" and "civilization."
First, the English held that the Indians, however benighted, were capable of conversion. "It is not the nature of men," they believed, "but
the education of men, which make them barbarous and uncivill."
Moreover, the English were confident that the Indians would want to
be converted once they were exposed to the superior quality of English
life. The strength of these beliefs was reflected in Cotton Mather's astonishment as late as 1721 that

> Tho' they saw a People Arrive among them, who were Clothed in
> *Habits* of much more Comfort and Splendour, than what there
> was to be seen in the *Rough Skins* with which they hardly cov-
> ered themselves; and who had *Houses full of Good Things*, vastly
> out-shining their squalid and dark *Wigwams*; And they saw this
> People Replenishing their *Fields*, with *Trees* and with *Grains*,
> and useful *Animals*, which until now they had been wholly Stran-
> gers to; yet they did not seem touch'd in the least, with any *Am-
> bition* to come at such Desireable Circumstances, or with any
> *Curiosity* to enquire after the *Religion* that was attended with
> them.

The second article of the English faith followed from their fundamental belief in the superiority of civilization, namely, that no civilized
person in possession of his faculties or free from undue restraint would
choose to become an Indian. "For, easy and unconstrained as the sav-

From the *William and Mary Quarterly* 32 (January 1975): 55–88. Reprinted
with permission from the author and the publisher.

age life is," wrote the Reverend William Smith of Philadelphia, "certainly it could never be put in competition with the blessings of improved life and the light of religion, by any persons who have had the happiness of enjoying, and the capacity of discerning, them."

And yet, by the close of the colonial period, very few if any Indians had been transformed into civilized Englishmen. Most of the Indians who were educated by the English—some contemporaries thought *all* of them—returned to Indian society at the first opportunity to resume their Indian identities. On the other hand, large numbers of Englishmen had chosen to become Indians—by running away from colonial society to join Indian society, by not trying to escape after being captured, or by electing to remain with their Indian captors when treaties of peace periodically afforded them the opportunity to return home.

Perhaps the first colonist to recognize the disparity between the English dream and the American reality was Cadwallader Colden, surveyor-general and member of the King's council of New York. In his *History of the Five Indian Nations of Canada*, published in London in 1747, Colden described the Albany peace treaty between the French and the Iroquois in 1699, when "few of [the French captives] could be persuaded to return" to Canada. Lest his readers attribute this unusual behavior to "the Hardships they had endured in their own Country, under a tyrannical Government and a barren Soil," he quickly added that "the *English* had as much Difficulty to persuade the People, that had been taken Prisoners by the *French Indians*, to leave the *Indian* Manner of living, though no People enjoy more Liberty, and live in greater Plenty, than the common Inhabitants of *New-York* do." Colden, clearly amazed, elaborated:

> No Arguments, no Intreaties, nor Tears of their Friends and Relations, could persuade many of them to leave their new *Indian* Friends and Acquaintance[s]; several of them that were by the Caressings of their Relations persuaded to come Home, in a little Time grew tired of our Manner of living, and run away again to the *Indians*, and ended their Days with them. On the other Hand, *Indian* Children have been carefully educated among the *English*, cloathed and taught, yet, I think, there is not one Instance, that any of these, after they had Liberty to go among their own People, and were come to Age, would remain with the *English*, but returned to their own Nations, and became as fond of the *Indian* Manner of Life as those that knew nothing of a

civilized Manner of living. What I now tell of Christian Prisoners among *Indians* [he concluded his history], relates not only to what happened at the Conclusion of this War, but has been found true on many other Occasions.

Colden was not alone. Six years later Benjamin Franklin wondered how it was that

> When an Indian Child has been brought up among us, taught our language and habituated to our Customs, yet if he goes to see his relations and makes one Indian Ramble with them, there is no perswading him ever to return. [But] when white persons of either sex have been taken prisoners young by the Indians, and lived a while among them, tho' ransomed by their Friends, and treated with all imaginable tenderness to prevail with them to stay among the English, yet in a Short time they become disgusted with our manner of life, and the care and pains that are necessary to support it, and take the first good Opportunity of escaping again into the Woods, from whence there is no reclaiming them.

In short, "thousands of Europeans are Indians," as Hector de Crèvecoeur put it, "and we have no examples of even one of those Aborigines having from choice become Europeans!"

The English captives who foiled their countrymen's civilized assumptions by becoming Indians differed little from the general colonial population when they were captured. They were ordinary men, women, and children of yeoman stock, Protestants by faith, a variety of nationalities by birth, English by law, different from their countrymen only in their willingness to risk personal insecurity for the economic opportunities of the frontier. There was no discernible characteristic or pattern of characteristics that differentiated them from their captive neighbors who eventually rejected Indian life—with one exception. Most of the colonists captured by the Indians and adopted into Indian families were children of both sexes and young women, often the mothers of the captive children. They were, as one capitivity narrative observed, the "weak and defenceless."

The pattern of taking women and children for adoption was consistent throughout the colonial period, but during the first century and one-half of Indian-white conflict, primarily in New England, it coexisted with a larger pattern of captivity that included all white colo-

nists, men as well as women and children. The Canadian Indians who
raided New England tended to take captives more for their ransom
value than for adoption. When Mrs. James Johnson gave birth to a
daughter on the trail to Canada, for example, her captor looked into
her makeshift lean-to and "clapped his hands with joy, crying two
monies for me, two monies for me." Although the New England legislatures occasionally tried to forbid the use of public moneys for "the
Ransoming of Captives," thereby prolonging the Indians' "diabolical
kidnapping mode of warfare," ransoms were constantly paid from both
public and private funds. These payments became larger as inflation
and the Indians' savvy increased. Thus when John and Tamsen Tib-
betts redeemed two of their children from the Canadian Indians in
1729, it cost them £105 10s. (1,270 livres). "Being verry Poore,"
many families in similar situations could ill afford to pay such high
premiums even "if they should sell all they have in the world."

When the long peace in the Middle Atlantic colonies collapsed in
1753, the Indians of Pennsylvania, southern New York, and the Ohio
country had no Quebec or Montreal in which to sell their human chat-
tels to compassionate French families or anxious English relatives. For
this and other reasons they captured English settlers largely to replace
members of their own families who had died, often from English mus-
ketballs or imported diseases. Consequently, women and children—the
"weak and defenceless"—were the prime targets of Indian raids.

According to the pattern of warfare in the Pennsylvania theater, the
Indians usually stopped at a French fort with their prisoners before
proceeding to their own villages. A young French soldier captured by
the English reported that at Fort Duquesne there were "a great number of English Prisoners," the older of whom "they are constantly
sending . . . away to Montreal" as prisoners of war, "but that the Indians keep many of the Prisoners amongst them, chiefly young People
whom they adopt and bring up in their own way." His intelligence was
corroborated by Barbara Leininger and Marie LeRoy, who had been
members of a party of two adults and eight children captured in 1755
and taken to Fort Duquesne. There they saw "many other Women
and Children, they think an hundred who were carried away from the
several provinces of P[ennsylvania] M[aryland] and V[irginia]." When
the girls escaped from captivity three years later, they wrote a narrative
in German chiefly to acquaint "the inhabitants of this country . . .

with the names and circumstances of those prisoners whom we met, at the various places where we were, in the course of our captivity." Of the fifty-two prisoners they had seen, thirty-four were children and fourteen were women, including six mothers with children of their own.

The close of hostilities in Pennsylvania came in 1764 after Col. Henry Bouquet defeated the Indians near Bushy Run and imposed peace. By the articles of agreement reached in October, the Delawares, Shawnees, and Senecas were to deliver up "all the Prisoners in [their] Possession, without any Exception, Englishmen, Frenchmen, Women, and Children, whether adopted in your Tribes, married, or living amongst you, under any Denomination, or Pretence whatever." In the weeks that followed, Bouquet's troops, including "the Relations of [some of] the People [the Indians] have Massacred, or taken Prisoners," encamped on the Muskingum in the heart of the Ohio country to collect the captives. After as many as nine years with the Indians, during which time many children had grown up, 81 "men" and 126 "women and children" were returned. At the same time a list was prepared of 88 prisoners who still remained in Shawnee towns to the west: 70 were classified as "women and children." Six months later, 44 of these prisoners were delivered up to Fort Pitt. When they were captured, all but 4 had been less than sixteen years old, while 37 had been less than eleven years old.

The Indians obviously chose their captives carefully so as to maximize the chances of acculturating them to Indian life. To judge by the results, their methods were hard to fault. Even when the English held the upper hand militarily, they were often embarrassed by the Indians' educational power. On November 12, 1764, at his camp on the Muskingum, Bouquet lectured the Shawnees who had not delivered all their captives: "As you are now going to Collect all our *Flesh*, and *Blood*, . . . I desire that you will use them with Tenderness, and look upon them as Brothers, and no longer as Captives." The utter gratuitousness of his remark was reflected—no doubt purposely—in the Shawnee speech when the Indians delivered their captives the following spring at Fort Pitt. "Father—Here is your *Flesh*, and *Blood* . . . they have been all tied to us by Adoption, although we now deliver them up to you. We will always look upon them as Relations, whenever the *Great Spirit* is pleased that we may visit them . . . Father—we have taken as much Care of these Prisoners, as if they were [our] own Flesh, and blood; they are become unacquainted with your Customs, and manners, and therefore, Father we request you will use them tender, and kindly, which will be a means of inducing them to live contentedly with you.

The Indians spoke the truth and the English knew it. Three days after his speech to the Shawnees, Bouquet had advised Lt.-Gov. Francis Fauquier of Virginia that the returning captives "ought to be treated by their Relations with Tenderness and Humanity, till Time and Reason make them forget their unnatural Attachments, but unless they are closely watch'd," he admitted, "they will certainly return to the Barbarians." And indeed they would have, for during a half-century of conflict captives had been returned who, like many of the Ohio prisoners, responded only to Indian names, spoke only Indian dialects, felt comfortably only in Indian clothes, and in general regarded their white saviors as barbarians and their deliverance as captivity. Had they not been compelled to return to English society by militarily enforced peace treaties, the ranks of the white Indians would have been greatly enlarged.

From the moment the Indians surrendered their English prisoners, the colonists faced a series of difficult problems. The first was the problem of getting the prisoners to remain with the English. When Bouquet sent the first group of restored captives to Fort Pitt, he ordered his officers there that "they are to be closely watched and well Secured" because "most of them, particularly those who have been a long time among the Indians, will take the first Opportunity to run away." The young children especially were "so completely savage that they were brought to the camp tied hand and foot." Fourteen-year-old John McCullough, who had lived with the Indians for "eight years, four months, and sixteen days" (by his parents' reckoning), had his legs tied "under the horses belly" and his arms tied behind his back with his father's garters, but to no avail. He escaped under the cover of night and returned to his Indian family for a year before he was finally carried to Fort Pitt under "strong guard." "Having been accustomed to look upon the Indians as the only connections they had, having been tenderly treated by them, and speaking their language," explained the Reverend William Smith, the historian of Bouquet's expedition, "it is no wonder that [the children] considered their new state in the light of a captivity, and parted from the savages with tears."

Children were not the only reluctant freedmen. "Several women eloped in the night, and ran off to join their Indian friends." Among them undoubtedly were some of the English women who had married Indian men and borne them children, and then had been forced by the English victory either to return with their half-breed children to a country of strangers, full of prejudice against Indians, or to risk escaping under English guns to their husbands and adopted culture. For Bouquet had "reduced the Shawanese and Delawares etc. to the most Humiliating Terms of Peace," boasted Gen. Thomas Gage. "He has Obliged them to deliver up even their Own Children born of white women." But even the victorious soldier could understand the dilemma into which these women had been pushed. When Bouquet was informed that the English wife of an Indian chief had eloped in the night with her husband and children, he "requested that no pursuit should be made, as she was happier with her Chief than she would be if restored to her home."

Although most of the returned captives did not try to escape, the emotional torment caused by the separation from their adopted families deeply impressed the colonists. The Indians "delivered up their beloved captives with the utmost reluctance; shed torrents of tears over them, recommending them to the care and protection of the commanding officer." One young woman "cryed and roared when asked to come and begged to Stay a little longer." "Some, who could not make their escape, clung to their savage acquaintance at parting, and continued many days in bitter lamentations, even refusing sustenance." Children "cried as if they should die when they were presented to us." With only small exaggeration an observer on the Muskingum could report that "every captive left the Indians with regret."

Another problem encountered by the English was the difficulty of communicating with the returned captives, a great many of whom had replaced their knowledge of English with an Algonquian or Iroquoian dialect, and their baptismal names with Indian or hybrid ones. This immediately raised another problem—that of restoring the captives to their relatives. Sir William Johnson, the superintendent of Indian affairs, "thought it best to advertise them [in the newspapers] immediately, but I believe it will be very difficult to find the Friends of some of them, as they are ignorant of their own Names, or former places of abode, nay cant speak a word of any language but Indian." The only recourse the English had in such instances was to describe them "more particularly . . . as to their features, Complexion etc. That by the Publication of Such descriptions their Relations, parents or friends may hereafter know and Claim them."

But if several colonial observers were right, a description of the captives' physiognomy was of little help after they had been with the Indians for any length of time. Peter Kalm's foreign eye found it difficult to distinguish European captives from their captors, "except by their color, which is somewhat whiter than that of the Indians," but many colonists could see little or no difference. To his Maine neighbors twelve-year-old John Durell "ever after [his two-year captivity] appeared more like an Indian than a white man." So did John Tarbell. After thirty years among the Indians in Canada, he made a visit to his relatives in Groton "in his Indian dress and with his Indian complexion (for by means of grease and paints but little difference could be discerned)." When O. M. Spencer returned after only eight months with the Shawnees, he was greeted with a newspaper allusion "to [his] looks and manners, as slightly resembling the Indians" and by a gaggle of visitors who exclaimed "in an under tone, 'How much he looks like an Indian!' " Such evidence reinforced the environmentalism of the time, which held that white men "who have incorporated themselves with any of [the Indian] tribes" soon acquire "a great resemblance to the savages, not only in their manners, but in their colour and the expression of the countenance."

The final English problem was perhaps the most embarrassing in its manifestations, and certainly was so in its implications. For many Indians who had adopted white captives, the return of their "own Flesh, and Blood" to the English was unendurable. At the earliest opportunity, after bitter memories of the wars had faded on both sides, they journeyed through the English settlements to visit their estranged children, just as the Shawnee speaker had promised Bouquet they would. Jonathan Hoyt's Indian father visited him so often in Deerfield, sometimes bringing his captive sister, that Hoyt had to petition the Massachusetts General Court for reimbursement for their support. In 1760 Sir William Johnson reported that a Canadian Indian "has been since down to Schenectady to visit one Newkirk of that place, who was some years a Prisoner in his House, and sent home about a year ago with this Indians Sister, who came with her Brother now purely to see Said Newkirk whom she calls her Son and is verry fond of."

Obviously the feelings were mutual. Elizabeth Gilbert, adopted at the age of twelve, "always retained an affection toward John Huston, her Indian father (as she called him), for she remembered his kindness to her when in captivity." Even an adult who had spent less than six months with the Indians honored the chief who had adopted him. In 1799, eleven years after Thomas Ridout's release, his friend and father, Kakinathucca, "accompanied by three more Shawanese chiefs, came to pay me a visit at my house in York town (Toronto). He regarded myself and family with peculiar pleasure, and my wife and children contemplated with great satisfaction the noble and good qualities of this worthy Indian." The bond of affection that had grown in the Indian villages was clearly not an attachment that the English could dismiss as "unnatural."

Children who had been raised by Indian parents from infancy could be excused perhaps for their unwillingness to return, but the adults who displayed a similar reluctance, especially the women who had married Indian men and borne them children, drew another reaction. "For the honour of humanity," wrote Smith, "we would suppose those persons to have been of the lowest rank, either bred up in ignorance and distressing penury, or who had lived so long with the Indians as to forget all their former connections. For, easy and unconstrained as the savage life is, certainly it could never be put in competition with the blessings of improved life and the light of religion, by any persons who have had the happiness of enjoying, and the capacity of discerning, them." If Smith was struck by the contrast between the visible impact of Indian education and his own cultural assumptions, he never said so.

To find a satisfactory explanation for the extraordinary drawing power of Indian culture, we should begin where the colonists themselves first came under its sway—on the trail to Indian country. For although the Indians were known for their patience, they wasted no time in beginning the educational process that would transform their hostile or fearful white captives into affectionate Indian relatives.

Perhaps the first transaction after the Indians had selected their prisoners and hurried them into cover was to replace their hard-heeled shoes with the footwear of the forest—moccasins. These were universally approved by the prisoners, who admitted that they traveled with "abundant more ease" than before. And on more than one occasion the knee-deep snows of northern New England forced the Indians to make snowshoes for their prisoners in order to maintain their pace of twenty-five to thirty miles a day. Such an introduction to the superbly adapted technology of the Indians alone would not convert the English, but it was a beginning.

The lack of substantial food supplies forced the captives to accommodate their stomachs as best they could to Indian trail fare, which ranged from nuts, berries, roots, and parched corn to beaver guts, horse-flank, and semi-raw venison and moose, eaten without the customary English accompaniments of bread or salt. When there was nothing to eat, the Indians would "gird up their loins with a string," a technique that at least one captive found "very useful" when applied to himself. Although their food was often "unsavory" and in short supply, the Indians always shared it equally with the captives, who, being hungry, "relished [it] very well."

Sometimes the lessons learned from the Indians were unexpectedly vital. When Stephen Williams, an eleven-year-old captive from Deerfield, found himself separated from his party on the way to Canada, he "Hellowed" for his Indian master. When the boy was found, the Indian threatened to kill him because, as Williams remembered five years later, "the Indians will never allow anybody to Hollow in the woods. Their manner is to make a noise like wolves or any other wild creatures, when they call to one another." The reason, of course, was that they did not wish to be discovered by their enemies. To the young neophyte Indian this was a lesson in survival not soon forgotten.

Two other lessons were equally unexpected but instrumental in preparing the captives for even greater surprises when they reached the Indian settlements. Both served to undermine the English horror of the Indians as bloodthirsty fiends who defile "any Woman they take alive" before "putting her to Death." Many redeemed prisoners made a point of insisting that, although they had been completely powerless in captivity, "the Indians are very civil towards their captive women, not offering any incivility by any indecent carriage." Thomas Ridout testified that "during the whole of the time I was with the Indians I never once witnessed an indecent or improper action amongst any of the Indians, whether young or old." Even Smith admitted that "from every enquiry that has been made, it appears—that no woman thus saved is preserved from base motives, or need fear the violation of her honour." If there had been the least exception, we can be sure that this champion of civilization would have made the most of it.

One reason for the Indians' lack of sexual interest in their female captives was perhaps aesthetic, for the New England Indians, at least, esteemed black the color of beauty. A more fundamental reason derived from the main purpose of taking captives, which was to secure new members for their families and clans. Under the Indians' strong incest taboos, no warrior would attempt to violate his future sister or cousin. "Were he to indulge himself with a captive taken in war, and much more were he to offer violence in order to gratify his lust, he would incur indelible disgrace." Indeed, the taboo seems to have extended to the whole tribe. As George Croghan testified after long acquaintance with the Indians, "they have No [J]uri[s]diction or Laws butt that of Nature yett I have known more than onest thire Councils, order men to be putt to Death for Committing Rapes, wh[ich] is a Crime they Despise." Since murder was a crime to be revenged by the victim's family in its own way and time, rape was the only capital offense punished by the tribe as a whole.

Captive testimony also chipped away at the stereotype of the Indians' cruelty. When Mrs. Isabella M'Coy was taken from Epsom, New Hampshire, in 1747, her neighbors later remembered that "she did indeed find the journey [to Canada] fatiguing, and her fare scanty and precarious. But in her treatment from the Indians, she experienced a very agreeable disappointment. The kindness she received from them was far greater than she had expected from those who were so often distinguished for their cruelties." More frequent still was recognition of the Indians' kindness to children. Thomas Hutchinson told a common story of how "some of the children who were taken at Deerfield, they drew upon slays; at other times they have been known to carry them in their arms or upon their backs to Canada. This tenderness," he noted, "has occasioned the beginning of an affection, which in a few years has been so rivetted, that the parents of the children, who have gone to Canada to seek them, could by no means prevail upon them to leave the Indians and return home." The affections of a four-year-old Pennsylvania boy, who became Old White Chief among the

Iroquois, seem to have taken even less time to become "rivetted." "The last I remember of my mother," he recalled in 1836, "she was running, carrying me in her arms. Suddenly she fell to the ground on her face, and I was taken from her. Overwhelmed with fright, I knew nothing more until I opened my eyes to find myself in the lap of an Indian woman. Looking kindly down into my face she smiled on me, and gave me some dried deer's meat and maple sugar. From that hour I believe she loved me as a mother. I am sure I returned to her the affection of a son.

When the returning war parties approached the first Indian village, the educational process took on a new complexion. As one captive explained, "whenever the warriors return from an excursion against an enemy, their return to the tribe or village must be designated by warlike ceremonial; the captives or spoils, which may happen to crown their valor, must be conducted in a triumphant form, and decorated to every possible advantage." Accordingly, the cheek, chin, and forehead of every captive were painted with traditional dashes of vermillion mixed with bear's grease. Belts of wampum were hung around their necks, Indian clothes were substituted for English, and the men and boys had their hair plucked or shaved in Indian fashion. The physical transformation was so effective, said a twenty-six-year-old soldier, "that I began to think I was an Indian." Younger captives were less aware of the small distance between role-playing and real acceptance of the Indian lifestyle. When her captor dressed Frances Slocum, not yet five years old, in "beautiful wampum beads," she remembered at the end of a long and happy life as an Indian that he "made me look, as I thought, very fine. I was much pleased with the beautiful wampum."

The prisoners were then introduced to a "new school" of song and dance. "Little did we expect," remarked an English woman, "that the accomplishment of dancing would ever be taught us, by the savages. But the war dance must now be held; and every prisoner that could move must take its awkward steps. The figure consisted of circular motion round the fire; each sang his own music, and the best dancer was the one most violent in motion." To prepare for the event each captive had rehearsed a short Indian song on the trail. Mrs. Johnson recalled many years later that her song was "danna witchee natchepung; my son's was nar wiscumpton." Nehemiah How could not master the Indian pronunciation, so he was allowed to sing in English "I don't know where I go." In view of the Indians' strong sense of ceremonial propriety, it is small wonder that one captive thought that they "Seem[e]d to be Very much a mind I Should git it perfect."

Upon entering the village the Indians let forth with some distinctive music of their own. "When we came near the main Body of the Enemy," wrote Thomas Brown, a captive soldier from Fort William Henry, "the *Indians* made a Live-Shout, as they call it when they bring in a Prisoner alive (different from the Shout they make when they bring in Scalps, which they call a Dead-Shout)." According to another soldier, "their Voices are so sharp, shrill, loud and deep, that when they join together after one has made his Cry, it makes a most dreadful and horrible Noise, that stupifies the very Senses," a noise that naturally frightened many captives until they learned that it was not their death knell.

They had good reason to think that their end was near when the whole village turned out to form a gauntlet from the entrance to the center of the village and their captors ordered them to run through it. With ax handles, tomahawks, hoop poles, clubs, and switches the Indians flogged the racing captives as if to beat the whiteness out of them. In most villages, significantly, "it was only the more elderly People both Male and Female wh[ic]h rece[iv]ed this Useage—the young prisoners of Both Sexes Escaped without it" or were rescued from any serious harm by one or more villagers, perhaps indicating the Indian perception of the captives' various educability. When ten-year-old John Brickell was knocked down by the blows of his Seneca captors, "a very big Indian came up, and threw the company off me, and took me by the arm, and led me along through the lines with such rapidity that I scarcely touched the ground, and was not once struck after he took me."

The purpose of the gauntlet was the subject of some difference of opinion. A French soldier who had spent several years among the northeastern Indians believed that a prisoner "so unfortunate as to fall in the course of the bastonnade must get up quickly and keep on, or he will be beaten to death on the spot." On the other hand, Pierre de Charlevoix, the learned traveler and historian of Canada, wrote that "even when they seem to strike at random, and to be actuated only by fury, they take care never to touch any part where a blow might prove mortal." Both Frenchmen were primarily describing the Indians' treatment of other Indians and white men. Leininger and LeRoy drew a somewhat different conclusion from their own treatment. Their welcome at the Indian village of Kittanning, they said, "consisted of three blows each, on the back. They were, however, administered with great mercy. Indeed, we concluded that we were beaten merely in order to keep up an ancient usage, and not with the intention of injuring us."

William Walton came closest to revealing the Indians' intentions in his account of the Gilbert family's captivity. The Indians usually beat the captives with "great Severity," he said, "by way of Revenge for their Relations who have been slain." Since the object of taking captives was to satisfy the Indian families who had lost relatives, the gauntlet served as the first of three initiation rites into Indian society, a purgative ceremony by which the bereaved Indians could exorcise their anger and anguish, and the captives could begin their cultural transformation.

If the first rite tried to beat the whiteness out of the captives, the second tried to wash it out. James Smith's experience was typical.

> The old chief, holding me by the hand, made a long speech, very loud, and when he had done he handed me to three squaws, who led me by the hand down the bank into the river until the water was up to our middle. The squaws then made signs to me to plunge myself into the water, but I did not understand them. I thought that the result of the council was that I should be drowned, and that these young ladies were to be the executioners. They all laid violent hold of me, and I for some time opposed them with all my might, which occasioned loud laughter by the multitude that were on the bank of the river. At length one of the squaws made out to speak a little English (for I believe they began to be afraid of me) and said, 'No hurt you.' On this I gave myself up to their ladyships, who were as good as their word; for though they plunged me under water and washed and rubbed me severely, yet I could not say they hurt me much.

More than one captive had to receive similar assurance, but their worst fears were being laid to rest.

Symbolically purged of their whiteness by their Indian baptism, the initiates were dressed in new Indian clothes and decorated with feathers, jewelry, and paint. Then, with great solemnity, the village gathered around the council fire, where after a "profound silence" one of the chiefs spoke. Even a hostile captive, Zadock Steele, had to admit that although he could not understand the language spoken, he could "plainly discover a great share of native eloquence." The chief's speech, he said, was 'of considerable length, and its effect obviously manifested weight of argument, solemnity of thought, and at least human sensibility." But even this the twenty-two-year-old New Englander could not appreciate on its own terms, for in the next breath he denigrated the ceremony as "an assemblage of barbarism, assuming the appearance of civilization."

A more charitable account was given by James Smith, who through an interpreter was addressed in the following words:

> My son, you are now flesh of our flesh and bone of our bone. By the ceremony that was performed this day, every drop of white blood was washed out of your veins. You are taken into the Caughnewaga nation and initiated into a war-like tribe. You are adopted into a great family and now received with great seriousness and solemnity in the room and place of a great man. After what has passed this day you are now one of us by an old strong law and custom. My son, you have now nothing to fear. We are now under the same obligations to love, support and defend you that we are to love and to defend one another. Therefore you are to consider yourself as one of our people.

"At this time," admitted the eighteen-year-old Smith, "I did not believe this fine speech, especially that of the white blood being washed out of me; but since that time I have found that there was much sincerity in said speech; for from that day I never knew them to make any distinction between me and themselves in any respect whatever until I left them . . . we all shared one fate." It is a chord that sounds through nearly every captivity narrative: "They treated me . . . in every way as one of themselves."

When the adoption ceremony had ended, the captive was taken to the wigwam of his new family, who greeted him with a "most dismal howling, crying bitterly, and wringing their hands in all the agonies of grief for a deceased relative." "The higher in favour the adopted Prisoners [were] to be placed, the greater Lamentation [was] made over them." After a threnodic memorial to the lost member, which may have "added to the Terror of the Captives," who "imagined it to be no other than a Prelude to inevitable Destruction," the mood suddenly shifted. "I never saw . . . such hug[g]ing and kissing from the women and crying for joy," exclaimed one young recipient. Then an interpreter introduced each member of the new family—in one case "from brother to seventh cousins"—and "they came to me one after another," said another captive, "and shook me by the hand, in token that they considered me to stand in the same relationship to them as the one in whose stead I was placed."

Most young captives assumed the place of Indian sons and daughters, but occasionally the match was not exact. Mary Jemison replaced a brother who had been killed in "Washington's war," while twenty-six-year-old Titus King assumed the unlikely role of a grandfather. Although their sex and age may not always have corresponded, the adopted captives succeeded to all the deceased's rights and obligations—the same dignities, honors, and often the same names. "But the one adopted," reported a French soldier, "must be prudent and wise in his conduct, if he wants to make himself as well liked as the man he is replacing. This seldom fails to occur, because he is continually reminded of the dead man's conduct and good deeds."

So literal could the replacement become at times that no amount of exemplary conduct could alter the captive's reception. Thomas Peart, a twenty-three-year-old Pennsylvanian, was adopted as an uncle in an Iroquois family, but "the old Man, whose Place [he] was to fill, had never been considered by his Family as possessed of any Merit." Accordingly, Peart's dress, although in the Indian style, was "in a meaner Manner, as they did not hold him high in Esteem after his Adoption." Since his heart was not in becoming an Indian anyway, and "observing that they treated him just as they had done the old worthless Indian . . . he therefore concluded he would only fill his Predecessor's Station, and used no Endeavours to please them."

When the prisoners had been introduced to all their new relatives and neighbors, the Indians proceeded to shower them with gifts. Luke Swetland, taken from Pennsylvania during the Revolution, was unusually feted with "three hats, five blankets, near twenty pipes, six razors, six knives, several spoons, gun and ammunition, fireworks, several Indian pockets [pouches], one Indian razor, awls, needles, goose quills, paper and many other things of small value"—enough to make him the complete Indian warrior. Most captives, however, settled for a new shirt or dress, a pair of decorated moccasins, and abundant promises of future kindness, which later prompted the captives to acknowledge once again that the Indians were "a[s] good as their word." "All the family was as kind to me," related Thomas Gist, "as if I had really been the nearest of relation they had in the world." The two women who adopted Jemison were no less loving. "I was ever considered and treated by them as a real sister," she said near the end of a long life with them, "the same as though I had been born of their mother."

Treatment such as this—and it was almost universal—left an indelible mark on every captive, whether or not they eventually returned to English society. Although captives like Mrs. Johnson found their adoption an "unnatural situation," they had to defend the humanity of the practice. "Those who have profited by refinement and education," she argued, "ought to abate part of the prejudice, which prompts them to look with an eye of censure on this untutored race. . . . Do they ever adopt an enemy," she asked, "and salute him by the tender name of brother?" It is not difficult to imagine what effect such feelings must have had in younger people less habituated to English culture, especially those who had lost their own parents.

The formalities, purgations, and initiations were now completed. Only one thing remained for the Indians: by their daily example and instruction to "make an Indian of you," as the Delawares told Brickell. This required a steady union of two things: the willingness and gratitude of the captives, and the consistent love and trust of the Indians. By the extraordinary ceremonies through which they had passed, most captives had had their worst fears allayed. From a state of apprehension or even terror they had suddenly emerged with their persons intact and a solemn invitation to begin a new life, as full of love, challenge, and satisfaction as any they had known. For "when they [the Indians] once determine to give life, they give every thing with it, which, in their apprehension, belongs to it." The sudden release from anxiety into a realm of affirmative possibility must have disposed many captives to accept the Indian way of life.

According to the adopted colonists who recounted the stories of their new lives, Indian life was more than capable of claiming their respect and allegiance, even if they eventually returned to English society. The first indication that the Indians were serious in their professions of equality came when the adopted captives were given freedom of movement within and without the Indian villages. Naturally the degree of freedom and its timing depended on the captive's willingness to enter into the spirit of Indian life.

Despite his adult years, Ridout had earned his captor's trust by the

third night of their march to the Shawnee villages. Having tied his prisoner with a rope to himself the first two nights, the Indian "never after-
wards used this precaution, leaving me at perfect liberty, and frequently
during the nights that were frosty and cold," Ridout recalled, "I found
his hand over me to examine whether or not I was covered." As soon
as seventeen-year-old John Leeth, an Indian trader's clerk, reached his
new family's village, "my father gave me and his two [Indian] sons our
freedom, with a rifle, two pounds of powder, four pounds of lead, a
blanket, shirt, match-coat, pair of leggings, etc. to each, as our freedom
dues; and told us to shift for ourselves." Eleven-year-old Benjamin
Gilbert, "considered as the [Indian] King's Successor," was of course
"entirely freed from Restraint, so that he even began to be delighted
with his Manner of Life." Even Steele, a somewhat reluctant Indian at
twenty-two, was "allowed the privilege of visiting any part of the village, in the day time, and was received with marks of fraternal affection,
and treated with all the civility an Indian is capable to bestow."

The presence of other white prisoners complicated the trust relationship somewhat. Captives who were previously known to each other,
especially from the same family, were not always allowed to converse
"much together, as [the Indians] imagined they would remember their
former Situation, and become less contented with their present Manner of Life." Benjamin Peart, for example, was allowed the frequent
company of "Two white Men who had been taken Prisoners, the one
from Susquehanna, the other from Minisinks, both in Pennsylvania,"
even though he was a Pennsylvanian himself. But when he met his
captive wife and infant son by chance at Fort Niagara, the Indians
"separated them again the same Day, and took [his] Wife about Four
Miles Distance."

Captives who were strangers were permitted not only to visit frequently but occasionally to live together. When Gist suddenly moved
from his adopted aunt's house back to her brother's, she "imajined I
was affronted," he wrote, and "came and asked me the reason why I
had left her, or what injury she or any of the family had done me that
I should leave her without so much as leting her know of it. I told her
it was the company of my fellow prisoners that drew me to the town.
She said that it was not so far but I mite have walked to see them every
two or three days, and ask some of them to come and see me those days
that I did not chuse to go abroad, and that all such persons as I thought

proper to bring to the house should be as welcom[e] as one of the family, and made many promises how kind she would be if I would return. However," boasted the twenty-four-year-old Gist, "I was obstinate and would not." It is not surprising that captives who enjoyed such autonomy were also trusted under the same roof. John Brickell remarked that three white prisoners, "Patton, Johnston, and Mrs. Baker [of Kentucky] had all lived with me in the same house among the Indians, and we were as intimate as brothers and sisters."

Once the captives had earned the basic trust of their Indian families, nothing in Indian life was denied them. When they reached the appropriate age, the Indians offered to find them suitable marriage partners. Understandably, some of the older captives balked at this, sensing that it was calculated to bind them with marital ties to a culture they were otherwise hesitant to accept. When Joseph Gilbert, a forty-one-year-old father and husband, was adopted into a leading family, his new relatives informed him that "if he would marry amongst them, he should enjoy the Privileges which they enjoyed; but this Proposal he was not disposed to comply with, . . . as he was not over anxious to conceal his Dislike to them." Elizabeth Peart, his twenty-year-old married sister, was equally reluctant. During her adoption ceremony "they obliged her to sit down with a young Man an Indian, and the eldest Chieftain of the Family repeating a Jargon of Words to her unintelligible, but which she considered as some form amongst them of Marriage," she was visited with "the most violent agitations, as she was determined, at all events, to oppose any step of this Nature." Marie LeRoy's honor was even more dearly bought. When "it was at length determined by the [Indians] that [she] should marry one of the natives, who had been selected for her," she told a fellow captive that "she would sooner be shot than have him for her husband." Whether her revulsion was directed toward the act itself or toward the particular suitor was not said.

The distinction is pertinent because the weight of evidence suggests that marriage was not compulsory for the captives, and common sense tells us that any form of compulsion would have defeated the Indians' purpose in trying to persuade the captives to adopt their way of life. Mary Jemison, at the time a captive for two years, was unusual in implying that she was forced to marry an Indian. "Not long after the Delawares came to live with us, at Wiisho," she recalled, "my sisters told me that I must go and live with one of them, whose name was

She-nin-jee. Not daring to cross them, or disobey their commands, with
a great degree of reluctance I went; and Sheninjee and I were married
according to Indian custom." Considering the tenderness and kindness
with which most captives reported they were treated, it is likely that
she was less compelled in reality than in her perception and memory
of it.

For even hostile witnesses could not bring themselves to charge that
force was ever used to promote marriages. The Puritan minister John
Williams said only that "great *essays* [were] made to get [captives]
married" among the Canadian Indians by whom he was captured. Elizabeth Hanson and her husband "could by no means obtain from their
hands" their sixteen-year-old daughter, "for the squaw, to whom she
was given, had a son whom she intended my daughter should in time
be prevailed with to marry." Mrs. Hanson was probably less concerned
that her daughter would be forced to marry an Indian than that she
might "in time" want to, for as she acknowledged from her personal
experience, "the Indians are very civil towards their captive women, not
offering any incivility by any indecent carriage." An observer of the
return of the white prisoners to Bouquet spoke for his contemporaries
when he reported—with an almost audible sigh of relief—that "there
had not been a solitary instance among them of any woman having her
delicacy injured by being compelled to marry. They had been left liberty of choice, and those who chose to remain single were not sufferers
on that account."

Not only were younger captives and consenting adults under no compulsion, either actual or perceived, to marry, but they enjoyed as wide
a latitude of choice as any Indian. When Gist returned to his Indian
aunt's lodge, she was so happy that the "dress'd me as fine as she could,
and . . . told me if I wanted a wife she would get a pretty young girl
for me." It was in the same spirit of exuberant generosity that Spencer's
adopted mother rewarded his first hunting exploit. "She heard all the
particulars of the affair with great satisfaction," he remembered, "and
frequently saying, 'Enee, wessah'" (that is right, that is good), said I
would one day become a great hunter, and placing her forefingers together (by which sign the Indians represent marriage) and then pointing to Sotonegoo' (a thirteen-year-old girl whom Spencer described as
"rather homely, but cheerful and good natured, with bright, laughing
eyes") "told me that when I should become a man I should have her

for a wife." Sotonegoo cannot have been averse to the idea, for when Spencer was redeemed shortly afterward she "sobbed loudly as [he] took her hand, and for the moment deeply affected, bade her farewell."

So free from compulsion were the captives that several married fellow white prisoners. In 1715 the priest of the Jesuit mission at Sault-au-Recollect "married Ignace shoetak8anni [Joseph Rising, aged twenty-one] and Elizabeth T8atog8ach [Abigail Nims, aged fifteen], both English, who wish to remain with the Christian Indians, not only renouncing their nation, but even wishing to live *en sauvages*." But from the Indians' standpoint, and perhaps from their own, captives such as John Leeth and Thomas Armstrong may have had the best of all possible marriages. After some years with the Indians, Leeth "was married to a young woman, seventeen or eighteen years of age; also a prisoner to the Indians; who had been taken by them when about twenty months old." Armstrong, an adopted Seneca, also married a "full blooded white woman, who like himself had been a captive among the Indians, from infancy, who unlike him, had not acquired a knowledge of one word of the English language, being essentially Indian in all save blood." Their commitment to each other deepened their commitment to the Indian culture of which they had become equal members.

The captives' social equality was also demonstrated by their being asked to share in the affairs of war and peace, matters of supreme importance to Indian society. When the Senecas who had adopted Thomas Peart decided to "make a War Excursion," they asked him to go with them. But since he was in no mood—and no physical condition—to play the Indian, "he determinately refused them, and was therefore left at Home with the Family." The young Englishman who became Old White Chief was far more eager to defend his new culture, but his origins somewhat limited his military activity. "When I grew to manhood," he recalled, "I went with them [his Iroquois kinsmen] on the warpath against the neighboring tribes, but never against the white settlers, lest by some unlucky accident I might be recognized and claimed by former friends." Other captives—many of them famous renegades—were less cautious. Charlevoix noticed in his travels in Canada that adopted captives "frequently enter into the spirit of the nation, of which they are become members, in such a manner, that they make no difficulty of going to war against their own countrymen." It was behavior such as this that prompted Sir William Johnson to praise Bou-

quet after his expedition to the Ohio for compelling the Indians to give
up every white person, even the "Children born of White Women.
That mixed Race," he wrote, referring to first-generation captives as
well, "forgetting their Ancestry on one side are found to be the most
Inveterate of any, and would greatly Augment their numbers."

It is ironic that the most famous renegade of all should have introduced ten-year-old Spencer to the ultimate opportunity for an
adopted captive. When he had been a captive for less than three weeks,
Spencer met Simon Girty, "the very picture of a villain," at a Shawnee
village below his own. After various boasts and enquiries, wrote Spencer,
"he ended by telling me that I would never see home; but if I should
'turn out to be a good hunter and a brave warrior I might one day be a
chief.' " Girty's prediction may not have been meant to tease a small
boy with impossible delusions of grandeur, for the Indians of the Northeast readily admitted white captives to their highest councils and offices.

Just after Ridout was captured on the Ohio, he was surprised to meet
an English-speaking "white man, about twenty-two years of age, who
had been taken prisoner when a lad and had been adopted, and now
was a chief among the Shawanese." He need not have been surprised,
for there were many more like him. John Tarbell, the man who visited
his Groton relatives in Indian dress, was not only "one of the wealthiest" of the Caughnawagas but "the eldest chief and chief speaker of
the tribe." Timothy Rice, formerly of Westborough, Massachusetts,
was also made one of the clan chiefs of Caughnawaga [Québec], partly
by inheritance from his Indian father but largely for "his own Super[io]r
Talents" and "warlike Spirit for which he was much celebrated."

Perhaps the most telling evidence of the Indians' receptivity to
adopted white leadership comes from Old White Chief, an adopted
Iroquois.

> I was made a chief at an early age [he recalled in 1836] and as my
> sons grew to manhood they also were made chiefs. . . . After
> my youngest son was made chief I could see, as I thought, that
> some of the Indians were jealous of the distinction I enjoyed and
> it gave me uneasiness. This was the first time I ever entertained
> the thought of leaving my Indian friends. I felt sure that it was
> displeasing to the Indians to have three of my sons, as well as
> myself, promoted to the office of chief. My wife was well pleased
> to leave with me, and my sons said, 'Father, we will go wherever
> you will lead us.'

I then broke the subject to some of my Indian relatives, who were very much disturbed at my decision. They immediately called the chiefs and warriors together and laid the plan before them. They gavely deliberated upon the subject for some hours, and then a large majority decided that they would not consent to our leaving. They said, 'We cannot give up our son and brother (meaning myself) 'nor our nephews' (meaning my children). 'They have lived on our game and grown strong and powerful among us. They are good and true men. We cannot do without them. We cannot give them to the pale faces. We shall grow weak if they leave us. We will give them the best we have left. Let them choose where they will live. No one shall disturb them. We need their wisdom and their strength to help us. If they are in high places, let them be there. We know they will honor us.

"We yielded to their importunity," said the old chief, and "I have never had any reason to regret my decision." In public office as in every sphere of Indian life, the English captives found that the color of their skin was unimportant; only their talent and their inclination of heart mattered.

Understandably, neither their skill nor their loyalty was left to chance. From the moment the captives, especially the young ones, came under their charge, the Indians made a concerted effort to inculcate in them Indian habits of mind and body. If the captives could be taught to think, act, and react like Indians, they would effectively cease to be English and would assume an Indian identity. This was the Indians' goal, toward which they bent every effort in the weeks and months that followed their formal adoption of the white captives.

The educational character of Indian society was recognized by even the most inveterately English captives. Titus King, a twenty-six-year-old New England soldier, spent a year with the Canadian Indians at St. Francis trying—unsuccessfully—to undo their education of "Eight or tin young [English] Children." What "an awfull School this [is] for Children," he wrote. "When We See how Quick they will Fall in with the Indians ways, nothing Seems to be more takeing in Six months time they Forsake Father and mother Forgit thir own Land Refuess to Speak there own toungue and Seemin[g]ly be Holley Swollowed up with the Indians." The older the person, of course, the longer it took to become fully Indianized. Mary Jemison, captured at the age of twelve, took three or four years to forget her natural parents and the home she had once loved. "If I had been taken in infancy," she said, "I should have been contented in my situation." Some captives, commonly those over fifteen or sixteen years old, never made the transition from English to Indian. Twenty-four-year-old Gist, soldier and son of a famous scout and Indian agent, accommodated himself to his adoption and Indian life for just one year and then made plans to escape. "All curiosity with regard to acting the part of an Indian," he related, "which I could do very well, being througherly [thoroughly] satisfied, I was determined to be what I really was."

Children, however, took little time to "fall in with the Indians ways." Titus King mentioned six months. The Reverend John Williams witnessed the effects of eight or nine months when he stopped at St. Francis in February 1704. There, he said, "we found several poor children, who had been taken from the eastward [Maine] the summer before; a sight very affecting, they being in habit very much like Indians, and in manners very much symbolizing with them." When young Joseph Noble visited his captive sister in Montreal, "he still belonged to the St. François tribe of Indians, and was dressed remarkably fine, having forty or fifty broaches in his shirt, clasps on his arm, and a great variety of knots and bells about his clothing. He brought his little sister . . . a young fawn, a basket of cranberries, and a lump of sap sugar." Sometime later he was purchased from the Indians by a French gentleman who promptly "dressed him in the French style; but he never appeared so bold and majestic, so spirited and vivacious, as when arrayed in his Indian habit and associating with his Indian friends."

The key to any culture is its language, and the young captives were quick to learn the Indian dialects of their new families. Their retentive memories and flair for imitation made them ready students, while the Indian languages, at once oral, concrete, and mythopoeic, lightened the task. In less than six months ten-year-old Spencer had "acquired a sufficient knowledge of the Shawnee tongue to understand all ordinary conversation and, indeed, the greater part of all that I heard (accompanied, as their conversation and speeches were, with the most significant gestures)," which enabled him to listen "with much pleasure and sometimes with deep interest" to his Indian mother tell of battles, heroes, and history in the long winter evenings. When Jemima Howe was allowed to visit her four-year-old son at a neighboring Indian village in Canada, he greeted her "in the Indian tongue" with "Mother, are you come?" He too had been a captive for only six months.

The early weeks of captivity could be disquieting if there were no English-speaking Indians or prisoners in the village to lend the comfort of a familiar language while the captives struggled to acquire a strange one. If a captive's family left for their winter hunting camp before he could learn their language, he might find himself, like Gist, "without any com[p]any that could unders[t]and one word that I spake." "Thus I continued, near five months," he wrote, "sometimes reading, other times singing, never melancholy but when alone. . . . About the first of April (1759) I prevailed on the family to return to town, and by the last of the month all the Indians and prisoners returned, when I once more had the pleasure to talk to people that understood what I said."

Younger captives probably missed the familiarity of English less than the adult Gist. Certainly they never lacked eager teachers. Mary Jemison recalled that her Seneca sisters were "diligent in teaching me their language; and to their great satisfaction I soon learned so that I could understand it readily, and speak it fluently." Even Gist was the recipient of enthusiastic, if informal, instruction from a native speaker. One of his adopted cousins, who was about five or six years old and his "favorite in the family," was always "chattering some thing" with him. "From him," said Gist affectionately, "I learn'd more than from all the rest, and he learn'd English as fast as [I] did Indian."

As in any school, language was only one of many subjects of instruction. Since the Indians generally assumed that whites were physically inferior to themselves, captive boys were often prepared for the hardy life of hunters and warriors by a rigorous program of physical training. John McCullough, aged eight, was put through the traditional Indian course by his adoptive uncle. 'In the beginning of winter," McCullough recalled, "he used to raise me by day light every morning, and make me sit down in the creek up to my chin in the cold water, in order to make me hardy as he said, whilst he would sit on the bank smoking his pipe until he thought I had been long enough in the water, he would then bid me to dive. After I came out of the water he would order me not to go near the fire until I would be dry. I was kept at that till the water was frozen over, he would then break the ice for me and send me in as

before." As shocking as it may have been to his system, such treatment
did nothing to turn him against Indian life. Indeed, he was transpar-
ently proud that he had borne up under the strenuous regimen "with
the firmness of an Indian." Becoming an Indian was as much a challenge and an adventure for the young colonists as it was a "sore trial,"
and many of them responded to it with alacrity and zest. Of children
their age we should not expect any less.

The captives were taught not only to speak and to endure as Indians
but to act as Indians in the daily social and economic life of the community. Naturally, boys were taught the part of men and girls the part
of women, and according to most colonial sources—written, it should be
noted, predominantly by men—the boys enjoyed the better fate. An
Ohio pioneer remembered that the prisoners from his party were "put
into different families, the women to hard drudging and the boys to run
wild with the young Indians, to amuse themselves with bow and arrow,
dabble in the water, or obey any other notion their wild natures might
dictate." William Walton, the author of the Gilbert family captivity
narrative, also felt that the "Labour and Drudgery" in an Indian family
fell to "the Share of the Women." He described fourteen-year-old
Abner Gilbert as living a "dronish Indian life, idle and poor, having
no other Employ than the gathering of Hickory-Nuts; and although
young," Walton insisted. "his Situation was very irksome." Just how
irksome the boy found his freedom from colonial farm chores was revealed when the ingenuous Walton related that "Abner, having no useful Employ, amused himself with catching fish in the Lake. . . . Not
being of an impatient Disposition," said Walton soberly, "he bore his
Captivity without repining."

While most captive boys had "nothing to do, but cut a little wood
for the fire," draw water for cooking and drinking, and "shoot Black-
birds that came to eat up the corn," they enjoyed "some leisure" for
"hunting and other innocent devertions in the woods." Women and
girls, on the other hand, shared the burdens—onerous ones in English
eyes—of their Indian counterparts. But Jemison, who had been taught
English ways for twelve years before becoming an Indian, felt that the
Indian women's labor "was not severe," their tasks "probably not
harder than that [sic] of white women," and their cares "certainly
. . . not half as numerous, nor as great." The work of one year was
"exactly similar, in almost every respect, to that of the others, without

that endless variety that is to be observed in the common labor of the white people. . . . In the summer season, we planted, tended and harvested our corn, and generally had all our children with us; but had no master to oversee or drive us, so that we could work as leisurely as we pleased. . . . In the season of hunting, it was our business, in addition to our cooking, to bring home the game that was taken by the [men], dress it, and carefully preserve the eatable meat, and prepare or dress the skins." "Spinning, weaving, sewing, stocking knitting," and like domestic tasks of colonial women were generally unknown. Unless Jemison was correct, it would be virtually impossible to understand why so many women and girls chose to become Indians. A life of unremitting drudgery, as the English saw it, could certainly hold no attraction for civilized women fresh from frontier farms and villages.

The final and most difficult step in the captives' transition from English to Indian was to acquire the ability to think as Indians, to share unconsciously the values, beliefs, and standards of Indian culture. From an English perspective, this should have been nearly an impossible task for civilized people because they perceived Indian culture as immoral and irreligious and totally antithetical to the civilized life they had known, however briefly. "Certainly," William Smith assumed, "it could never be put in competition with the blessings of improved life and the light of religion." But many captives soon discovered that the English had no monopoly on virtue and that in many ways the Indians were morally superior to the English, more Christian than the Christians.

As early as 1643 Roger Williams had written a book to suggest such a thing, but he could be dismissed as a misguided visionary who let the Narragansetts go to his head. It was more difficult to dismiss someone like Brickell, who had lived with the Indians for four and one-half years and had no ax to grind with established religion. "The Delawares are the best people to train up children I ever was with," he wrote. "Their leisure hours are, in a great measure, spent in training up their children to observe what they believe to be right. . . . [A]s a nation they may be considered fit examples for many of us Christians to follow. They certainly follow what they are taught to believe right more closely, and I might say more honestly, in general, than we Christians do the divine precepts of our Redeemer. . . . I know I am influenced to good, even at this day," he concluded, "more from what I learned among them, than what I learned among people of my own color." After many decades with them, Jemison insisted that "the moral character of the Indians was . . . uncontaminated. Their fidelity was perfect, and became proverbial; they were strictly honest; they despised deception and falsehood; and chastity was held in high veneration." Even the tory historian Peter Oliver, who was no friend to the Indians, admitted that "they have a Religion of their own, which, to the eternal Disgrace of many Nations who boast of Politeness, is more influential on their Conduct than that of those who hold them in so great Contempt." To the acute discomfort of the colonists, more than one captive maintained that the Indians were a "far more moral race than the whites."

In the principled school of Indian life the captives experienced a decisive shift in their cultural and personal identities, a shift that often fostered a considerable degree of what might be called "conversion zeal." A French officer reported that "those Prisoners whom the Indians keep with them . . . are often more brutish, boisterous in their Behaviour and loose in their Manners than the Indians," and thought that "they affect that kind of Behaviour thro' Fear of and to recommend themselves to the Indians." Matthew Bunn, a nineteen-year-old soldier, was the object of such behavior when he was enslaved—not adopted— by the Maumee in 1791. "After I had eaten," he related, "they brought me a little prisoner boy, that had been taken about two years before, on the river called Monongahela, though he delighted more in the ways of the savages than in the ways of Christians; he used me worse than any of the Indians, for he would tell me to do this, that, and the other, and if I did not do it, or made any resistance, the Indians would threaten to kill me, and he would kick and cuff me about in such a manner, that I hardly dared to say my soul was my own." What Bunn experienced was the attempt of the new converts to pattern their behavior after their young Indian counterparts, who, a Puritan minister observed, "are as much to be dreaded by captives as those of maturer years, and in many cases much more so; for, unlike cultivated people, they have no restraints upon their mischievous and savage propensities, which they indulge in cruelties."

Although fear undoubtedly accounted for some of the converts' initial behavior, desire to win the approval of their new relatives also played a part. "I had lived in my new habitation about a week," recalled Spencer, "and having given up all hope of escaping . . . began to regard it as my future home. . . . I strove to be cheerful, and by my ready obedience to ingratiate myself with Cooh-coo-cheeh [his Indian mistress], for whose kindness I felt grateful." A year after James Smith had been adopted, a number of prisoners were brought in by his new kinsmen and a gauntlet formed to welcome them. Smith "went and told them how they were to act" and then "fell into one of the ranks with the Indians, shouting and yelling like them." One middle-aged man's turn came, and "as they were not very severe on him," confessed the new Indian, "as he passed me I hit him with a piece of pumpkin—which pleased the Indians much." If their zeal to emulate the Indians sometimes exceeded their mercy, the captives had nonetheless fulfilled their new families' expectations: they had begun to act as Indians in spirit as well as body. Only time would be necessary to transform their conscious efforts into unconscious habits and complete their cultural conversion.

"By what power does it come to pass," asked Crèvecoeur, "that children who have been adopted when young among these people, . . . and even grown persons . . . can never be prevailed on to re-adopt European manners?" Given the malleability of youth, we should not be surprised that children underwent a rather sudden and permanent transition from English to Indian—although we might be pressed to explain why so few Indian children made the transition in the opposite direction. But the adult colonists who became Indians cannot be explained as easily, for the simple reason that they, unlike many of the children, were fully conscious of their cultural identities while they were being subjected to the Indians' assiduous attempts to convert them. Consequently, their cultural metamorphosis involved a large degree of personal choice.

The great majority of white Indians left no explanations for their choice. Forgetting their original language and their past, they simply disappeared into their adopted society. But those captives who returned to write narratives of their experiences left several clues to the motives of those who chose to stay behind. They stayed because they found Indian life to possess a strong sense of community, abundant love, and uncommon integrity—values that the English colonists also honored, if less successfully. But Indian life was attractive for other values—for social equality, mobility, adventure, and, as two adult converts acknowledged, "the most perfect freedom, the ease of living, [and] the absence of those cares and corroding solicitudes which so often prevail with us." As we have learned recently, these were values that were not being realized in the older, increasingly crowded, fragmented, and contentious communities of the Atlantic seaboard, or even in the newer frontier settlements. By contrast, as Crèvecoeur said, there must have been in the Indians' "social bond something singularly captivating." Whatever it was, its power had no better measure than the large number of English colonists who became, contrary to the civilized assumptions of their countrymen, white Indians.

4

The "Second Sex" in Baltimore

KATHRYN ALLAMONG JACOB

• When one seeks to analyze a certain historical period or a specific event, the usual practice is to turn to written sources. The problem with this approach is that it tends to perpetuate the notion that history is the record of the actions of adult white men—and especially those who were also wealthy or powerful. Because newspapers biographies, and government documents have typically been dominated by entries dealing with only one portion of the population, it has been exceedingly difficult to get at the history of women or of blacks or of any other group that has had little written about it.

Kathryn Allamong Jacob has set about the difficult task not only of reconstructing the lifestyle of the "Second Sex," but also of doing it in a colonial city. Some of the problems of that period—such as bastardy, adultery, employment, and education—have a decidedly modern ring. Similarly, the opinion that woman's sphere is the home has apparently been a constant for over two centuries. Even today, when women make up 45 per cent of the work force, the belief that women are defined primarily by their domestic activities remains strong. Attempts to change sex-role definitions are viewed by many as an attack on the very fabric of religious and family life.

Other problems with which eighteenth-century women had to deal—such as the constant threat of infant death—have, thankfully, been mitigated in the intervening years. As you read the essay, you should note the ways in which the lives of ordinary women in 1780 differed from those in 1980. You might also ask yourself how compelling is the argument that the essential functions and roles of women are biologically determined and are not susceptible to change over time. Or is the evidence too fragmentary to make sweeping generalizations about the lives of the inarticulate?

When speaking of women in history, Arthur Schlesinger, Sr., once noted, "From reading history textbooks, one would think half of our population made only a negligible contribution to history. . . ." He precisely described the standard histories of Baltimore. One finds lamentably few references to women in the town's traditional chronicles. Those few women who do appear are the lovely belles who captured the hearts of young men at home and abroad and the women who gained recognition by virtue of being the wife, mother, or daughter of a famous gentleman. The widowed mothers of a dozen or more children who built up prosperous businesses and the anonymous women who donated long-labored-over quilts to the war effort are consistently overlooked. Yet these, and even the women accused of horsethievery or bearing bastards, represent the very essence of Baltimore Town's social history.

Created by legislative fiat in 1729, Baltimore was officially called Baltimore Town until it received its city charter in 1797. Rising from almost empty acres along the Patapsco, it lacked the sophistication of its older and more glamorous neighbor, Annapolis. The majority of Baltimore's women were more expert at wielding a needle than a pen. Theirs were the skills of cookery, not composition, and consequently they left few written accounts of themselves. Fortunately, records about these early women were kept by others. Tax, court, land, and church records, wills and inventories, censuses, newspapers, and private papers provide a wealth of information about Baltimore's first women citizens.

The wide variety of information gleaned from this data permits a partial reconstruction of various facets of the Baltimore woman's life, her birth, her marriage, and her legal status. Several specific threads run through the data, creating unity on several levels. One such thread, and one of the most striking, is the very real way in which economics was related to every aspect of the woman's life, from whom and how she would marry to the kinds of problems that resulted in her appearance before the courts. Dependent in childhood upon her father, in middle age upon her husband, and, often, in old age upon her sons, with few exceptions the Baltimore woman's whole life style and social status was largely determined by the wealth of the men in her life.

The wealth of her father or husband determined whether she would

From *Maryland Historical Magazine* 71 (Fall 1976): 283–95. Reprinted by permission of the author and the publisher.

wear silks and damasks of coarse linen and osnaburg; whether her food would be sweetened with expensive sugar or plain honey. Her house might be an elegant, multi-story brick dwelling or a two room, readily combustible wooden structure. For amusement, she might attend the gay assemblies and banquets or gossip with a neighbor while they made soap together—it all depended on her economic status.

Aside from such tangible and obvious evidence of economic differences as dress, diet, and housing, economic considerations clearly affected the woman's prospects in the marriage market. Colonial society exerted great pressure on both men and women to marry. Though matrimony was held up to men as a pleasant duty, the bachelor's tax levied by Maryland reflected the widespread belief that the unmarried man was evading his moral and civic responsibility. While merely one, albeit an important one, of the many facets of the man's life, marriage and procreation were thought to be the only role for which women were suited.

In 1666 promoter George Alsop sought to lure women to Maryland by promising them that they would soon find "copulative matrimony" and have no fears lest their "virginity turn moldy." A poem in Dunlap's *Maryland Gazette* exhorted women to accept their fate:

> Reserved the stern decrees of fate,
> Do everything—but get a mate.

And get mates they did. As marriage and birth records show, most Baltimore women, rich and poor alike, did marry. From the town's beginning, women were outnumbered by men, making theirs a "seller's market."

The English laws forbidding marriage between persons related by "consanguinity or affinity" were in effect in colonial Maryland. They forbade, for example, a woman from marrying her late husband's grandfather. However, a far more effective regulator of marriage than such laws was the social convention which required parental consent to a match. The considerations which governed the decisions of parents were both prudent and shrewd—the more money involved, the harder the bargaining. As Charles Carroll of Carrollton's father pointed out to him, there were certain qualities a man of breeding should look for in a wife. She should be virtuous, sensible, good-natured, complacent, neat and cheerful, of a good size, well-proportioned, and free from hereditary disorders. She should also, of course, be wealthy, or, as the elder Carroll cautioned, "at the very least, of a good family."

A prospective bride's share, or expected share, of worldly goods was carefully scrutinized by both the potential groom and his father. Marriage announcements unabashedly referring to Baltimore brides as "Miss Jane Low, a most agreeable lady with a large and handsome fortune" were common. When the lady's fortune was "handsome," a pre-nuptial agreement often culminated her courtship. In such contracts, the bride was guaranteed a certain standard of living and rights to certain property in the event that her husband died before she did, and the groom was given a complete inventory of the property to come his way in the form of the dowry.

Though of paramount importance to the town's wealthiest citizens, the need for a firm economic foundation for a marriage was also recognized by the less affluent. Whether a multiacre estate or a set of linen sheets, nearly every bride brought certain material goods to the union. Similarly, the groom, no matter how humble, usually gave assurances of bed and board to his bride. Evidence suggests that among Baltimore's lower classes, love and marriage were more spontaneous than they were for the wealthy. Where there was little of either prestige or property to inherit, parental blessings were less coveted.

Once courtship was officially under way, thoughts could realistically turn to the wedding. Despite such notable exceptions as the marriage of fourteen-year-old Sophia Gough to James Maccubin Carroll, the years between eighteen and twenty appear to be the most popular ones for the first marriages of Baltimore's young women of all classes. For the middle and lower classes, evidence points toward a near parity in ages of spouses at first marriage. A typical union was that of twenty-one-year-old William Brown, a currier, and nineteen-year-old Mary Mattox in June 1795. Among the wealthy, cases such as that of forty-year-old Charles Carroll, the Barrister, marrying nineteen-year-old Margaret Tilghman, and thirty-one-year-old Charles Carroll of Carrollton marrying fourteen-year-old Mary Darnall were not uncommon.

As it still does today, the lavishness of the eighteenth-century Baltimore wedding depended on the wealth of the bride's father. Though the weddings of the rich were splendid and lengthy affairs, most Baltimoreans visited their church for a simple ceremony followed by a family dinner. Such must certainly have been what William Duncan, a cooper who had seven attractive daughters to marry off, hoped for.

While most Baltimore couples appear to have lived together peacefully, conjugal felicity was far from universal. One finds husbands expressing great confidence in their wives by naming them as their executrixes. In his will, John Smithson lovingly wrote of his wife, "All I have I leave her and if I had more she should enjoy it." On the other hand, nearly every issue of Baltimore's weekly *Maryland Journal* contained notices like the following:

> As Elizabeth Marken hath absconded from her husband's bed, I do forewarn all persons not to trust her on my account.
>
> Samuel Marken

In addition to protecting themselves from debts incurred by their runaway wives, some husbands sought publicly to embarrass their spouses, often to the point of admitting to be cuckolds, by declaring them to be "harlots" and "unworthy persons." Not all such repudiations went unchallenged. After her husband had renounced her as his wife, Mary McLaughlin countered, "His assertion is false; and altho' I do not think he is worthy the name of husband, yet he is certainly mine." The couples who resorted to such damning rhetoric were never members of "society." City directories reveal them to be common laborers and generally unskilled. This is not, however, to imply that the wealthy lived in constant harmony, but rather that they preferred to keep their marital problems more private.

Though a few husbands claimed their wives had been lured away by other men or were "disordered in the mind," one is left to ponder the reasons which prompted several dozen wives to leave their homes. Though under Maryland law physical punishment was a husband's prerogative, there is no evidence that abuse of this privilege caused wives to flee.

After a brief period, several absconding wives returned home. Indeed, for some wives, running away seems to have been a way of getting a vacation from the monotony of domesticity. A postscript to one of Mr. Starr's advertisements in 1756 for his wife Susanna indicated that this was her fourth elopement.

Though certainly more vocal when vexed, husbands were not the only harried spouses in Baltimore Town. Other evidence suggests that

the wife's patience was equally tried. The numerous cases of women
arraigned before the court on charges of keeping a "disorderly" or
"bawdy house" indicate that there was ample opportunity for husbands
to philander. That several accepted the invitation is suggested by the
bastardly cases in which the mother named a married man as the father
of her illegitimate child.

Like those who advertised their spouses, the offenders named in
adultery and bastardy cases were rarely individuals of high social standing. However, this is not to say that wealthy gentlemen were models of
fidelity. Money, not morality, brought the unwed mother to court. The
object was to charge someone with the bastard's support. Gentlemen
usually had sufficient funds to make private compensation for their
indiscretions, thus avoiding public censure.

A woman was not only expected to wed, despite uncertain prospects
for happiness, but to bear children as well—legitimate ones, of course.
Baltimore's women were very "fruitful vines." According to the 1790
census, the average Baltimore family consisted of a mother, father, and
five children. However, such an average family is hard to find. Compris-
ing this figure are families of nine, eleven, and even thirteen children
and couples who had only one child.

Large families were common among both the rich and poor. Ellin
North, reputedly the first baby born in Baltimore Town, married John
Moale and became the mother of thirteen. The town's original sur-
veyor, Philip Jones, was the father of fifteen: his first wife bore him two
children before her death, and his second thirteen more. William Pat-
terson and his wife, the former Dorcus Spear, had thirteen children,
one of whom was the famous Betsy. Cooper William Duncan and his
wife Rebecca had eleven children in twenty-four years.

While some local women were prevented from having more babies
only by old age, others sadly found themselves unable to bear any at all.
Though wealthy women seem particularly plagued with barrenness,
they may simply have been more noteworthy because of the inheritance
problems they created. Rebecca Dorsey Ridgely could produce no heirs
for her husband, Charles Ridgely, the builder. He left Hampton to his
nephew, Charles Ridgely Carnan, but required him to change his name
to Charles Carnan Ridgely, in hopes that the family name would live
on. The builder would have been gratified to know that his nephew
and his wife, Priscilla Dorsey Ridgely, younger sister of Rebecca, the

builder's barren wife, had several children, including future male heirs.

Margaret Tilghman Carroll produced no heir for the Barrister's Mount Clare, and he too left his estate to a nephew, James Maccubin, also requiring him to change his name. James Maccubin Carroll and his young bride, Sophia Gough, realized the elder Carroll's hopes by having four sons and two daughters, three of whom married the offspring of Charles and Priscilla Ridgely.

Birth records reveal an interesting trend among Baltimore's prolific mothers. In many families there is apparent a great regularity in the spacing of children. The two year interval was most common. For example, the seven children of shipfitter James Biays and his wife Mary were born in 1786, 1788, 1790, 1792, 1794, 1796, and 1798. This regularity in the spacing of births is especially interesting in light of recent studies on the effects of nursing on conception. These studies suggest that, for many women, unsupplemented breast feeding acts as a natural birth control, altering the mother's hormonal balance in such a way as to make conception unlikely until the first child is weaned.

Most middle and lower class Baltimore mothers did nurse their own infants. Indeed, the question of the suckling of infants was receiving much attention in the contemporary women's guides. To the considerable dismay of moralists, wealthy women throughout the colonies were beginning to turn their infants over to wet nurses, who were often black, in order to return to the social whirl unhindered. As the following advertisement indicates, Baltimore's wealthy women were following the fashionable trend: "Wanted: a nurse with a good breast of milk, of a healthy constitution and good character, that is willing to go into a gentleman's family."

Wealthy women were also scandalizing many townspeople by having their babies delivered by male doctors rather than by one of several local midwives. The presence of a male doctor at the delivery was considered by many to be a terrible compromise of female modesty, one which "sullied the chastity and tainted the purity of the clients." Despite the attendance of midwives or doctors, mothers both rich and poor died in childbirth with shocking frequency. Even if the mother survived, she often never fully recovered her health. All too frequently, tombstone inscriptions tell of mothers succumbing to the strain well before middle age.

Time and time again, Baltimore mothers laid down their lives or ruined their health only to bring forth babies for the grave. While church records reveal many births, the wills of the period show few large families. The tiny graves in local churchyards explain the difference. For example, next to their mother's grave in the Westminister Presbyterian Church cemetery lie the graves of three of her daughters who died at ages eight months, eleven months, and twelve years. Infant mortality knew no class boundaries. Charles and Mary Carroll lost four of their seven children before adulthood.

Not all Baltimore Town mothers were wives as well. Several bastardy cases were brought before the court each year, and these probably represented only a fraction of the actual illegitimate births. But since court records are one of the few sources for the study of women in early Baltimore, and of course only illegitimate children would figure in such records, any account based on the sources will document a disproportionate number of bastards. Almost without exception, these unwed mothers were indentured servants.

Indentured servants were prevented by law from marrying without the consent of their masters. Masters were naturally reluctant to approve of a relationship which would probably result in childbearing, loss of service during pregnancy, and the real possibility of death or permanent damage to health. Though the framers of the law must have thought it an effective deterrent to marriage and pregnancy, it merely served to create some quite prolific unwed mothers. For example, the town was barely three years old when two servant women were charged with bearing bastards. One Abigail Geer confessed to giving birth to four illegitimate children in as many years.

The master's main concern in prosecuting his servant was finding a culprit to reimburse him for the loss of her labor during pregnancy. Townspeople, who did not want the bastard to become a public tax burden, were equally concerned that the father be found. If she refused to divulge the father's name under routine questioning, and if she had not yet been delivered of her child, the question of paternity was often put to the unwed mother in the midst of her labor pains—a method which proved most effective.

If she named a man and he was found guilty, he was ordered to maintain his offspring. Servant Margaret Hollyday swore that Daniel Hare was the father of her bastard son, Isaac. Hare was convicted and fined. A few months later, he was also charged with keeping a disorderly house. If the unwed mother refused to reveal the father's name, she could be fined or physically punished. The aforementioned Agibail Geer was whipped "on her bare back with twenty lashes well laid until the blood appeared," and fined as well.

Most of the illegitimate children born to servant women were mulattoes. Their mothers, who had names like Bridget Kelly and Margaret Yerby, appear to have been white, suggesting that sexual relations between white women and black men of low status were somewhat commonplace.

Black slave women appear to have given birth to bastards as frequently as did white servant women. However, instead of being punished, in some cases slave women were encouraged to be fruitful. Unlike the servant woman, the female slave was owned for life and her offspring was valuable enough in trade that the time lost during her pregnancy was but a little inconvenience. Though the cohabitation of white men with "women of color" was forbidden by law, visitors' observations of slave women with broods of mulatto children suggest that such laws were frequently broken.

Infant bastards were almost always taken from their servant mothers and sold into servitude for a customary period of thirty-one years. However, unwed mothers were not the only poor Baltimore women to be parted from their young children. Newspapers and court records suggest that among large, poor families, children were often bound out at an early age as apprentices and helpers. For example, nine-year-old Elizabeth Powell was bound out by her father for seven years, and the penniless Widow Robins bound out her young son to a carpenter for ten years.

For the little girls who remained at home, family finances determined what type of education, if any, they would receive. Even in the wealthiest of families, while sons were well educated, daughters received no formal education. Many of their fathers subscribed to the belief that a woman needed only domestic talents to find happiness. Some wealthy young women, such as Catherine Carroll, whom the Signer sent to England to be educated, received excellent training in the sciences and literature. Most, however, simply learned genteel, drawing-room accomplishments.

Schools like those of Mary Anne March of Annapolis which offered "young misses all sorts of embroidery, Turkey work and all sorts of rich stitches," and Mary Salisbury's, which offered "French, tapestry, embroidery with gold and silver and all education fit for young ladies," lured several Baltimore girls to the colony's capital. Other fashionable boarding schools in Philadelphia and Charlestown advertised for pupils in Baltimore's newspapers and promised to teach all manner of subjects from silhouette cutting to clear-starching.

For the many middle-class Baltimore girls whose fathers could not afford expensive finishing schools, opportunities for education were few. Though four Baltimore women listed themselves as schoolmistresses in 1796, their modest schools were not free and offered little more than the barest rudiments of education. No free schools existed for Baltimore girls in this period. For the poorest girls, the servants, education was nearly nonexistent. Unlike Virginia and North Carolina, Maryland's apprentice laws did not require a master to teach his charge to read and write, and thus few did.

Under these circumstances, it is not surprising to find that many of Baltimore's women were illiterate. Even women of prominent families could not write their names. For example, wealthy widow Letticia Raven, executrix of a large estate and guardian of nine children, signed official documents with her mark—a large carefully drawn "L."

While homemaking was the sole employment of a majority of Baltimore Town women, several women were employed outside the home. They did not venture into the business world because time hung heavy on their hands; they did so out of financial necessity. To cut expenses, the wives of storekeepers and tradesmen often helped their husbands in their shops. Though often illiterate, by close association these wives learned enough of their husbands' trades to continue on alone in the event their husbands predeceased them and left behind a large family for the mothers to support. Other women, who did not inherit shops, began their own. These were generally spinsters or recent widows who found themselves suddenly penniless. Either unable or unwilling to live with parents or siblings, such women sought to support themselves.

Whatever her reasons, there seems to have been nothing in the eighteenth-century social or economic code of Baltimore to prevent a woman from working outside the home. Indeed, local poor laws encouraged single women to work lest they become recipients of tax-funded relief. While the number of women engaged in business never exceeded 5 per cent of all local women, they are a very significant group. In 1796, 259 of the city's nearly six thousand women were heads of households and made up 8 per cent of the total number of house-holders. Two-thirds of these women were widows, and the remainder were spinsters. Two-thirds of these women also had outside occupa-tions, but the proportion of business women was not evenly distributed between widows and spinsters. Only 45 per cent of the widows had occupations, compared to 92 per cent of the spinsters. Such discrepan-cies are often explained by the widow's substantial inheritance, which enabled her to forgo outside employment.

Baltimore Town's working women were engaged in more than twenty-five different professions ranging from baking to watchmaking to millinery. By far the largest number of working women were in-volved in some facet of the clothing trade. Fifty-five women listed themselves as seamstresses in 1796, and they clearly monopolized the trade. Several local women earned small fortunes as proprietresses of "tasteful" shops, and some even employed assistants. In 1774 Barbara Bence was advertising for a "sober, industrious person" to aid her in the tailor's business.

Laundering was popular among poor women with little money to invest. The laundress's trade, however, required more than merely soap, water, and stamina. Various local washerwomen advertised themselves as accomplished practitioners of dyeing, glazing, silk cleaning, clear-starching, and lace blocking. The boarding house proprietress was an-other common figure. She ranged from the woman who furnished a modest room and simple meals to the elegant hostess whose genteel accommodations were known throughout the colonies. When the Con-tinental Congress fled to Baltimore in 1777, John Adams stayed at the fashionable inn owned by Mrs. Ross. He wrote Abigail that his accom-modations were excellent except "for the monstrous price of things here."

Another prominent innkeeper was Shinah Solomon Etting, matri-arch of one of the town's first Jewish families. After her husband's death in 1778, Mrs. Etting moved her family from Lancaster, Pennsyl-vania, to Baltimore Town. Using nearly all of her inheritance, she had a spacious home built to her own specifications on Market Street where she established her family and began to take in boarders. Mrs. Etting's business thrived. She used her profits to aid the business ven-tures of her two prominent sons: Reuben, who became a United States

marshal and noted military leader, and Solomon, who built up a prosperous shipping and wholesale business, became president of the city
council, and director of a local bank in which his mother and sisters
held stock.

Not all of the inns run by women were reputable establishments.
A good deal more than a night's sleep could be procured at some. Each
court session brought forth women arraigned for "keeping a bawdy
house" and "selling liquors without a license." One Ann Heron was
charged with three different counts of the former offense during one
session alone.

In addition to boarding houses and seamstress shops, Baltimore's
women ran grocery and dry goods stores, and pastry, crockery, and
bran meal shops. Two women were sausagemakers. The town's most
famous businesswoman was Mary Catharine Goddard, who not only
published the *Maryland Journal* throughout the war years but served
as the town's first postmistress as well. Other women who, like Miss
Goddard, were engaged in "unwomanly" businesses included Widow
Hudson, who ran a thriving brick factory on the edge of town, and
Widow Ann Rawlins, who took over her late husband's ornamental
plaster works.

Tax and land records reveal other ways in which the independent
female heads of households with no listed occupations supported
themselves. Several women grew wealthy as land speculators and land-
lords, and by hiring out their slaves at a considerable profit. Of course,
such careers required a substantial outlay of either earned or inherited
capital. For women who could afford to enter it, the land market re-
paid them handsomely.

When Baltimore Town was first laid out, many wealthy men hesi-
tated to buy lots, fearing the enterprise would collapse as had two
other attempts at founding towns called Baltimore. However, wealthy
women who were either less cautious or more shrewd soon appeared to
purchase and speculate in prime lots. Mary Hanson, a widow, became
the first woman to purchase town lots when in 1740 she bought lots
five and six from the commissioners. She sold them seven years later,
unimproved, at a profit.

Among the displaced French Acadians who found their way to Baltimore Town in the 1750s were single women with both an eye for
property and the wealth to purchase it. Within two years of their ar-

rival, four French women had bought lots in the area of the town that came to be known as French Town. On board the ships which arrived in Baltimore in 1793 full of planters fleeing revolt-torn San Domingo were other French women whose wealth and independence rivaled that of their male shipmates. By 1796, ten San Domingan women, eight widows and two spinsters owned town lots.

The detailed records of the federal tax assessment of 1798 provide a wealth of information about Baltimore's landed women. In that year, over four hundred of the approximately six thousand free white women in the city were property owners. While many women owned only the tiny plot of ground upon which their modest frame houses stood, several women owned a dozen or more residential and commercial properties. Mary Nichols owned nine commercial lots and two residential lots valued at over $6,000. Some of these land-wealthy women qualify for the modern title of "slum lords" or "ladies." They apparently owned a number of houses in poor neighborhoods which they did not improve but rented at high rates—all the while living in comfortable three-story brick mansions some distance away.

Many of these female lot owners undoubtedly inherited rather than purchased their property. Whether they bought or inherited, the women of Baltimore were responsible for the same taxes and fines as local men. In 1786 a Mrs. Clifton was fined for not tending to her chimney. In 1787 a Mrs. Agnes Thompson was assessed five pounds for paving the street in front of her home on Light Street. Civic responsibility was also shouldered by Baltimore's women. When a subscription was taken up in 1748 to erect a fence to enclose local pigs, one of the subscribers was property owner Hannah Hughes, a midwife.

Wills and inventories of the period reveal the wide variety of other types of property owned by the women of Baltimore Town. A few appear to have found livestock to be a profitable investment. Mary Bowen left a variety of farm animals plus hams and sides of beef to her children. The seemingly endless inventory of articles in Ellin North Moale's house on Pratt Street included a half-dozen beds, four dozen chairs, and a large quantity of silver. In the absence of banks, money was invested in property.

The same wills that yield information about household goods provide clues to another type of property owned by Baltimore's wealthy women—human property. After dispensing with her sugar bowls and candlesticks, Mrs. Moale's will stipulated "that my mulatto woman Lydia shall not be sold—but choose which of my children to live with. . . . My negro woman Henny shall be given freedom at my death." Several other local women who owned slaves bequeathed them along with their furniture and jewelry to close friends and children.

By the census of 1790 there were 1,255 black slaves among Baltimore's 13,503 inhabitants. In that year, twenty-two Baltimore women were slaveowners and together they owned sixty-six slaves or .5 percent of the town's slave population. Several of these slaves were women. Nothing states quite so dramatically the vast differences in status among Baltimore's women as do the advertisements like the following by Mary Porter, in which one woman is literally selling another: "To be sold: a negro wench and three girls from three to eleven, a wagon, horses, hogs and cattle."

Female indentured servants were also common in early Baltimore. Though they would someday be free, while in bondage they were at the mercy of their masters and mistresses. Occasionally, a servant woman would be sold before her term expired. Curiosity-arousing notices like the following appeared with some regularity: "To be sold: a healthy servant girl with three and one-half years to serve. A good spinner. The reason why her time is to be sold the purchaser will be informed of. Inquire—John McCabe." Mr. McCabe was not very successful in selling his servant. His advertisement ran almost three months. One can only guess that the spinner's secret must have been a dastardly one.

Slave and servant women had almost no legal rights, but in this respect they were not unlike their married mistresses. Almost without exception, both rich and poor married women, the *femes covert*, were legal non-entities. The husband had the right physically to chastise his wife and had exclusive rights to any property she might have owned as a single woman, to her dower, and to any wages or property that might come to her while his wife. Only by the prenuptial contracts of the wealthy or specific provisions in wills could a married woman own anything at all.

Married women in Maryland could make no wills or valid contracts, nor could they sue or be sued. While in most colonies married women could conduct business in the courts as agents for their husbands, this right had been abruptly revoked in Maryland in 1658 by Governor

Fendall. Single women and widows, the *femes sole*, on the other hand, had considerable legal rights. They were considered competent enough to own land, enter into contracts and deeds, write wills, execute estates, bring suit, and be sued.

Local court and land records indicate that many of Baltimore Town's *femes sole* vigorously exercised all the rights and privileges to which they were entitled. The women of the prominent Fell family emerge from deeds and bills of sale as particularly shrewd land owners. Ann, Jannett, and Catherine Fell, daughters of William Fell, the founder of Fell's Point, each owned considerable acreage which they leased or sold in their own names at considerable profit. Their brother Edward died a young man and left behind his widow Ann to execute his very large estate and hold it in trust for their son, William. Though she soon remarried, by a prenuptial contract Mrs. Ann Fell Giles retained the right to manage the estate free from Mr. Giles's interference, and she passed it on to young William undiminished.

Several *femes sole* frequently appeared before the court of common pleas as defendants and plaintiffs in cases involving debts. Such women were generally the widows of middle-class tradesmen who, as executrixes, were trying to recoup debts owed to their late husbands. Gender apparently carried little weight with local judges. Every one of the women who brought suit for outstanding debts won her case. Similarly, every man who brought suit, even if against a woman, won his.

The docket of the criminal court reveals the more serious crimes with which local women were charged. Of all the women brought before this court, the female indentured servant was the most common. An early case was that of servant Elizabeth Green, convicted of arson for setting fire to Mr. William Bosley's corn crib and hen house. Though the crimes of the female indentured servants ranged from "uttering imparlances" to brawling in the streets, they were most often in court on charges of bastardy. Indeed, in the early years, such cases nearly overwhelmed all others.

The most common offense of non-servant women was running a "bawdy" or "disorderly" house and the companion charge of selling liquors without a license. Rebecca Hall was charged with four such counts in just one year. Other felonies with which such women were charged ranged from bigamy to horse thievery to receiving stolen goods. The women who committed these crimes were neither wealthy nor of high social standing. The names of the town's socially prominent women do not appear on felony records.

Though Baltimore's chronicles give the impression that the contributions made by local women were negligible, primary sources prove otherwise. Baltimore's women came in all varieties, each of which has made unique contributions to local culture. One important factor in determining the type of life the Baltimore woman would lead was her share, or, more accurately, her father's and husband's share, of worldly goods.

Aside from such tangible evidence of wealth as dress, diet, and the number and quality of household goods, the woman's desirability as a marriage partner, the quality of her life, and her own self-image were all determined by her place on the economic ladder. While all free married women, both rich and poor, were virtually legal non-entities and all women were politically powerless, life for the woman who was free, no matter what her social status, was very different from that of the woman in bondage. Superficially, one might wear brocades, while the other wore coarse linen. More significantly, one might own property, while the other was someone's property. We are just beginning to understand the woman's lot in Baltimore Town, and the social history of Maryland will be incomplete until we know more about the distaff side of the past in every region and period.

5

"Never Out of Step": Colonial New York

MILTON M. KLEIN

• Historians are generally great partisans of their own area of study. Whether it be a particular city, state, region, event, or individual, the historian almost invariably regards his subject as of major significance. And this desire seems to increase as the subject of one's labor becomes more narrowly defined, in part because the author must justify the importance of his topic not only to himself but also to his reader.

It is not surprising, therefore, that historians of specific regions like New England or the South hold up their own areas as the incubators of major American traditions and freedoms. What is surprising is that so few partisans have arisen for the colonies between those two areas—the present states of New York, New Jersey, and Pennsylvania.

The absence of Middle Colonies defenders is particularly unusual in view of the dominance of Philadelphia and New York City over American economic and cultural life after 1740. Prior to that time, Boston had been the first city of the New World, but the lack of a productive agricultural hinterland prevented the Massachusetts capital from competing effectively with her more southerly rivals. Nevertheless, most scholars have chosen to view colonial culture through the perspective of either "Southern agrarianism" or "New England" democracy. This neglect of the Middle Atlantic region exists not only in studies of colonial times but in works on subsequent periods as well. Even in the last quarter of the twentieth century, New York and Philadelphia continue to be ignored by most urban historians.

Professor Milton M. Klein of the University of Tennessee rectifies this neglect by examining in detail the pivotal role of the future "Empire State" before the American Revolution.

On every occasion of the anniversary of the founding of Jamestown or the landing at Plymouth, heated debate occurs—more often among amateur than among professional historians—as to which of these two events more properly marks the beginning of the American epic. On the 350th commemoration of the arrival of the *Susan Constant* and her sister ships, a southern partisan, Virginius Dabney, was especially vocal in raising the query: "Why have historians underrated the Virginia Fathers?" Justice for the Southern colonies, was his cry! New Englanders ignored the plea and arranged to have a reconstruction of the *Mayflower* brought to Plymouth on its 350th birthday. The "war" promises to be one of those unending historical conflicts. What I propose to do is not settle the question but confuse it further—by simply suggesting that we correct the myopia of both sides, reject the claims of each, and offer a new contender for the honor of initiating the American tradition: the Middle Colonies in general and New York in particular.

The early neglect of Americans in turning elsewhere than New York for their national image is not hard to understand. The American colonies were founded once by the first settlers, and as Wesley Craven has observed, the process was repeated over and over again as succeeding generations redrew the portrait of the founding fathers to suit their own moods. But whatever the angle of vision of these varying re-creations of the nature of our colonial origins, New York was ignored. A perceptive explanation of this neglect has been offered by two sociologists, in a recent book on New York City:

> History, or perhaps historians, keep passing New York by. . . . By preference, but also in some degree by necessity, America has turned elsewhere for its images and traditions. Colonial America is preserved for us in terms of the Doric simplicity of New England, or the pastoral symmetry of the Virginia countryside. . . . But who can summon an image of eighteenth-century New York that will still hold in the mind?

There are other explanations, historical and historiographical. The earliest American historians reflected the regional consciousness of New England and Virginia. Historical accounts of these geographic

From *New York History* 53 (April 1972): 132–56. Reprinted by permission of the New York State Historical Association, Cooperstown, New York, and of the author.

areas appeared within seventy-five years of their founding, even if "New England" was more often synonymous with Massachusetts and the term "Virginia" was broadly construed. The histories of the Southern colonies stressed the great achievement of the Virginia charters in bringing English liberties and common law to these shores at so early a date. New Englanders emphasized the divine Providence which had guided Pilgrims and Puritans and thereby set the providential tone for all future American development. New York's beginnings as a conquered province and the proprietary of the King's brother could stir few patriotic breasts and arouse little native emotion. As the Revolution approached, the polemicists of Boston and Williamsburg found solid precedent for their claims to English liberties in their first charters and in the images they created of their first settlers, whom they represented as early exponents of liberty and opponents of tyranny. New York had no such charter to cite as comparable example.

After independence, the earliest national histories joined Virginians and New Englanders as common progenitors of "the just and genuine principles" of the new republican society. Portraying our national origins as rooted in the rising of a free people, "not led by powerful families," and "under no general influence, but that of their personal feelings and opinions," who had already achieved a republican society before the separation from England, these historians steered clear of New York, with its aristocratic manor lords, great estates, and quasi-feudal tenantry as illustrations of the indigenous republican spirit. That New York was one of the least militant and most hesitant of the provinces in casting its vote for independence did not improve its standing with future historians from New England. William Gordon's *History*, published in 1789, specifically disavowed the role of New York, with its "party of aristocracy," in the glorious struggle against tyranny.

Local historians of New York did little to help its reputation. Washington Irving's *New York* was a caricature which infuriated the state's better citizenry. Thomas Jones's loyalist *History of New York*, appearing in 1879, proved no better, since it represented the province's "golden age" as those halcyon days of the mid-eighteenth century just before the evil triumvirate of Presbyterians and lawyers—William Livingston, William Smith, Jr., and John Morin Scott—began their conspiracy to turn the colony on its head by its agitation against church and state. When biography replaced history as the favorite literary medium for recalling the nation's heritage, again New York suffered. It had no heroes of the stature of Washington and Patrick Henry to eulogize.

In creating a "usable past" for a new people, the homogeneous English communities of New England and the South had far more appeal than New York's (or New Jersey's or Pennsylvania's) disordered, complex, heterogeneous population. Indeed, the more ethnically varied America became in the years that followed, the more attractive did Anglo-Saxon Jamestown and Plymouth appear to historians who themselves were disturbed by, and hostile to, the influx of masses of European immigrants from outside the British Isles or its northern neighbors. Thus, John Fiske, a convert to the theory of Teutonic origins of American democracy and of Aryan race supremacy, traced the roots of our political heritage from the primitive Saxons through the English middle class and then to America in the veins of Virginia Cavaliers and New England Puritans. A limited degree of heterogeneity was acceptable, since the English race had a "rare capacity for absorbing slightly foreign elements and molding them into conformity" with Anglo-Saxon political ideals. Hence, Fiske was prevented from rejecting the Dutch, Huguenots, Jews, Germans, and Scotch-Irish who comprised so much of the population of the Middle Colonies. It is quite clear, however, from Fiske's strong hostility to late nineteenth-century immigration—he was President of the Immigration Restriction League —that New York's mongrel people took only second place in his roll of proper Americans.

Even when the study of immigration was made professionally respectable by Marcus Lee Hansen, the focus was on the immigrants who peopled the rural Midwest, not those who crowded New York's urban ghettos. Popular rhetoric glorified the country as a melting pot of different peoples, but in actuality what was meant was the degree to which immigrants conformed to Anglo-Saxon characteristics.

Geography, also, had something to do with the neglect of the Middle Colonies. They could not be clearly defined, nor were the Middle Atlantic States much easier afterward. At times, British administrators simply swallowed up the middle region into the other two, using the term "Northern colonies" to include New England, New York, New

Jersey, and Pennsylvania. Cartographers confused the matter similarly. Lewis Evans, in his famous map of 1755, depicted the Middle Colonies as including everything from Virginia to Rhode Island! With the Middle Atlantic region undefinable physically, it is not surprising that historians failed to write about it. Except for Fiske's two volumes on the Dutch and Quaker colonies, published in 1899, nothing appeared on the subject until Wertenbaker's volume in his *Founding of American Civilization* series, in 1938; and no study of the Middle Atlantic States found its way into print until 1956.

Richard Shryock has raised the provocative question of whether historians have neglected the Middle Atlantic region—either as colonies or as states—because it does not exist or whether the region has been lost to view because historians have failed to write about it. One interesting suggestion he offers for the blurred focus of historians is that the inhabitants of the area have never developed the kind of regional self-consciousness which arises from the nursing of a grievance. Certainly there is nothing in Middle Atlantic history comparable to C. Vann Woodward's "Burden of Southern History"—the brooding sense of racial guilt and consciousness of military defeat. Nor is there evidence of anything like the anguished cry of an alienated social elite —such as David Donald's New England Abolitionists. In recalling its origins, the Middle Colonies could not draw upon the knowledge of a "starving time" which its first settlers had overcome by stubborn will or divine intervention. Nor could the Middle Colonies attribute the formation of their collective character to the forge of bitter encounters with savages during their earliest years. There were no counterparts to the New Englander's fierce conflicts with the Pequots and Narragansetts, in 1637 and 1675–76, nor to Virginia's Indian massacres of 1622 and 1644 in the recollection of New Yorkers and Pennsylvanians. Conflict with the Indians was not entirely absent in the history of these colonies, but the diplomatic skill of a Penn and the business acumen of the Dutch had secured a peace through trade and diplomacy which kept the Middle Colonies free from the worst horrors of Indian warfare—and made them the object of suspicion and envy. Economically, New York and its neighbors, by the eve of the Revolution, enjoyed so large a measure of prosperity that one historian offers this condition, along with the colonies' social and cultural diversity, as an explanation of their indecision for independence, in contrast to New

England and Virginia, whose impaired economic fortunes propelled them the more rapidly toward a separation which their socially homogeneous populations could be asked to accept.

Clearly, however, it was the urban character of the Middle Colonies, symbolized by the great cities of New York and Philadelphia, and their polyglot populations which played a major role in the historical amnesia of Americans, who preferred to remember their homogeneous, rural Arcadia even as it disappeared before their eyes. The paradox, of course, was that colonies like New York represented, in germinal form, the very nation that had come into existence by the late nineteenth century. The paradox is heightened by the discovery that the historian who, more than any other, was responsible for focusing the nation's attention on its rural West as the home of its distinctive traits of collective character should also have been the one to most emphatically stress the Middle Atlantic origins of those traits.

A year before his famous essay on the significance of the frontier, Frederick Jackson Turner directed the notice of historians to the "middle region" of the Atlantic coast and deplored the fact that it had "never been studied with the care due to its importance." With its wide mixture of nationalities, he noted, its varied society and economic life, its multiplicity of religions, and its mixed pattern of town and county government, the region between New England and the South represented for Turner "that composite" which was the America of 1892, even the patterns of its settlement reflecting the map of Europe in variety. The region was also "typical of the modern United States" in its ideas and ideals: democratic, national, easy, tolerant, and strongly materialistic. In the frontier address itself, Turner repeated his sentiments in more explicit fashion. It was the very non-Englishness of the middle region which made it "typically American." It "mediated" between East and West, between Puritan New England and the slaveholding South; and it was the least sectional of all the sections. The men of the frontier, whom Turner eulogized, "had closer resemblances to the Middle region than to either of the other sections."

The more Turner wrote about the West and on sectionalism, the more he seemed to return to the importance of the Middle Atlantic area. In two subsequent essays, he reiterated the prototypicality of the

Middle Colonies and States for their composite nationality and democratic social structure:

> The middle region was so complex in its composition that it had
> little social self-consciousness as a section. Nevertheless this re-
> gion of many nationalities, creeds, and industries became, during
> a considerable part of its history, a more characteristically demo-
> cratic region than any of the others. Tolerance of difference of
> opinion was pronounced, and, in the course of time, individual-
> ism and lack of social control became marked features of the
> section.

In a florid metaphor, Turner painted the West as a land of new "national hue," a composite coloration of all of its Eastern ingredients
and its local environment, but one section gave the distinctive tint to
the new color: "This section was the Middle Region." In the post-
humous volume *The United States, 1830–1850*, Turner again stressed
the special "national destiny" of the Middle Atlantic, its leadership by
1830 in urban growth, manufacturing, and shipping, its perfect reflection of the American "melting pot," and its pivotal role in the nation's
politics—all of which made it for him "typical of the deep-seated
tendencies of America in general."

One of Turner's colleagues, Woodrow Wilson, agreed that the region between New England and the South was more than merely a
blurred middle ground between two more important extremes. In out-
lining the course of American development, Wilson challenged the
notion that the country's history comprised the working out of Puritan
and Southern ideals, each striving for predominance. It was, in fact,
New York, New Jersey, and Pennsylvania which by their composite
character and origins presaged later complex America. Here, according
to Wilson, occurred the experiments that most resembled the methods
by which the American continent was peopled; in the Middle Atlantic
States, from the beginning, life reflected the pattern of living of the
nation itself.

Turner and Wilson were exceptional, and none of Turner's students except Carl Becker were attracted either to the Middle Colonies
or the Middle States as fields of research. Becker himself found trouble
blending the frontier thesis of his mentor into his own interpretation
of the urban origins of colonial democracy. For other American his-

torians, the very resemblance of the Middle Atlantic region to the nation as a whole produced a familiarity that bred only indifference, not scholarly attraction. Still others were baffled by the very qualities of life and culture in the Middle Colonies that did not set them apart from the rest of the nation. A region that appeared to be "everyman's" became "no man's" in literature and history.

Present-day historians undertaking to achieve a synthesis of the colonial period have yet to spell out New York's role satisfactorily. In the most recent such effort, Daniel Boorstin illustrates his underlying theme of practical adaptation by reference to the experiences of Massachusetts, Virginia, Pennsylvania, and Georgia. New York, despite its overridingly accommodative political and religious structure and its pragmatic society and culture, is unmentioned. The elements in synthesizing New York (and the Middle Colonies) into the stream of early American history are perfectly visible; and it is the purpose of this paper to point out some directions which such inquiry should logically take.

The central fact in the colony's history, so well observed even by historians who have slighted it, is the heterogeneity of its population. This circumstance arose from the nature of the colony's beginning as an English province, the absorption of some 10,000 residents of New Netherland. But the population had already developed a diversity under Dutch rule which adumbrated its later heterogeneity. There were in New Netherland—besides Hollanders—Walloons, Swedes, English, Norwegians, Germans, Scotch-Irish, and Negroes. The visiting Jesuit, Father Jogues, was astonished to be told in 1644 that eighteen languages were spoken in the province. This diversity was a cause for continued amazement by English officials and visitors, the substitution of English for Dutch rule doing nothing to improve the homogeneity of the colony's population. One traveler in 1760 abandoned any attempt to generalize about New Yorkers: "Being . . . of different nations, different languages and different religions, it is almost impossible to give them any precise or determinate character." On the eve of the Revolution, the population of the colony was estimated to be still only half English, making New York the most polygenetic of all the British dependencies in North America. The consequences of this diversity were enormous for the religious, political, and cultural life of the province, as it was for the later United States.

It is now clear that while this country can take credit for its faith in freedom of religion, the prize did not come as a free gift or as an act of love from our earliest forebears. The English came with established ideas of religious orthodoxy and conformity in their intellectual and spiritual baggage, nor was this heritage changed much by the New England Protestantism which Burke hailed as "the dissidence of dissent." Religious liberty was rather extorted step-by-step from an unwilling majority and accorded ultimately less out of commitment than as a result of social and economic necessity. Nowhere did the process evolve more typically than in New York. With its social complexity came religious diversity almost from the beginning. The domines of the Dutch Reformed Church were no more liberal in matters of religion than the spiritual representatives of the English conquerors. Toleration became the New Netherland way because of the pragmatic outlook of the Dutch West India Company. When crusty Peter Stuyvesant recommended, shortly after the arrival of the first Jews, that these "blasphemers of Christ" be barred from the colony, he was advised to allow them and the Lutherans, whom the Director-General found almost as objectionable, to "peacefully carry on their business" and to treat both sects "quietly and leniently." That Jews in Amsterdam reminded the company of the loyal support extended by their coreligionists in defense of the Dutch settlement in Brazil was helpful, but what was even more persuasive was the capital which Dutch Jews had invested in the company and the knowledge that the American plantation was underpopulated. "The more of loyal people that go to live there, the better it is in regard to the population of the country . . . and in regard to the increase of trade," the Amsterdam Chamber was reminded. So the Jews were permitted to stay and by struggle wrested from the government the right to a burial ground, exemption from Sabbath business laws and service in the militia.

When Stuyvesant, undaunted, turned his intolerance against Quakers, he prompted not only a stiffer rebuke from home but also evoked one of the most moving expressions of the principle of religious freedom in our history. With Quakers swarming over Long Island, the governor thought to hound them away by prohibiting the other inhabitants from admitting them into their homes. Whereupon thirty-one shocked residents of Flushing subscribed to the following remonstrance [on December 27, 1657]:

Right Honorable
You have been pleased to send up unto us a certain prohibition or command that we should not receive or entertain any of
those people called Quakers because they are supposed to be by
some seducers of the people. For our part we cannot condemn
them in this case neither can we stretch out our hands against
them to punish, banish, or persecute them, for out of Christ
God is a consuming fire, and it is a fearful [thing] to fall into
the hands of the living God.

We desire therefore in this case not to judge least we be
judged, neither to condemn least we be condemned, but rather
[to] let every man stand and fall to his own Master. We are
bound by the law to do good unto all men. . . . And though
for the present we seem to be unsensible of the law and the law
giver, yet when death and the Law assault us, if we have our advocate to seek, who shall plead for us in this case of conscience
betwixt God and our own souls. . . .

The law of love, peace and liberty in the states [extends] to
Jews, Turks, and Egyptians, as they are considered the sons of
Adam, which is the glory of the outward state of Holland. So
love, peace and liberty, extending to all in Christ Jesus, con-
demns hatred, war and bondage. . . . Our desire is not to of-
fend one of his little ones, in whatsoever form, name, or title
he appears in, whether Presbyterian, Independent, Baptist, or
Quaker, but shall be glad to see anything of God in any of them,
desiring to do unto all men as we desire all men should do unto
us, which is the true law both of Church and state. . . .

Therefore if any of these said persons come in love unto us,
we cannot in conscience lay violent hands upon them, but give
them free egress and regress into our town and houses, as God
shall persuade our consciences. . . .

Only the residents of today's Flushing, in Queens, appear to commemorate the eloquence of the town's founders and to render tribute
to the writers of one of the earliest statements on religious liberty of
such broad character in all of the colonies.

Stuyvesant's response was quick and expected. He arrested the
sheriff of Flushing who bore the remonstrance to him and dismissed
him from office. A few years later, he arrested and banished one of the
Quakers, John Bowne, who promptly went to Amsterdam to plead his
case. After much deliberation, the Amsterdam Chamber sent Stuyvesant another reminder of the practical value of religious toleration:

Although we heartily desire, that these and other sectarians remained away from there, yet as they do not, we doubt very much whether we can proceed against them rigorously without diminishing the population and stopping immigration, which must be favored at a so tender stage of the country's existence. You may therefore shut your eyes, at least not force people's consciences, but allow everyone to have his own belief, as long as he behaves quietly and legally, gives no offence to his neighbors and does not oppose the government. As the government of this city has always practised this maxim of moderation and consequently has often had a considerable influx of people, we do not doubt that your Province too would be benefitted by it.

It was the "maxim of moderation" which became the practice of English New York, as well, not because policy so dictated but because circumstances compelled it. The assumption of English control did not homogenize the colony's religious complexion. "There are religions of all sorts," complained Governor Andros in 1678. A few years later, another governor was more caustic: he found thirteen denominations in the province, "in short of all sorts of opinions there are some," but for the most part, there were "none at all." In Pennsylvania and New Jersey, the absence of an established church reflected the intention of their founders; in New York, the indeterminate character of the Anglican Church developed from the complexity of the colony's population. The first proprietor, the Duke of York, granted religious toleration as a recognition of this diversity and of the need to pursue moderate policies if trade and profits were to be promoted. In any case, the Articles of Capitulation by which the Dutch surrendered specified that the Reformed Church should remain undisturbed. The first English governor, Richard Nicolls, went further, providing that the majority of the population in any town could establish a public church but that other congregations should be permitted to conduct their own services. The prescription was repeated to Andros after the reacquisition of the province from the Dutch in 1674 and was incorporated in the Charter of Liberties drawn up in 1683.

The Glorious Revolution, which advanced the cause of religion in England by the Toleration Act, actually represented a backward step for New York. The province had already gone beyond the notion of one public church and second-class concessions to Dissenters. New

Yorkers had come to see "the necessity of leaving religion to each man's conscience in the interest of getting on." The feeble effort during the remainder of the colonial period to elevate the Anglican Church in status proved a failure. A Ministry Act of 1693 provided for public support of "a good sufficient Protestant Minister" in the four lower counties, but this is as close as the colony ever got to a church establishment; and the effort to interpret the law as an exclusive benefit to the Anglican Church was vigorously opposed by New York's many Dissenters. If the law of 1693 established any church, as Clinton Rossiter observed facetiously, "no one was quite sure what church it was."

What developed in the province of New York was neither a clear separation of church and state nor a well-defined state church. In communities where non-Anglicans were in a majority, the proceeds of the Ministry Act could be used to support dissenting churches; in New York City, where the diversity of religions was most pronounced, the principle of voluntarism was followed. Ministers of the Anglican and Dutch churches continued to lament the "spirit of confusion" that resulted from New York's "perfect freedom of conscience," where everybody could "do what seems right in his own eyes, so long as he does not disturb the public peace." New York's churchgoers were always more latitudinarian than their ministers. They were not strict in keeping the Sabbath, as one dismayed Bostonian discovered in 1704; and among the Dutch, even in Albany, where the domines ministered to a population that was largely Dutch, there was very little religion, as another visitor noted in 1744, and "not a grain" of enthusiasm. Some New Yorkers saw virtue in the colony's confusion of religious voices: "the Variety of Sects" in the province was "a Guard against the Tyranny and Usurpation of one over another." Even the Deists, it was claimed, served a useful purpose by forcing casual Christians to reexamine the tenets of their own faith.

Well before the Great Awakening constrained other colonists to recognize the danger of church establishments to their own new programs of spiritual regeneration, well before Isaac Backus and the Separatist Baptists preached the cause of religious voluntarism, and years before Jefferson expressed his fear of the danger to civil peace of state control of religion, New Yorkers had learned in the crucible of day-to-day living in a multifarious society the value of a neutral state which permitted creeds to compete for the spiritual affection of the citizenry. In New York, competition had strengthened freedom, not atheism; and the "natural right" of religious liberty was supported not by political theory so much as by long experience. Prejudice and mutual religious suspicions were not exorcised by the New York accommodation. Germans and Dutch eyed each other with distrust in the Mohawk Valley as did Presbyterians and Anglicans in New York City, but the state was not expected to create love, only harmony. Its role was neither to force its own orthodoxy on others nor to allow any denomination to try to do so. Its jurisdiction in religious matters was legitimate, as one of the colony's most vigorous polemicists put it, only when denominational opinion was converted into "Actions prejudicial to the Community," and then it was not the opinion but the action which was punishable. New York entered the republic with a model to offer its neighbors which gave the lie to the sectarian argument that diversity bred only religious strife and immorality.

Tolerance in New York, as in the other colonies and in the future United States, had its limits; and the outer edge was passed where blacks were concerned. If racial violence is as American as cherry pie, then New York was typically American in this ugly respect, too, setting an example by its harsh repression of blacks suspected of crimes that were magnified in the public mind largely by the color of the perpetrators. Slavery in New York was more humane under the Dutch than under the English, resulting from a peculiar practice of granting Negroes half-freedom as well as freedom, while others were held in bondage. No clear institutionalization of slavery could be developed midst such confusion; and none was. Under the English, slavery expanded so that there were more bondsmen in New York than in any other northern colony; and one of the concomitants of the increase was the most severe violence against Negroes of any of the colonies. In 1712 nineteen blacks were executed after an uprising in which about two dozen fired a building and killed five whites. The reprisals were grisly; the forms of execution included burning, starvation, and use of the medieval wheel. In 1741 a far more imaginary plot resulted in a witch hunt comparable in blind savagery to that at Salem a half-century earlier. The reprisals this time included eighteen Negroes hanged, thirteen burned at the stake, and seventy-one deported.

What is prototypical about the racial violence is not so much the severity of the punishment as the confusion of the white population. It had learned cosmopolitanism as a way of life but had never fitted the black man into this scheme of accommodation. Unwilling or unable to enlarge their vision of diversity beyond the color line, white New Yorkers responded with a rationale that was to become more familiar in the succeeding century: The colony's slaves were treated with "great indulgence" and were better cared for than were the poor in Europe; those who had participated in the "villainous plot" were exceptional, and their "senseless" and "wicked enterprise" must be attributable to their seduction by the Devil. Even in the twentieth century, northern, urban cosmopolitanism proved to be no guarantor of color blindness. Indeed, race prejudice was to become worse in the very centers of ethnic diversity which bred tolerance for whites. Colonial New York mirrored the national disease.

On the more favorable side, New York's slaves were employed not in gangs on great estates but in a variety of crafts, trades, and domestic service, ameliorating their lot to that extent and providing them with skills for freedom. And the colony appears to have produced America's earliest black poet, one Jupiter Hammon, whose first work appeared in 1760 but whose name and verse disappeared thereafter from the pages of our color-conscious histories. Colonial New York's failure, like that of other colonies, was not that it neglected to cultivate the talents of its black men but that it made no provision for employing those talents after slavery ended.

To pursue in similar detail other evidences of New York's prototypicality in the American colonies would go beyond the confines of a paper intended to be no more than suggestive. The illustrations are numerous enough to provide grist for many doctoral mills. New York, it is said today, is not the United States; yet many Europeans think it is. So in the eighteenth century, New York somehow conveyed the impression of its typicality. The city's shipping was well below that of the other colonial seaports, but Peter Kalm, the Swedish naturalist, visiting in 1750, was sure that New York's commerce was more extensive than that of any other place in British North America. New York was not the largest city in the colonies in the 1760s—Philadelphia exceeded it by 5,000—but the visiting Lord Adam Gordon was surprised to discover the fact on his arrival. The city of New York, he commented, had "long been held at home, the first in America." When that adopted American, Crèvecoeur, raised the question of what an American was, the answer he gave in a nation still almost three-quarters English was that "they are a mixture of English, Scotch, Irish, French, Dutch, Germans, and Swedes." From his observation post in Orange County, New York, he had made of the "new man" he saw in that colony the larger American. The misimpressions may have been the result of sheer ignorance, but it is curious how already New York was taken to be the image of greater America.

Colonial New York can boast of its firsts: the first school supported by public funds, although under church control, and now the oldest private school in the country with a continuous existence (the Collegiate School in New York City); the first chamber of commerce not organized under governmental auspices; the first play to be written and printed in America—the farce, *Androborus*, written by Governor Robert Hunter and presented in 1714; the first licensing of doctors, in New York City in 1760; the first legislative proceedings to be printed in any of the colonies, in 1695, at least fifteen years before any of its neighbors followed suit; as well as the enrichment of American popular culture by such Dutch innovations as Santa Claus, New Year's Eve celebrations, ten-pin bowling; words such as skipper, sloop, and yacht; culinary delights like crullers and cookies and waffles; political terms like boss and boodle; and inimitable place names like Brooklyn, Harlem, and the Catskills.

Apart from the boost to local pride, firsts are probably of less significance than New York's seconds—or thirds. When the province did not lead, it was not very far behind. Culture was not New York's forte, since the "Art of getting Money" seemed to be the provincial preoccupation and, as Cadwallader Colden viewed it, "the only principle of life propagated among the young People"; but a corps of the province's young intellectuals tried hard in the mid-eighteenth century to compensate for the defect. Philadelphia organized its first philosophical society in 1743; five years later, New York City had a "Society for the Promotion of Useful Knowledge." In 1731, the Quaker City organized a public library; three years later, the Corporation of New York City was operating one with a librarian paid out of public monies (the salary was three pounds a year but was raised to four pounds after three years). The Philadelphians established the colonies' first hospital; New York was responsible for the second. The first medical school was opened in Philadelphia in 1765; New York began the second within three years. Boston had an informal medical society in 1736; New York followed—thirteen years later. The Bay City had a legal discussion group operating in 1765; New York had a larger, better organized, and more professional one—the Moot—five years later. New Yorkers were rarely in the van, but their cultural aspirations always exceeded their grasp. When the New York Society Library was organized in 1754, the elaborate bookplate prepared for its volumes depicted New York City as the Athens of America!

New York's evening schools were not the only ones in the colonies, but by the Revolution the province had more of them than any of its neighbors. Philadelphia's Academy (later College) was the first institution of higher education in the colonies that was strictly secular in purpose and character; but when King's College was founded in 1754, a group of New York's intellectuals fought hard to make that province's equally secular. The effort failed, but the arguments for state control of education advanced in that controversy inspired the post-Revolutionary creation of the University of the State of New York, a model followed by other states similarly committed to the proposition that the supervision of education was the proper business of the public.

New York's press was not as numerous as those of either Massachusetts or Pennsylvania—although not far behind; but in the twenty-two newspapers published at one time or another between 1725 and 1776 appeared some of the most lively and contentious political literature of all the colonial presses. Withal, the literary output of the Middle Colonies exhibited the kind of balance to which Turner had alluded. Of the South's literary productions during the period 1638–1783, more than half comprised statutes, laws, and executive proclamations. New England's output during this same period was preponderantly theological. The press of the Middle Colonies shows a remarkable balance of interests among the fields of politics, law, theology, education, social science, and literature. If this analysis represents accurately the intellectual interests of the three sections, the Middle Colonies were truly the mediators between the two outer extremes.

The shape of the colonial economy of the Middle Atlantic region has yet to be drawn accurately, but even by rough and ready yardsticks, it was more varied, more stable, and less dependent upon single staples or industries than either of the other two regions. Agriculture in New York, as in Pennsylvania, was not a supplementary activity wrung from a barren soil to assist in supporting a trading population but was rather interlaced with trade, New York City providing the outlet for the products of the colony's farms. New York's paper money was better managed and less inflated than the currency of any of the colonies for which adequate statistics are available. The trade of the Middle Colonies reflects the mediating character of which Turner had written. In contrast with the South's dominantly bilateral and New England's heavily triangular trade patterns, the commerce of the middle region was partly triangular but more largely direct with Europe. Conceivably, this was at the root of the region's prosperity on the eve of the Revolution and explains its hesitation in drawing the sword against England.

The French and Indian War provided New York with the largest boost to its economy, headquartering the British Army as it did, but the war points up even more the strategic and diplomatic significance of New York in the colonial and imperial structure. When Herbert L. Osgood wrote his four-volume *American Colonies in the Eighteenth Century*, he felt compelled to apologize in the preface for the extensive treatment given to New York. But, he explained, the four volumes dealt heavily with the Anglo-French Wars and, "of course, in all military relations in which Canada was involved New York was the strategic centre of the colonial territory. In a period of wars, therefore, it necessarily holds a prominent place, while in all that pertained to Indian relations its position was a leading one." "Of course," indeed! What is surprising in Osgood's volumes is not the attention paid to New York but the need of an explanation for doing so. New York was the pivot of empire. It was the only colony in which British regular troops were stationed throughout virtually the entire colonial period. The four independent companies were woefully neglected, it is true, but their mere presence was symbolic of Whitehall's recognition of the strategic importance of New York and of its alliance with the Iroquois. It was on the New York frontier that the rivalry between France and England was pursued most enduringly during the eighteenth century; and it was from New York's militant imperialists—Robert Livingston, Cadwallader Colden, Archibald Kennedy, James Alexander, William Livingston, and William Smith—that Britain received the most repeated suggestions for strengthening the Empire and turning it to the mutual benefit of colonies and mother country. It was in New York, significantly, that the most serious attempt to produce a colonial union was made; and the interest of both the colony's leaders and British officials was prompted by their recognition of the crucial role which New York, its Indian connections, and its fur trade bore in the imperial framework. And it was in New York, as the strategic center of empire, that the British Post Office in North America established its headquarters and to which it organized its packet service from England, in 1755, in order to provide the Crown with "early and frequent intelligence" of what was "in agitation" in its American colonies.

Finally, there is politics, which in New York almost defies comprehension in the colonial period as it does today. The nature of New York's political structure and the mechanisms by which it operated are still being debated; but a number of conclusions seem acceptable even to the most contentious historians. There was no simple oligarchy of home-grown aristocrats; no politically mute masses; no clearly discernible clash between democrats and aristocrats, conservatives and radicals. What emerges is a complex, dynamic, and, in part, sophisticated preformation of the later political scene. Political factions reflected the heterogeneity of the colony's economy, its ethnic and religious composition, its geographic sectionalism, and its social structure. Parties were broad coalitions, and programs were necessarily diffuse enough to appeal to the colony's cosmopolitan population, often in a variety of languages. If there was deference, there was also democracy. If there was aristocracy, there was also public accountability. If there were family rivalries, there were also popular issues. If there were local concerns, there were also Anglo-American interests. If there was social stratification and monopoly of office-holding, there was also mobility and considerable rotation in office. If there was Whig ideology imported from England, there was also the uniquely American idiom in which it was couched by provincial politicians to suit the colony's special political dynamic. If the articulate were spokesmen of conservatism and status, there were also inarticulate believers in liberty and equality.

Even before the returns are in and while the historians still debate, one may hazard the proposition that the infrastructure of New York's politics was for more complex and interesting than its superstructure, and that the intensity of dialogue disclosed in the polemical literature flowing from the New York presses did not camouflage a mere shadow system of politicking. There surely must have been a contest over who should rule at home, but we are not yet certain who the contestants were or just what they wanted or whether they were always the same people or were consistent in their objectives. Somehow, New Yorkers learned during the colonial period to play the game of politics in the style which conditions dictated that later America should play it and which a future America came to expect. Somehow, its inhabitants learned to be, as a confused Henry Adams put it in 1899, "democratic by instinct" despite the colony's aristocratic tone. Perhaps the clue is provided by J. H. Plumb's astute observation concerning eighteenth-century English politics, that it was "always richer, freer, more open than the oligarchical nature of its institutions might lead one to believe." In those days neither suffrage nor even elections were at the heart of politics, Plumb says, but rather decision-making and "the turmoil they aroused" and the steady growth of "political consciousness."

New York's colonial experience validates the conclusion perfectly. By 1775, New Yorkers were accustomed to what the country would become so adept in during the years ahead. Only a non-New Yorker could be astonished to hear in New York City, on the eve of the Revolution, nothing but "Politics, politics, politics! . . . Men, women, children, all ranks and professions mad with Politics."

When an English visitor in 1800 said of the Middle States that they seemed "never out of step in the national march," always about to become or being what the rest of the country was, he cast the region in its proper role. The role had already been played out while the states were still colonies. As for New York, that amateur historian Theodore Roosevelt may have been more perspicacious than he intended when he wrote in his little history of New York in 1891: "The most important lesson taught by the history of New York City is the lesson of Americanism."

6

Roots: Search for an Ancestor

ALEX HALEY

• Many years ago the black poet Langston Hughes asked, "What is Africa to me?" The significance of Africa to black Americans has not been constant. Africa is the homeland, the point of origin. Yet throughout the eighteenth and nineteenth centuries Africa was considered by white America an unknown and barbaric continent. It was difficult, therefore, for American blacks to feel proud of their ancient homeland. True, there were some blacks who looked to Africa as a place of refuge and possible resettlement, but most plans to send blacks back to Africa in the nineteenth century originated with whites eager to eliminate the black population and avoid the problems of how the two races could live together. In the twentieth century two notable blacks, W. E. B. DuBois, an intellectual of outstanding caliber, and Marcus Garvey, a charismatic, popular leader of the 1920s, encouraged their fellow blacks to be proud of the historical connection with Africa. Later on in the century, members of the black power movement of the 1960s, inspired by the all-black leadership in the newly independent African states, donned dashikis and wore Afros and, at a deeper level, looked with new interest at the historical connection of their lives to the African past.

Alex Haley shows in this article how one man embarked on a personal quest for his origins in the remote African past of his ancestors. Reading more like an adventure story than a research report, Haley's article describes how a few African words passed down through generations in his family led him to the very African village where his forebears lived before he was sold into slavery. Haley's effort is heartening, not only as one man's search for his historical roots but also because it offers both inspiration and method for further research into the history of American blacks which for too long has been cut off from the richness of its African past.

From *The Listener* (January 10, 1974), pp. 43–47.

I grew up in a little town called Henning, Tennessee, about fifty miles west of Memphis, and I lived there in the home of my grandmother, my mother's mother. Every summer my grandmother would have visitors come to our home. They would be older women of the family, her nieces, aunts and cousins, and every single evening that I can remember, they would sit out on the front porch in rocking-chairs, and I would sit behind my grandmother's rocking-chair and listen to them talking. They would tell about things that had happened to the family when they had been slaves, and they went back and back and back. The furthest-back person they would ever talk about was someone they described as "the African," and they would tell how this African had been brought on a ship to a place they pronounced as "Napalis." They told how he had been bought off that ship by a man whose name was John Waller, who had a plantation in a place called Spotsylvania County, Virginia, and they told how the African had kept trying to escape. The first three times he escaped he was caught, brought back, given a worse beating each time, and then, the fourth time he escaped, he had the misfortune to be caught by a professional slave-catcher. I have since done some peripheral research on the profession of slave-catching and I think there's never been a more bestial one in the United States. This particular man brought the African back, and it was decided on the spot that he would be given a punishment at the decision of the slave-catcher. I grew up hearing how the slave was offered the punishment either of being castrated or of having a foot cut off. He chose the foot, and it was cut off with an axe against a tree stump. It was a very hideous act and as it turned out it was to play a major role in keeping the African's story alive in a black family. In the middle of the 1700s, slaves, particularly male slaves, were sold back and forth so frequently that there was very little sense of family continuity among them. In that part of Virginia they were sold at auction and, on the average, each would bring around eight dollars. At the end of every slave auction there would be what they called a "scrap sale": slaves who were ill, or otherwise incapacitated, would bring in smaller amounts, generally one dollar or less. When this particular slave managed to survive and then to convalesce, he posed an economic question to his master: slavery, after all, was an economic matter. Although he was crippled and hobbled around, he could do limited work around the house and yard-area of the plantation, so the master decided he would be worth more kept to do this limited work than he would be just sold away for less than one dollar in cash. And so he was kept on one plantation for what turned out to be quite a long period of time.

On that plantation, this slave met and mated with another slave. My grandmother and the others said that she was named Belle, the Big House cook, and of that union was born a little girl, who was given the name Kissy. When Kissy got to be four or five, and could begin to understand things, this African, whenever he got a chance, would take her by the hand (he knew her to be his daughter, she knew him to be her father—an unusual thing in slavery at that point) and lead her round the plantation. He would point out to her various natural objects and tell her the names for them in his native tongue: some sounds for *tree, rock, cow.* In the slave-cabin area, he would point out a banjo or a guitar and he would say one syllable, *ko,* and in time the little girl came to associate the sound *ko* with a banjo or a guitar. On the outer edges of the plantation there was a small river, and when they were out in that area, he would say to her something like *Kamby-Bolongo,* and the little girl came to know that this sound meant river.

All the Africans who were brought to the United States as slaves gradually learned a word here, a phrase there, of the new language, English. As this began to happen with this particular African, he would tell his daughter more involved things, little anecdotes about himself. He seemed to have a passion for trying to communicate to her a sense of his past. For instance, he would tell her how he had been captured. He told her he had not been far away from his village, chopping wood, when he had been set upon by four men, kidnapped and taken into slavery. The first thing that happened to slaves when they got to a plantation was that they were given an Anglicised name: that was the first step in the psychic dehumanisation of an individual—the removal from that individual of the name he had carried all his life, with which went, as it goes for us today, the sense of who we are. The master had given this African the name of "Toby" but, whenever any of the other slaves used the word "Toby," he would strenuously reject it and tell them his name was Kin-Tay.

Kissy stayed directly exposed to her father from Africa until she was 16 years old. She had quite a considerable repertoire of knowledge about him, when she herself was sold away to a man named Tom Lea who had a much smaller plantation in North Carolina. It was on that plantation that Tom Lea became the father of Kissy's first child, a boy who was given the name of George. When George got to be about four or five, Kissy began to tell him the things she had learned from her father. Among the other slave children, his peers, he began to run into the common phenomenon that slave children rarely knew who their fathers were. He had something that made him singular: he had direct knowledge of a grandfather. The boy grew up and, when he got into his teens, became a gamecock fighter: that was a great sport in the Ante-Bellum South. When he was about seventeen, he gained the nickname that he would take to his grave—"Chicken George."

When he was about eighteen, Chicken George took a mate, another slave, whose name was Matilda, and in time Matilda gave birth to seven children. On another plantation, a generation later, in another section of North Carolina, Chicken George would tell his children the story which had come down from his mother Kissy. Those children grew up, took mates and had children. One of them was named Tom. He became an apprentice blacksmith and was sold to a man named Murray who had a tobacco plantation in Alamance County, North Carolina. He met and mated with a slave whose name was Irene, the weaver on the plantation, and she bore him seven children. Tom the blacksmith would tell his seven children about something virtually unique among the slaves: direct knowledge of a great-great-grandfather. The youngest of his seven children was a little girl whose name was Cynthia, and Cynthia was to become my maternal grandmother. That was how it happened that I grew up in my grandmother's home in Tennessee, hearing from her that story which had passed down the family about all the rest of the family going back to that African who said his name was Kin-Tay, who called the river *Kamby-Bolongo*, and the guitar *ko*, and who said he had been chopping wood when he was captured. By the time I was in my mid-teens, I knew this story pretty well, having heard it for fully a decade.

I went to school briefly at small black land-grant colleges around the South where my father was teaching, and when World War Two came along I went into the U.S. Coastguard. It was the time when if you were black and you went into one of the Naval Services in the United States, you went into the Stewards' Department. You were mess-boy, you cleaned up the state rooms, waited on tables, washed the dishes, and, if you did well, advanced to cook. I became cook on a ship in the southwest Pacific during the war. It was boring. We would be put to sea for two or three months at a time before we could get ashore in Australia or New Zealand. My most precious possession was a portable typewriter. I had learned to type when I was in high school, and I would write letters to everybody I could think of: I would get thirty or forty letters at a time, simply because I wrote so much. Then I began trying to write marine dramas, sea stories. They didn't sell for a long time, but I kept writing for eight years, until finally a small magazine began to buy some of my stories. I stayed on in the Service, began to write for somewhat larger magazines, and finally, when I was 37, I retired from the Coastguards with 20 years service. At that time, something happened that seems to me to have been the first of a series of miracles that were to make it possible to pull together a document, a book of which I am now at the finishing stages, having to do in an unusual way with black history, black culture, black pride, relating to the whole area of blackness in Africa and the United States and the continuities.

The first thing that happened could scarcely have seemed to have less to do with blackness. *Playboy* asked me if I would fly over to London to do an interview with a film actress, Julie Christie. There were long gaps when I couldn't get to see her. One morning I was in the British Museum, and I came upon the Rosetta Stone. I had read how the French scholar, Champollion, had matched the unknown characters on the stone with the Greek, and had finally been able to prove that the demotic and the hieroglyphics had the same text as the Greek. That fascinated me: I would go round in London doing other things, but I would find my mind going back to that Rosetta Stone.

I was on a plane going back to the United States when an idea hit me. What Jean Champollion really did was to match the unknown with the known, and so find the meaning of what hitherto had been unknown. In that story always told in our family there had been a language: the sounds that this African always said when he pointed to different objects. Obviously, many sounds would have been lost in the transmission down the generations, but I could see that the sounds which had survived tended to be hard, angular sounds of the sort that would survive: like *ko*, Kin-Tay, *Kamby-Bolongo*. They had to be fragments of some native tongue. Could I possibly find out where these sounds had come from? My research assistant George Simms, came up with a list of people who were very knowledgeable in the field of African linguistics. One of them was at the University of Wisconsin. His name was Doctor Jan Vansina. He had been trained in his native Belgium, and then at the University of London's Oriental and African Studies department. He had worked in Africa, living in African villages, and had written a book called *The Oral Tradition*. In the Vansinas' living-room that evening I told Dr Vansina everything I could remember from the time I was a little boy: every bit of the stories, the sounds, the names of the people, the chronology of the family. As an oral historian, he was particularly interested in the physical transmission of the story from one generation to another. The following morning, Dr Vansina came down with a very serious expression on his face. I learned that he had already been on the phone to knowledgeable colleagues of his. He said that they felt that the greatest possibility was that the sounds represented the Mandinka dialect. I had never heard of such a thing as Mandinka. From his knowledge of it, he began to guess-translate what those sounds had meant. There was a sound that probably meant the *beobab tree*, generic in West Africa: there was a sound that probably meant *cow*. I heard about something that could be said to look like a banjo, an instrument called the *kora*, well-known where Mandinka was spoken. Finally, we came to *Kamby-Bolongo*: I heard that in Mandinka *bolongo* would mean *river* or *stream*. Preceded by *Kamby*, very probably it would mean *Gambia River*. I tend to be, if something hits me just right, very impulsive. It was Thursday morning when I heard the words *Gambia River*. On Monday morning I was in Africa.

On the Friday morning, I had looked among the names of African students in the United States. From that small country, the Gambia, the one I found who was physically closest to where I was was a fellow called Ebon Manga, attending Hamilton College at Clinton, New York. I hit that campus around 3.30, Friday afternoon, and practically snatched Ebon Manga out of an economics class. We got onto a Pan-American that night and flew to Dakar. From there we got a light plane and flew over to Yanda, near Bathurst. We took a van into Bathurst. Ebon and his father helped to assemble a group of about eight members of the Gambian Government, mature men who met me in the patio of the Hotel Atlantic in Bathurst. There I sat with them, telling them the stories that had been passed down. It gives me the quivers sometimes when I reflect how tissue-thin have been the hinges upon which this whole adventure has swung at one time or another. What these men in the Gambia reacted to most was a sound which I had no idea had any particular meaning. They said: "There may be great significance in the fact that your forefather said his name was Kin-Tay. In our country, our older villages are often named from the families which founded those villages centuries ago." And they showed me a little map, with names of villages like Kinte-Kundah Janneh-Ya. They also told me about men of whom I had never heard called *griots*, who were like walking, living archives. A line of *griots* would know the history of one village, they told me, or of one large family clan. They told me that they would look about to see what *griot* might be able to help me.

I went back to the United States. About six weeks later, a letter came to me from the Gambia saying that when I was able it might be worth-while for me to return—as casually as that. In about a week I was back in Bathurst. The same men with whom I had talked at the Atlantic Hotel told me that the word had been put out in the back-country, and a *griot* knowledgeable about the history of the Kinte clan had been found. "Where is he?" I asked. I would have figured, from my experience as an American magazine writer, that the Government should have had him there with a public relations man for me to talk to. They said: "He's in his village." In order to see this man, I had to get together a total of 14 people, three of which were interpreters, and four musicians—they told me that, in the back-country, the *griots* wouldn't talk without music in the background.

Mud walls, conical-roofed huts, thatched roofs: there were only about seventy people in the village. As soon as I saw a man, I knew somehow that he was the man we had come to see. Small of build with a pill-box hat and off-white robe: I was later to learn that his name was Kebba Kanga Fofana. The interpreter with me went straight to him. Meanwhile I had stepped into a succession of events that were almost traumatic in their emotional effect upon me. First, the people, about seventy of them, crowded very closely around me. I began to notice how they were staring at me. Their brows were forward and the intensity of the eyes was just raking. It was as if they wanted to know me in corpuscular detail. I dropped my eyes: I had this sensation of looking at my own hands, my own complexion, and I had a tremendous feeling within me, like a gale-force wind. I was looking at a crowd of people and, for the first time in my life, everybody in the crowd was jet-black in colour. That just hit me like a sledge-hammer. And then, I had this second sledgehammer-type feeling: a kind of guilt, a feeling of being hybrid, of being impure among pure. Then the old man, Kebba Kanga Fofana, began to tell me, through the interpreters, the history of the Kinte clan.

Griots can talk for hours on end, telling the stories they have learned. Every now and then when the *griot* was spilling out lineage details of who married whom, who had what children and in what order, a couple of centuries ago, he would stop: a translation would come of some little detail about an individual—for example, that in the year of the Big Water he slew a water buffalo. Kebba Kanga Fofana said that the Kinte clan had begun in the country called Old Mali, and a branch of the clan had moved into Mauretania. In Old Mali, the clan had been characterized by the men being blacksmiths as a rule; the women were habitually potters and weavers. There had come out of Mauretania a son of the clan whose name was Kairaba Kunta Kinte. He came from Mauretania to the country of the Gambia. He stopped first in a village called Pakali N'Ding. He went next to a village called Jiffarong, and then to a village called Juffure. It was in Juffure that he took his first wife, a Mandinka maiden whose name was Sireng. By her he begot two sons whose names were Janneh and Saloum. Then he took (Moslem men, plural marriages) a second wife. Her name was Yaisa, and by Yaisa he begot a son whose name was Omoro.

The three sons grew up in the village of Juffure, and when they came of age the older two, Janneh and Saloum, went away and founded a new village called to this day Kinte-Kundah Janneh-Ya. The young-est son, Omoro, stayed there until he had 39 rains; and at the age of 30 rains he took a wife whose name was Binta Kebba. Between 1750 and 1760, there were born four sons to Omoro and Binta Kebba: Kunta, Lamin, Suwadu and Madi. When he named those four brothers, the old man stopped and the interpreter said: "about the time the King's soldiers came." That was one of the time-fixing references which *griots* use. Later, in London, I found the British Parliamentary records, be-cause I had to know the date. He was talking about a group called Colonel O'Hare's Forces, which had been sent from London to the

Gambia River to guard the then British-held fort, James Slave Fort, and the date was right on.

Then Kebba Kanga Fofana said: "About the time the King's soldiers came, the eldest of these four sons, Kunta, went away from this village to chop wood, and he was never seen again." I sat there with goose-pimples the size of lemons popping over me. He had no way of knowing that what he had told me meshed with what I had heard as a little boy on the front porch of my grandmother's home in Tennessee.

I suddenly became aware that the people of the village had formed a circle and were moving counter-clockwise around me. They were chanting: up, down, loud, soft. I had been sitting on a chair, and I popped up as if I had been full of helium. All I could do was stand up. Then there came the music that was always in the background. I remember my ears slowly becoming aware that I was hearing sounds I had to recognize from a *kora* player, who was singing. I was hearing in a way I could understand. I could distinguish the words "Alex Haley." I could understand Kinte. I didn't know then that, in the way of *griots*, my having come to that village, my having been found to be a descendant of that village, was there and then being recorded as part of the village's history. They carried me into the mosque, and there was a prayer. It was translated as: "Praise be to Allah for one lost long from us whom God has returned."

We finally had to go back. I had to return to America and, on the road going out, I was full of the emotion of it. We got to the first village, and I saw people lined up on either side of the road. The people in this village already knew what had happened in the village of Juffure. As we came close with the Land-Rover, the driver slowed down, and I was looking down at these people standing on either side waving, a great cacophony of sound coming out of them, from wizened elders to little naked youngsters. I thought it was nothing but caprice: they were there, never having left Africa, and I, symbolizing to them all of us in America, happened to be standing up in there simply because of the caprice—which of our forefathers had been taken out. That was the only thing which had made the difference. Then I gradually became aware what the sound was they were crying out: "Mr Kin-Tay, Mr Kin-Tay." I'm a man, but a sob rolled up from foot-level, and I just flung up my hands and cried as I never had in my life. It seemed to me that if you knew the story of how the black people in

America had come there, taken as slaves from all those countries, and you knew the continuity of us as a people, then, whatever else you might do, you really needed to start by weeping, because there were no words and no actions which could ever assuage what had happened in that terrible time in the history of both countries.

That's the saga of the black people in America, and I had to write it. I had to know everything I could to put into this book. I wanted to find, if I could, the symbolic boat that, it is said, brought 1,500,000 of our forefathers to the USA. To be the proper ship, it had to be the one that brought Kunta-Kinte out of the Gambia River. I knew now about the time "the King's soldiers had come," and I had found that Colonel O'Hare's Forces were his reference. I knew that it had happened in mid-1767. I went to Lloyds of London and I got help from them with the marine records of the 1700s. I searched for seven weeks. One afternoon in the Public Records Office, I was on the 123rd set of slaveship records when I found a sheet with 30 ships' movements on it. Number 18 was moving out of Gambia River, James Fort. Number 18 was a ship that had stated her destination as Annapolis, Maryland. I knew that Kunta-Kinte had been taken to Annapolis.

In the next ten days I crossed the Atlantic Ocean three times, patching together little things I had to find out about that ship. I found she was called the *Lord Ligonier*, named after a British field-marshal. She had been built in 1765 in the New England Colonies. She set sail in 1766, with a cargo of rum, as a new slaveship to Gravesend. There she sold the rum. The profits were used to buy a cargo, the slaving hardware—the chains, the shackles, the other restraining objects to put on the extra crew—and the extra foodstuffs she would need, and she started sailing to Africa, to the source of what was called the "black gold" of Africa. I was able to follow the ship from the records along the Channel, and it became almost like running along the Channel, watching her. I knew her timbers, I knew her planking was loblolly pine and hackmatack cedar. I knew she had red oak timbers. I knew that the flax in her sails was out of New Jersey. I knew the kind of nails that held her together, how the black lopes were held together with a wedge of oak. I could almost read the captain's mind as he was driving to get to the African coast.

She went southerly across the Bay of Biscay, down past the Canaries, the Cape Virgins, into the mouth of the Gambia River. She was to spend the next ten months in the Gambia River, slaving. In the course of that ten months she got a cargo of 3,265 elephant tusks, 3,700 pounds of beeswax, 800 pounds of rough raw Gambian cotton, 32 ounces of Gambian gold and 140 slaves. She set sail on Sunday, 5 July 1767, headed directly for Annapolis. Her crossing voyage of about 5,000 miles took two months, three weeks and two days. She arrived in Annapolis, Maryland, on the morning of 29 September 1767.

29 September 1967: I was standing on a pier in Annapolis looking seaward, drenched in tears. It was two hundred years to the day since my forebear had come to that city, and there in Annapolis I went into the tax records to find out what she had come in with. I found she came in with a cargo. She declared the same cargo she had leaving James Fort, Gambia River, except that her original 140 slaves had become 98. Forty-two had died on the crossing, which was about average for the ships making that trip in that period. I knew that when slaves were brought in they were always advertised, and I went down to the microfilm records of the Annapolis media of the time, the *Maryland Gazette*, and in the issue of 1 October 1967, on page three, was the ad of the agents of the ship, saying that the *Lord Ligonier* had just arrived under Captain Davies from the River Gambia, with a cargo of fresh, choice, healthy slaves for sale, to be sold the following Wednesday at Meg's Wharf. Among them was Kunta-Kinte, who had come from the village of Juffure.

One thing remained to complete it. I knew that my grandmother and the others had always said that he had been named Toby by his master, and I knew that every kind of deal involving slaves was a matter of legal records. I went to Richmond, Virginia, and went into the legal deeds of the transactions of the 1760s. I found a deed dated 5 September 1768 between two brothers, John and William Waller, transferring goods between them: on the second page were the words "and also one Negro man slave named Toby."

7

The American Revolution: Yesterday and Today

DON HIGGINBOTHAM

• *The word "revolution," whether used by labor organizers, college students, or statesmen, arouses misgivings and even terror in the minds of most people. Perhaps this is due to the normal human preference for the comfort of the tried and the true rather than the uncertainty of a new situation. The idea of revolution was also disturbing to the founders of the United States. They believed in John Locke's notion of natural right—that just governments rested on the consent of the governed—and that the colonial cause was just. But a large number of the citizenry, including Benjamin Franklin, hoped for some kind of settlement, short of an open break, of their quarrel with the mother country. This is contrary to the popular stereotype of a people united from the beginning in a desire for independence from England and imbued with the vision of a continental destiny.*

In the following essay, originally given as a lecture to the New Hampshire Historical Society, Professor Don Higginbotham writes of the power and prestige of Great Britain in the eighteenth century and of the reluctance of most colonists to realize their ambitions outside the Empire. From the British perspective, war with the Colonies was a frustrating experience, not unlike that encountered by the United States in Vietnam almost two centuries later. In both instances the conflict pitted the most powerful nation in the world against a weak and undeveloped foe. King George III and his advisers feared that if the American colonies gained independence then the whole British Empire might fall away like a series of dominos. Once the battle had been joined at Lexington and Concord and Bunker Hill, the English discovered the difficulties of fighting a distant wilderness war, where it was difficult to tell the friendly natives from the rebels. And at every important juncture, Lord North and his sovereign had

to weigh the consequences of possible intervention by hostile
powers.

   As you read Professor Higginbotham's essay, you might ask
yourself whether Presidents John F. Kennedy, Lyndon B.
Johnson, and Richard M. Nixon might have profited by examining the ghostly footsteps of America's last king.

As we continue with our Bicentennial festivities, it might be well for
us to remember that we were the first people to celebrate national
birthdays. Before 1776 nations had evolved, the result of tradition and
history, geography and circumstance. I have no quarrel in principle
with such commemorations. My opportunity to be here—to visit your
state for the first time—is tied to the Bicentennial. I am not as cynical
as a former teacher of mine who wrote in the *South Atlantic Quarterly*
in 1960 of the Civil War Centennial—which was just then getting up
steam—that he was heading for the hills, not to return until 1965 when
it was all over.

   But I do suggest that—along with the Sunday afternoon military
units, minted coins, dramas like "1776," to say nothing of fireplugs
painted like Continental soldiers—we endeavor to obtain a deeper and
fuller meaning of the events we are observing.

   Unfortunately, such a serious, reflective approach to our national beginnings was almost wholly absent from America's Centennial celebra-
tion. Whatever else one may say of Gore Vidal's best-selling *1876*,
that novel reveals the crass materialism which then permeated American society to the almost total exclusion of any form of idealism. That
period was one of boisterous confidence and enthusiasm. The paramount themes of the Philadelphia Exposition all saluted our new industrial prowess. It was fitting, given the national mood, that President
Grant highlighted the fair by pulling a lever to release a jet of steam;
and that William Dean Howells exclaimed, "It is in these things of
iron and steel that the national genius most freely speaks."

   Let us hope that our mood is somewhat more serious and reflective
in 1976, in a world far more complex and strained than that of the

From *Historical New Hampshire* 31, nos. 1 and 2 (Spring/Summer 1976):
1–15.

Grant Administration and the Gilded Age. With this belief in mind, I wish to contribute some of my own ideas about the meaning of the American Revolution, both for that time and for later generations, particularly our own. Hero worship is not part of my objective. Our Revolutionary forebearers were themselves healthy skeptics; they definitely saw a danger in elevating mortals to the status of deities. They wanted no Cromwell or Caesar to emerge from their struggle. And all of the accolades heaped upon Washington got on the nerves of some of them; they did not want to replace George III with George I.

On the other hand, we need not go to the other extreme as did some debunkers earlier in this century. They castigated the Revolutionary leadership as overly conservative or reactionary, intent only on kicking the British out and otherwise maintaining the status quo on all fronts. According to this view, the rebel grandees were a repressive lot: they held back the lower orders of society and they shaped the Federal Constitution to meet their own selfish personal and class needs.

Then, too, there are those who, while admiring the principles of 1776, maintain that we have exaggerated their uniqueness and originality. No doubt the charge contains some truth. Such American ideas as sovereignty of the people, bills of right, written constitutions, and separation of powers were all notions associated with the European Enlightenment, the so-called Age of Reason. It was the American Revolution, however, that transformed theories into political realities, and that in itself was a development of such magnitude that it made our upheaval a profound catalytic agent for the revolutionary movements of the nineteenth century.

Of course, it is crucial that we acknowledge that no revolution can be fully exported. A vast array of factors that include the political experience and social structure of a people will determine the exact course of any and all revolutions. Some revolutionists preferred the model of the French Revolution of 1789; but others, recalling that the French Revolution ended in Napoleonic despotism, found more to emulate in the American outburst that culminated in republicanism and individual freedom.

More recently, as William H. McNeill has phrased it, our kind of revolution has had to compete with newer models. To some, ours appears to be dated, a "horse-and-buggy revolution" if you will, com-

pared to brighter, newer models—particularly the "Russian Marxmo-
bile of 1917 and the Chinese Mao–Marx II of 1949." The statement
is beyond refute. Yet revolutionary Marxism is not a monolith; it
contains about as many shades and degrees as other political ideologies. Even in "the Third World" of Africa and Asia, where Marxism
has assuredly had its impact, the new or revitalized states of the post-
1945 era have also not infrequently seen relevance in the American
Revolution, which, after all, was an anti-colonial movement in the
name of freedom. For example, in 1955 the keynote speaker at the
first conference of non-aligned nations found an inspiring theme in
"The Midnight Ride of Paul Revere." Ironically, our government in
Washington, thinking the event too radical, turned down an invitation to send an observer. Of 280 business, educational, and political
leaders from 86 foreign countries who recently spent several months
in the United States examining our way of life, 85 per cent of them
thought America to be generally unsympathetic to revolutionary governments abroad. The first modern revolutionaries have become, in
the words of former Senator William Fulbright, "the most unrevolu-
tionary nation on earth."

Why the paradox in Americans, a people who, according to historian Arthur Schlesinger, Sr., have bestowed no contribution to world
civilization equal that of "the right of revolution"? Is it the distance
in time from 1776? Is it owing to the long-time stability of our own
institutions? Is it possible too that the America of 1976 is more analo-
gous in some ways to the Great Britain of 1776 than to the thirteen
embattled states of 1776?

In 1776 Britain was the superpower of Europe. Her star stood at
Zenith, her reputation and her prosperity the envy of all nations. The
Industrial Revolution was well advanced in England compared to her
neighbors. She had humiliated her ancient foes, France and Spain, in
the Seven Years' War which had ended in 1763; she had not only
beaten them on land and sea, but had taken from them valuable colonies. Now the British Empire rivaled ancient Rome in its territorial
expansiveness: it included North America and the dependencies in India; glittering if smaller island jewels that studded the Caribbean Sea;
outposts in central America and Africa; Minorca and Gibraltar in the
western Mediterranean.

Britain's state of mind corresponded to her lofty status. Pax Romana would pale in comparison to Pax Britannica, to a "prosperity and glory unknown to any former age." She felt that she no longer needed her former continental European allies. For what nation could threaten her? She no longer required the good will of her American colonies. Neither France nor Spain, nor those combined Bourbon monarchies, could any longer pose a threat to the thirteen provinces, whose men and other resources had in fact helped her to victory in 1763.

Britain's was a mentality unable to relate to the aims and aspirations of her own colonial people. Superpowers, all too often, are not much given to introspection, to questioning their values and assumptions. And it had been a long time since the English people themselves had felt their liberties threatened, either by a foreign danger or by an internal menace from a tyrannical king. Now I am not suggesting that Britain embarked upon a conscious policy of robbing the Americans of their liberty when Parliament enacted laws designed to tax the colonists and to reorganize and restructure the empire along ways that seemed, in London at least, more systematic and more economical. But the point is that the colonists were not really consulted; they were given no alternatives; and when they raised objections, most royal politicians rejected the idea that the Americans were genuinely concerned and alarmed. Instead, they only concluded that the colonists were devious and irresponsible, merely trying to escape making a contribution to the welfare of the empire.

Some Londoners interpreted the protests from Boston, Philadelphia, Williamsburg, and so on as covert desires to cast loose from imperial moorings, to become politically independent. Nothing was farther from the truth. Although the colonists had grown up, had reached a level of maturity that called for less restraint, not more controls, they were British and proud of it. They wished to realize their ambitions within the Empire; in many respects each colony had more in common with England—the source of trade and culture—than with its neighboring provinces. Strange to say, British policies drove them together, not a conscious desire to unite. Therefore, in one respect the history of American nationalism was different from the self-identification characterized by most of the Third World nations: our nationalism was a result of the Revolution and not the cause of it.

The pre-1763 empire had, for all practical purposes, been of a federal nature, with governmental powers separated and distributed. King and Parliament had dealt with the regulation of commerce and other external matters, and the colonists had been left largely alone to manage their internal affairs through their representative assemblies. Time and again American writers urged a return to that concept of empire, but it fell upon deaf ears in Whitehall and Parliament. So did a later and final American offer at compromise when the possibility of no recourse but independence was becoming a painful reality on the western side of the Atlantic: that was for what we would today call a commonwealth conception of empire—to continue a tie held in place by mutual interest and by a common king, George III, but one which denied to Parliament any jurisdiction in American affairs. But the Hanoverian monarch rejected it as disdainfully as did Parliament. Thus the position that would one day be accorded to Canada, Australia, and New Zealand was denied to the North American colonies in the eighteenth century.

Men and women do sometimes learn from history, although the process may be slow and the price painful. In 1976 Queen Elizabeth II, reigning monarch in direct line of descent from King George III, said as much on her Bicentennial visit to Philadelphia. The American Revolution "taught Britain a very valuable lesson," she said. "We learned to respect the right of others to govern themselves in their own ways; this was the outcome of experience learned the hard way in 1776."

The Queen, of course, would acknowledge that the lesson in question did not sink in for a long time. In fact, in 1776 most Britons were supremely confident that the might of the mother country would quickly crush the American rebellion. That notion was the product of the superpower mentality. When had Britain ever lost a war? Hers was a winning tradition, as much of a winning tradition as America could boast of in the post World War II era—when for instance in 1945 *Life* magazine bragged of the coming "American Century" in which Americans would call the shots on the world scene as had the Romans and the British in other ages.

British soldiers and political leaders held Americans in utter contempt. Lord Jeffrey Amherst said that with 5,000 men he could sweep from one end of America to the other. Lord Sandwich of the Admiralty exclaimed that the provincials would run at "the very sound of cannon . . . as fast as their feet could carry them." Only a small mi-

nority in Parliament and throughout the Kingdom asked the hard
questions. What would be the problems of transporting and provision-
ing armies across a three-thousand-mile ocean; of conducting campaigns in rugged, forested country; of contesting an armed population
over a vast area from New Hampshire to Georgia; of the probability of
France and Spain entering the fray to redress the international balance
of power? And, even if royal arms prevailed, what would be the value
of an American empire that lay in smouldering ruin?

Whether one goes so far as to characterize the War of Independence as "England's Vietnam," there are nonetheless striking parallels,
such as in the growing opposition to the Revolutionary War in Britain
as the home country's losses mounted and as the struggle dragged on
to a final length of eight and one-half years. An eloquent if small band
of Englishmen likewise opposed the war on moral grounds. Philoso-
phers such as Richard Price and Joseph Priestley publicly championed
the rebel side. Lord Effingham told the King that "I could not, without reproach from my conscience, consent to bear arms against my
fellow subjects in America." The dying William Pitt, Earl of Chat-
ham, thundered in the House of Lords: "If I were an American, as I
am an Englishman, while a foreign troop was landed in my country, I
never would lay down my arms—never—never—never. You cannot conquer America."

Was the Revolution a guerrilla war from the standpoint of how the
Americans fought it? Karl von Clausewitz, the nineteenth-century
Prussian military theorist, declared that when war is mainly carried on
by an armed citizenry rather than by professionals, "warfare introduces
a means of defense peculiar to itself." The Americans did resort to
guerrilla tactics when the British left the coastal plains and plunged
into the interior, a region mainly unsuited to European combat and
inhabited by backcountrymen who fought according to their own
rules. Furthermore, Nathanael Greene in the South played a brilliant
game of hit-and-run against Cornwallis by weakening His Lordship's
army and then, one by one, picking off British outposts in South Carolina; but neither Greene nor any other American general advanced a
theory of revolutionary or irregular warfare comparable to that enun-
ciated by a Mao Tse-Tung or a Vo Nguyen Giap.

Yet in the main the Revolution was conservative militarily. A war
that wrenched strongly to the left, that witnessed massive destruction

and devastation, that saw mass atrocities and wholesale executions—all this would burst the bonds of society and irreparably damage legal and political institutions. Such might well be the price for a full-scale guerrilla war. All that Washington and Congress wished to avoid. Instead they opted for a traditional army which in general fought according to the rules of the day. It was, moreover, an army that was a sign to foreigners of the Revolution's respectability and an indication to Americans of the country's gradually emerging nationalism, for it contained men from different states who were forging common bonds which transcended regional and local loyalties. In no sense, therefore, were the trustees of Revolution guerrilla chieftains. They saw the Revolution in all its dimensions, the relationship between the homefront and the battlefront, the relationship between the war years and the forthcoming years of peace. Ultimately, they wished posterity to hail them as builders rather than destroyers.

Here, in speaking of how the war was fought, we need to say something of civil-military relations. Unlike so many recent revolutions, the Army did not call the tune. It was thoroughly subordinate to Congress and the states. Military chieftains never made a grab for power, either during the conflict or in the post-war period. Only a handful of the one hundred or so nations born since World War II can claim such a record. Why the difference? Obviously, the English tradition of civil control was a factor, but so was the presence of effective, experienced civilian political leadership. Consequently, the military element did not have a bureaucratic function to perform, as has been true in some of the new underdeveloped nations since 1945. There the armies—with their officers graduates of Sandhurst and St. Cyr—have sometimes been almost alone in their administrative and managerial know-how. In America, the generals were ready to relinquish their authority, to shape their ploughshares into swords, to melt into the civilian population from which they had come—or, as Washington liked to put it, to "return and sit under my own vine and fig tree."

This may well be an appropriate place for us to dwell a moment on Washington; for in one sense at least he was the real leader of our Revolution, and he has been compared to revolutionaries elsewhere at other times and other places. Fortunately, recent historians have discovered that Washington was a human being; he is down out of the clouds. We need no longer exclaim as did Nathaniel Hawthorne when he asked, "Did anybody ever see Washington nude? It is inconceivable," he responded; Washington "was born with his clothes on, and his hair powdered, and made a stately bow on his first appearance in the world."

It is a kind of universal that almost every great historical movement has had its unique leader, a William the Silent, a Cromwell, a Napoleon, a Bolivar, and more recently a Lenin, a Gandhi, a Castro, and so on. Freud considered the necessity of a father image so essential that men will unfailingly endow someone with leadership qualities regardless of whether such attributes exist. In the case of Washington, however, he possessed high qualities of leadership; and he departs from the company of certain famous revolutionaries in that he was not an extremist or fanatic by any definition; he does not fit the stereotype attributed to countless revolutionaries since the time of Robespierre, of being an ascetic and without libidinal ties—as, for example, Yasser Arafat of the Palestinian Liberation Movement is reputed to be. Often the revolutionary ascetic, according to psychohistorian Bruce Mazlish, becomes drunk with the wine of power and adulation; to himself, he is the movement, the revolution. Not so Washington, who never fell to the Narcissus complex that became the undoing of Nkrumah and Sukarno.

Still, as the head of the army and as a man of sterling character, Washington became during the times that tried men's souls, as Paine phrased it, a vital symbol of the Revolution and of emerging nationality. And as he reminded his army, patriotism took on a new meaning in this war, with free citizens fighting in defense of their own country. It was a conflict different from European contests, where a highly trained professional army (and not the productive elements of society) fought for pay or other emoluments in the service of a monarch's dynastic or territorial ambitions.

We sometimes forget how momentous were the tasks of the leaders of the American Revolution; they involved not only winning a war for independence but simultaneously writing constitutions for the states and putting new governments into operation. How could all these objectives be met simultaneously, especially when we are mindful that—in our own wars of the twentieth century—military preparations have so consumed the energies of the nation that domestic reform and all other internal needs were relentlessly pushed to the background? And, let us add parenthetically, that the Revolutionary War magnified the problem of coping with internal objectives since that struggle, unlike the others, was fought on our own soil. The military conservatism of the Americans helped, as did the willingness of Washington and other generals to follow civilian leadership and to accept civilian priorities. But let us not forget the remarkable political talent in the nation at that time, nor the fact that the colonists had a rich amount of experience in self-government before the Revolution; here the Americans' political background gave them a decided advantage over some of the creators of modern states, men who had not been given the right of serving in legislative assemblies and occupying local offices during their years of colonialism and subordination. Consequently, the Americans were able to build upon their past, to design instruments of government that borrowed the best and eliminated the worst features from their British colonial heritage.

Fortunately for the Americans, they had the natural resources—and they were accessible—to take care of most of their domestic economic needs, and that in itself eased appreciably their trek down the path to stability; just as it separated them from the grave problems of poverty and low gross national product that have afflicted many fledgling have-not states of late. Such was the point of one of the last columns by Walter Lippmann, who said of the great central mass of South America—and it might also be stated of Africa—that it was still a frontier, even a wilderness, in need of opening; that communications and trade were so lacking that the nations were disunited, oriented outward rather than inward, and dominated by trade relationships with other countries.

Partly for these reasons, the American Revolution compared to some present-day revolutions witnessed relatively little social experimentation. Besides, classes were fluid, legal privilege did not exist, and upward mobility was usually possible for those who would make the effort. Still, there were far-reaching democratic implications in the revolutionists' separation of Church and State and in their efforts to establish state-supported public education, to say nothing of the clearly expressed ideas in virtually every political document of the period that all men were entitled to certain basic rights and that government rested on the consent of the governed.

Slavery was another matter. On that subject all our lofty generalizations about idealism and principle must be brought up short. Our generation, guilt-ridden over our shortcomings in doing the black man justice in America, now seeks to remove that responsibility at the expense of the Founding Fathers, who are branded as racists or white supremacists. Jefferson has been the main target; and Fawn Brodie has attracted wide attention (although she may not have convinced the historical profession) out of attempting to prove that Jefferson was the father of his mulatto slave Sally Hemings's children. In truth, we need neither attack nor defend the Revolutionary generation. But we can explain how the problem looked to them. They differed considerably among themselves about whether the black man might, given a better environment, prove himself the intellectual equal of the white man; they also differed over whether the slaves, if freed, could ever live side by side in a society with their former masters. Even so, the Founding Fathers did see the peculiar institution as inconsistent with their ideals of human freedom. From their point of view, they believed that any measure to eradicate slavery where it currently existed would have been extremely divisive, would have wrecked any chance of building a cohesive nation.

Such a nation did not exist at the conclusion of the War of Independence in 1783. Congress, operating under the weak and inadequate Articles of Confederation, presided over thirteen sovereign states which cooperated with one another and with Congress itself only when it suited their interests; and their interests in doing so were less than ever after the shooting stopped. The next few years saw a political struggle. It was not a power struggle, a not uncommon phenomenon among revolutionaries; rather, it was a policy struggle over whether America should become one nation in the fullest sense—whether a capstone to the Revolution was needed in the form of a central government that would provide unity, order, and security.

If, as we know, the nationalists won out over the localists, if the Constitution of 1787 was the result, we should also remember that the Framers were concerned to see that the national Republic behaved responsibly and did not threaten the liberties of the people. One way of insuring against such developments was by dividing the powers of the central government between coequal executive, legislative, and judicial branches. If Presidential power has gone unchecked in the era of Vietnam and Watergate, it is not the fault of the architects at Philadelphia in 1787. At the Constitutional Convention James Madison warned his fellow delegates that the control of foreign affairs was more susceptible of abuse than all the other responsibilities entrusted to government. Congress, not the President, received the power to declare war. Although the Executive was named commander in chief of the Army and Navy, the Convention sought to restrain his authority through Congressional control of the purse. The Bicentennial, together with certain tragic, controversial events of recent times, is a fitting, even crucial, occasion for us to reassess the meaning of 1776 and 1787.

The separation of powers was not the only protection against tyranny built into the Constitution. That document also erected a federal system, dividing authority between national and state governments. Here was a problem, as we have seen earlier, that wrecked the first British empire in 1776; a problem that had also confounded statesmen in the Greek confederacies of antiquity, in medieval Italy, in the Holy Roman Empire, and elsewhere. The American achievement, the oldest and most successful form of federalism in history, has been seen from a variety of vantage points. Undoubtedly federalism may be a worthy subject of exploration for emerging nations troubled by ethnic, linguistic, and regional divisions, although the present internal fissures in Great Britain, Yugoslavia, and Canada demonstrate that the separatist phenomenon is scarcely confined to the fledgling countries. Following both twentieth-century world wars advocates of world government such as the Carnegie Endowment for International Peace and Federal Union Incorporated have also found analogies between the need of the thirteen states to secure "a more perfect union" and the necessity for some form of international political organization.

And yet, so far as the Founding Fathers themselves are concerned, we have been brought up on the notion that they were isolationists; that, in fact, Washington's Farewell Address was an appeal for us to remain aloof from the doings of the outside world. Nothing could be farther from the truth: the revolutionists spoke only against "entangling alliances" of a military nature that would involve us in wars where our vital interests were not at stake. Each one of us can judge for himself or herself the applicability of that idea to our own generation and the extent to which we have heeded it.

Actually, the designers of the new Republic gave considerable thought to the question of how the blood-drenched rivalries of Europe (into which England's former colonies had inexorably been drawn) might be terminated to the benefit of all mankind. In their most visionary moods, American diplomats went so far as to view the Revolutionary conflict in Wilsonian terms, as "a war to end all wars." For if mercantilism, that source of imperial struggles, could be replaced by free trade, by the laissez-faire principles of Adam Smith's *Wealth of Nations*, there would be far fewer tensions and rivalries between nations. By trading together openly and freely, people of all lands would find that their common interests exceeded their differences.

If Europe rejected the commercial principles of the American Revolution and scorned the idea of world cooperation, that goal of the Framers is well worth reviving during the Bicentennial, with America again taking the lead. A distinguished historian, Henry Steele Commager of Amherst College, has advanced a significant step in that direction. He has drafted "A Declaration of Interdependence," the central thrust of which is to carry the principles of 1776 to 1976; to remind us, in the words of Jefferson's earlier Declaration, that "a decent respect for the opinions of mankind" should propel us to bring the world closer together in an age of common dangers and common needs.

Let me conclude with a few remarks about the generation of Americans who led us through the pangs and joys of revolution and national birth—a generation which not only inspired mankind at large, but which, here at home, created the framework for future generations to spell out the far-reaching implications of the American Revolution for all Americans. Their numerous accomplishments were attained without going at each other's throats. Differences they had, sometimes bitter and acrimonious, but they resolved them in the political arena, not in the bloodbath of civil war or counterrevolution. There is slight exaggeration, if any, in the observation of Irving Kristol that "Alone among the revolutions of modernity, the American Revolution did not give rise to the pathetic and poignant myth of 'the revolution betrayed.' It spawned no literature of disillusionment; it left behind no grand hopes frustrated, no grand expectations unsatisfied, no grand illusions shattered." It tells us a great deal simply to recall that the American revolutionaries died in their beds. The poet Robert Penn Warren, with the sensitivity one expects of him, notes that the portraits of our Revolution's worthies—staring down at us from the walls of Independence Hall and elsewhere—are those of confident men; they knew who they were and where they were going. There is none of the sadness or uncertainty that Warren sees covering the faces of leaders in the American Civil War.

In the last analysis, the most striking characteristics of Revolutionary political leadership were that our helmsmen possessed the finest minds in America and that they exhibited an unusually high degree of dedication to public service. "Wise and good men are," observed Franklin, "the strength of a state, much more so than riches and arms." By any measurement, Franklin himself was one of six men of that generation who achieved greatness, displayed qualities of genuine statesmanship; the others were Washington, Jefferson, Madison, Hamilton, and John Adams. Why were our most intelligent, creative souls drawn to public service in the eighteenth century? Perhaps the reasons will remain at best speculative. At any rate, we would probably agree that this is much less the case today. There may well be as many talented individuals in proportion to the total population, but comparably fewer of them enter the political arena.

Nor, generally, do we encounter the dedication to service, often at the cost of personal inconvenience and economic distress, that marked the founders of the republic. Washington spent eight and a half years leading the Continental Army without ever taking a leave of absence. Both Franklin and Adams spent many years away from their families on business of state in Europe. Jefferson's final years were clouded by considerable financial misery, as were Hamilton's, both attributing their misfortunes in part to low pay and other personal sacrifices in behalf of the country.

From 1776 to 1976—a long time, but only in a linear sense. That is because the concerns of the Revolutionary generation were and remain fundamental ones, for old as well as new nations: self-preservation, effective but limited and honest government, subordination of the military to civilian authority, individual liberty and dignity, and world peace. There should be yet another timeless concern, frequently neglected, though not by the Founding Fathers. That is to view concerns beyond immediate, short-term solutions; to examine them rather in terms of the future. The word that Washington, Jefferson, and company reserved for this far-reaching outlook was *posterity*. They battled, designed, and constructed for posterity. Hear John Adams exclaim of the Declaration of Independence: "Through all the gloom I can see the rays of ravishing light and glory. Posterity will triumph in that day's transaction." Hear Benjamin Rush announce: "I was acting for the benefit of the whole world, and of future ages." Hear Jefferson in his twilight years assure Madison: "It has been a great solace to me to believe that you are engaged in vindicating to posterity the course we have pursued, of preserving to them, in all their purity, the blessings of self-government which we had assisted in acquiring for them."

Our generation too can meet our challenges, not only for our time but with an eye to our posterity if we conserve our natural resources, cease polluting the environment, and respond to other needs. We too can find statesmen, provided we recall the criteria for statecraft employed by our eighteenth-century ancestors. All of this is only to say that we cannot fully understand ourselves today without knowing the past that molded us. If we can do that, we will not play the eighteenth-century role of Britain in a twentieth-century world. Instead, we will choose the course outlined by President Millard Fillmore more than a century ago when he wrote: "The American Mission was not to impose upon other countries our form of government by artifice or force, but to teach by example and by our success."

8

Watermelon Armies and Whiskey Boys

GERALD CARSON

• Although Americans hold ambivalent views about alcoholic beverages, it cannot be denied that whiskey has played an important role in our culture from its very inception. The Pilgrims carried liquor with them on the Mayflower, and Congress itself voted to provide supplies of spirits to the American army during Revolutionary times. During the 1700s whiskey was said to be vital to the workers in the Southern states because of the hot climate.

To the Scotch-Irish of Pennsylvania, whiskey was not only an economic commodity but as necessary to their lives as Bibles and plows. Thus, when Alexander Hamilton proposed an internal revenue tax on distilled liquors, rumblings of dissatisfaction arose from the western Pennsylvania frontier. Because they based their livelihood on distilling grain rather than transporting the crop across the mountains, the farmers regarded the tax as discriminatory and leveled their shotguns at the revenue agents who came to collect. Public protests erupted, thousands marched on Pittsburgh, and there were talks of secession from the United States. Ultimately, President George Washington sent in federal troops.

Alexander Hamilton thought that the use of the army would illustrate the power of the newly created government to enforce the law. As you read Carson's witty and colorful account of the Whiskey Rebellion of 1794, consider the question of the use of federal troops to force compliance with a locally unpopular national policy. Does the use of military force, as Hamilton suggested, increase the citizen's respect for and adherence to the national laws? What similarities, if any, do you find between the quelling of the Whiskey Rebellion of 1794 and the use of the military to enforce integrated education in Little Rock, Arkansas, in 1957 and to dispel youthful protesters at the Democratic National Convention in Chicago in August 1968?

When one recalls that the President of the United States, the Secretary of War, the Secretary of the Treasury and the governors of four states once mobilized against the farmers of western Pennsylvania almost as large an army as ever took the field in the Revolutionary War, the event appears at first glance as one of the more improbable episodes in the annals of this country. Thirteen thousand grenadiers, dragoons, foot soldiers and pioneers, a train of artillery with six-pounders, mortars and several "grasshoppers," equipped with mountains of ammunition, forage, baggage and a bountiful stock of tax-paid whiskey, paraded over the mountains to Pittsburgh against a gaggle of homespun rebels who had already dispersed.

Yet the march had a rationale. President George Washington and his Secretary of the Treasury, Alexander Hamilton, moved to counter civil commotion with overwhelming force because they well understood that the viability of the United States Constitution was involved. Soon after he assumed his post at the Treasury, Hamilton had proposed, to the astonishment of the country, that the United States should meet fully and promptly its financial obligations, including the assumption of the debts contracted by the states in the struggle for independence. The money was partly to be raised by laying an excise tax upon distilled spirits. The tax, which was universally detested in the West—"odious" was the word most commonly used to describe it—became law on March 3, 1791.

The news of the passage of the measure was greeted with a roar of indignation in the back country settlements. The duty was laid uniformly upon all the states, as the Constitution provided. If the West had to pay more, Secretary Hamilton explained, it was only because it used more whiskey. The East could, if it so desired, forgo beverage spirits and fall back on cider and beer. The South could not. It had neither orchards nor breweries. To Virginia and Maryland the excise tax appeared to be as unjust and oppressive as the well-remembered Molasses Act and the tea duties of George III. "The time will come," predicted fiery James Jackson of Georgia in the House of Representatives, "when a shirt shall not be washed without an excise."

Kentucky, then thinly settled, but already producing its characteristic hand-made, whole-souled liquor from planished copper stills, was of the opinion that the law was unconstitutional. Deputy revenue collectors throughout the Bluegrass region were assaulted, their papers stolen, their horses' ears cropped and their saddles cut to pieces. On one wild night the people of Lexington dragged a stuffed dummy through the streets and hanged in effigy Colonel Thomas Marshall, the chief collector for the district.

Yet in no other place did popular fury rise so high, spread so rapidly, involve a whole population so completely, express so many assorted grievances, as in the Pennsylvania frontier counties of Fayette, Allegheny, Westmoreland and Washington. In these counties, around 1791, a light plume of wood smoke rose from the chimneys of no less than five thousand log stillhouses. The rates went into effect on July first. The whiskey maker could choose whether he would pay a yearly levy on his still capacity or a gallonage tax ranging from nine to eleven cents on his actual production.

Before the month was out, "committees of correspondence," in the old Revolutionary phrase, were speeding horsemen over the ridges and through the valleys to arouse the people to arm and assemble. The majority, but not all, of the men who made the whiskey decided to "forbear" from paying the tax. The revenue officers were thoroughly worked over. Robert Johnson, for example, collector for Washington and Allegheny counties, was waylaid near Pigeon Creek by a mob disguised in women's clothing. They cut off his hair, gave him a coat of tar and feathers and stole his horse.

The Pennsylvania troubles were rooted in the economic importance and impregnable social position of mellow old Monongahela rye whiskey. In 1825, for instance, when the Philadelphia Society for Promoting Agriculture offered a gold medal to the person in Pennsylvania who carried on large-scale farming operations without providing ardent spirits for his farm workers, the medal could not be awarded. There were no entries for the uncoveted honor.

The frontier people had been reared from childhood on the

family jug of farmer whiskey. They found the taste pleasant, the effect agreeable. Whiskey was usually involved when there was kissing or fighting. It beatified the rituals of birth and death. The doctor kept a bottle in his office for his own use under the deceptive label "Arsenic —Deadly poison." The lawyer produced the bottle when the papers were signed. Whiskey was available in the prothonotary's office when the trial-list was made up. Jurors got their dram, and the constable drew his ration for his services on election day. The hospitable barrel and the tin cup were the mark of the successful political candidate. The United States Army issued a gill to a man every day. Ministers of the gospel were paid in rye whiskey, for they were shepherds of a devout flock, Scotch Presbyterians mostly, who took their Bible straight, especially where it said: "Give strong drink unto him that is ready to perish, and wine unto those that be of heavy hearts."

With grain the most abundant commodity west of the mountains, the farmers could eat it or drink it, but they couldn't sell it in distant markets unless it was reduced in bulk and enhanced in value. A Pennsylvania farmer's "best holt," then, was whiskey. A pack-horse could move only four bushels of grain. But it could carry twenty-four bushels if it was condensed into two kegs of whiskey slung across its back, while the price of the goods would double when they reached the eastern markets. So whiskey became the remittance of the fringe settlements for salt, sugar, nails, bar iron, pewter plates, powder and shot. Along the Western rivers where men saw few shilling pieces, a gallon of good, sound rye whiskey was a stable measure of value.

The bitter resistance of the Western men to the whiskey tax involved both practical considerations and principles. First, the excise payment was due and must be paid in hard money as soon as the water-white distillate flowed from the condensing coil. The principle concerned the whole repulsive idea of an internal revenue levy. The settlers of western Pennsylvania were a bold, hardy, emigrant race who brought with them bitter memories of oppression under the excise laws in Scotland and Ireland, involving invasion of their homes, confiscation of their property and a system of paid informers. Revenue collectors were social outcasts in a society which warmly seconded Doctor Samuel Johnson's definition of excise: "a hateful tax levied upon commodities, and adjudged not by the common judges of property, but wretches hired by those to whom excise is paid."

The whiskey boys of Pennsylvania saw it as simply a matter of sound Whig doctrine to resist the exciseman as he made his rounds with Dicas' hydrometer to measure the proof of the whiskey and his marking iron to brand the casks with his findings. Earlier, Pennsylvania had taxed spirits. But whiskey produced for purely private use was exempt. William Findley of Westmoreland County, a member of Congress at the time and a sympathetic interpreter of the Western point of view, looked into this angle. To his astonishment, he learned that all of the whiskey distilled in the West was for purely personal use. So far as the state's excise tax was concerned, or any other tax, for that matter, the sturdy Celtic peoples of the Monongahela region had cheerfully returned to nature: they just didn't pay. About every sixth man made whiskey. But all were involved in the problem, since the other five took their grain to the stillhouse where the maste. distiller turned it into liquid form.

The state had been lenient. But now matters had taken a more serious turn. The new federal government in Philadelphia was dividing the whole country up into "districts" for the purpose of collecting the money. And the districts were subdivided into smaller "surveys." The transmontane Pennsylvanians found themselves in the grip of something known as the fourth survey, with General John Neville, hitherto a popular citizen and leader, getting ready to enforce the law, with a reward paid to informers and a percentage to the collectors, who appeared to be a rapacious set.

The first meeting of public protest against the 1791 federal tax was held at Redstone Old Fort, now Brownsville. The proceedings were moderate on that occasion, and scarcely went beyond the right of petition. Another meeting in August, more characteristic of others which were to follow, was radical in tone, disorderly, threatening. It passed resolves to the effect that any person taking office under the revenue law was an enemy of society.

When warrants were issued in the affair of Robert Johnson, the process server was robbed, beaten, tarred and feathered and left tied to a tree in the forest. As the inspectors' offices were established, they were systematically raided. Liberty poles reappeared as whiskey poles. The stills of operators who paid the tax were riddled with bullets in attacks sardonically known as "mending" the still. This led to a popular description of the Whiskey Boys as "Tom the Tinker's Men,"

an ironical reference to the familiar, itinerant repairer of pots and
kettles. Notices proposing measures for thwarting the law, or aimed at
coercing the distillers, were posted on trees or published in the *Pittsburgh Gazette* over the signature, "Tom the Tinker," nom de plume
of the insurgent John Holcroft and other anti-tax agitators. Findley,
who tried to build a bridge of understanding between the backwoods-
men and the central government, described the outbreak as not the
result of any concerted plan, but rather as a flame, "an infatuation
almost incredible."

An additional grievance grew out of the circumstance that offenders were required to appear in the federal court at Philadelphia,
three hundred miles away. The whiskey-makers saw this distant
government as being no less oppressive than one seated in London,
and often drew the parallel. The Scotch-Irish of western Pennsylvania
were, in sum, anti-federalist, anti-tax, and it may be added, anti-
Indian. West of Pittsburgh lay Indian country. The men of the west
held to a simple concept of how to solve the Indian problem: exter-
mination. The Indians had the same program, in reverse, and were
getting better results. The bungling campaigns, which generals Hamar
and St. Clair had conducted in the early 1790's made the people of
the fringe settlements despair of the ability of the Union to protect
them.

Congress amended the excise tax law in 1792 and again in 1794
to lighten the burden on country distillers. A further conciliatory step
was taken. To ease the hardships of the judicial process, Congress
gave to the state courts jurisdiction in excise offenses so that accused
persons might be tried in their own vicinity. But some fifty or sixty
writs already issued and returnable at Philadelphia resulted in men
being carried away from their fields during harvest time. This convinced the insurgents that the federalist East was seeking a pretext
to discipline the democratic West.

One day in July, while the papers were being served, William
Miller, a delinquent farmer-distiller, and political supporter of General Neville, saw the General riding up his lane accompanied by a
stranger who turned out to be a United States marshal from Philadelphia. The marshal unlimbered an official paper and began to read
a summons. It ordered said Miller peremptorily to "set aside all manner of business and excuses" and appear in his "proper person" before

a Philadelphia judge. Miller had been planning to sell his property and remove to Kentucky. The cost of the trip to Philadelphia and the fine for which he was liable would eat up the value of his land and betterments. The farm was as good as gone.

"I felt my blood boil at seeing General Neville along to pilot the sheriff to my very door," Miller said afterward. "I felt myself mad with passion."

As Neville and the marshal rode away, a party from the county militia which was mustered at Mingo Creek fired upon them, but there were no casualties. When the General reached Bower Hill, his country home above the Chartiers Valley, another party under the command of John Holcroft awaited him there and demanded his commission and official papers. The demand was refused and both sides began to shoot. As the rebels closed in on the main house, a flanking fire came from the Negro cabins on the plantation. The Whiskey Boys were driven off with one killed and four wounded.

The next day, Major James McFarlane, a veteran of the Revolution, led an attack in force upon Neville's painted and wall-papered mansion, furnished with such marvels as carpets, mirrors, pictures and prints and an eight-day clock. The house was now defended by a dozen soldiers from Fort Fayette at Pittsburgh. A fire-fight followed during which a soldier was shot and McFarlane was killed—by treachery, the rebels said, when a white flag was displayed. The soldiers surrendered and were either released or allowed to escape. Neville was not found, but his cabins, barns, outbuildings and finally the residence were all burned to the ground. Stocks of grain were destroyed, all fences leveled, as the victors broke up the furniture, liberated the mirrors and clock, and distributed Neville's supply of liquor to the mob.

The funeral of McFarlane caused great excitement. Among those present were Hugh Henry Brackenridge, author, lawyer and one of the western moderates, and David Bradford, prosecuting attorney for Washington County. The former wished to find ways to reduce the tension; the latter to increase it. Bradford was a rash, impetuous Marylander, ambitious for power and position. Some thought him a second-rate lawyer. Others disagreed. They said he was third-rate. But he had a gift for rough mob eloquence. Bradford had already robbed the United States mails to find out what information was being sent east against the conspirators. He had already called for the people to make a choice of "submission or opposition . . . with *head, heart, hand* and *voice*."

At Major McFarlane's funeral service Bradford worked powerfully upon the feelings of his sympathizers as he described "the murder of McFarlane." Brackenridge also spoke, using wit and drollery to let down the pressure and to make palatable his warning to the insurgents that they were flirting with the possibility of being hanged. But the temper of the throng was for Bradford, clearly revealed in the epitaph which was set over McFarlane's grave. It said "He fell . . . by the hands of an unprincipled villain in the support of what he supposed to be the rights of his country."

The high-water mark of the insurrection was the occupation of Pittsburgh. After the fight and the funeral, Bradford called out the militia regiments of the four disaffected counties. They were commanded to rendezvous at Braddock's Feld, near Pittsburgh, with arms, full equipment and four days' rations. At the field there was a great beating of drums, much marching and counter-marching, almost a holiday spirit. Men in hunting shirts practiced shooting at the mark until a dense pall of smoke hung over the plain, as there had been thirty-nine years before at the time of General Braddock's disaster. There were between five and seven thousand men on the field, many meditating in an ugly mood upon their enemies holed up in the town, talking of storming Fort Fayette and burning Pittsburgh as "a second Sodom."

Bradford's dream was the establishment of an independent state with himself cast as a sort of Washington of the West. Elected by acclaim as Major General, he dashed about the field on a superb horse in a fancy uniform, his sword flashing, plumes floating out from his hat. As he harangued the multitude, Bradford received applications for commissions in the service of—what? No one quite knew.

Marching in good order, strung out over two and a half miles of road, the rebels advanced on August first toward Pittsburgh in what was hopefully interpreted as a "visit," though the temper of the whiskey soldiers was perhaps nearer to that of one man who twirled his hat on the muzzle of his rifle and shouted, "I have a bad hat now, but I expect to have a better one soon." While the panic-stricken burghers buried the silver and locked up the girls, the mob marched

in on what is now Fourth Avenue to the vicinity of the present Baltimore and Ohio Railroad station. A reception committee extended
nervous hospitality in the form of hams, poultry, dried venison, bear
meat, water and whiskey. They agreed to banish certain citizens ob-
noxious to the insurrectionists. One building on a suburban farm was
burned. Another attempt at arson failed to come off. The day cost
Brackenridge four barrels of prime Monongahela. It was better, he
reflected, "to be employed in extinguishing the fire of their thirst
than of my house." Pittsburgh was fortunate in getting the main body
in and then out again without a battle or a burning.

All through the month of August armed bands continued to patrol
the roads as a "scrub Congress," in the phrase of one scoffer, met at
Parkinson's Ferry, now Monongahela, to debate, pass resolutions
and move somewhat uncertainly toward separation from the United
States. Wild and ignorant rumors won belief. It was said that
Congress was extending the excise levy to plows at a dollar each, that
every wagon entering Philadelphia would be forced to pay a dollar,
that a tax was soon to be established at Pittsburgh of fifteen shillings
for the birth of every boy baby, and ten for each girl.

With the terrorizing of Pittsburgh, it was evident that the crisis
had arrived. The President requisitioned 15,000 militia from Pennsylvania, New Jersey, Virginia and Maryland, of whom about 13,000
actually marched. Would the citizens of one state invade another to
compel obedience to federal law? Here one gets a glimpse of the larger
importance of the affair. Both the national government and the state
of Pennsylvania sent commissioners to the West with offers of pardon
upon satisfactory assurances that the people would obey the laws.
Albert Gallatin, William Findley, Brackenridge and others made a
desperate effort to win the people to compliance, though their motives
were often questioned by both the rebels and the federal authorities.
The response to the offer of amnesty was judged not to be sufficiently
positive. Pressed by Hamilton to have federal power show its teeth,
Washington announced that the troops would march.

The army was aroused. In particular, the New Jersey militia were
ready for lynch law because they had been derided in a western newspaper as a "Water-mellon Army" and an uncomplimentary estimate
was made of their military capabilities. The piece was written as a
take-off on the kind of negotiations which preceded an Indian treaty.

Possibly the idea was suggested by the fact that the Whiskey Boys were often called "White Indians." At any rate, in the satire the Indians admonished the great council in Philadelphia: ". . . Brothers, we have that powerful monarch, Capt. Whiskey, to command us. By the power of his influence, and a love to *his person* we are compelled to every great and heroic act. . . . We, the Six United Nations of White Indians . . . have all imbibed his principles and passions—that is a love of whiskey. . . . Brothers, you must not think to frighten us with . . . infantry, cavalry and artillery, composed of your water-mellon armies from the Jersey shores; they would cut a much better figure in warring with the crabs and oysters about the Capes of Delaware."

Captain Whiskey was answered hotly by "A Jersey Blue." He pointed out that "the water-melon army of New Jersey" was going to march westward shortly with "ten-inch howitzers for throwing a species of mellon very useful for curing a *gravel occasioned by whiskey!*" The expedition was tagged thereafter as the "Watermelon Army."

The troops moved in two columns under the command of General Henry (Light Horse Harry) Lee, Governor of Virginia. Old Dan Morgan was there and young Meriwether Lewis, five nephews of President Washington, the governors of Pennsylvania and New Jersey, too, and many a veteran blooded in Revolutionary fighting, including the extraordinary German, Captain John Fries of the Bucks County militia and his remarkable dog to which the Captain gave the name of a beverage he occasionally enjoyed—Whiskey.

The left wing marched west during October, 1794, over General Braddock's old route from Virginia and Maryland to Cumberland on the Potomac, then northwest into Pennsylvania, to join forces with the right wing at Union Town. The Pennsylvania and New Jersey corps proceeded via Norristown and Reading to Harrisburg and Carlisle. There, on October 4th, President Washington arrived, accompanied by Colonel Hamilton. The representatives of the disaffected counties told the President at Carlisle that the army was not needed but Hamilton convinced him that it was. Washington proceeded with the troops as far as Bedford, then returned to Philadelphia for the meeting of Congress. Hamilton ordered a roundup of many of the rebels and personally interrogated the most important

ones. Brackenridge, incidentally, came off well in his encounter with
Hamilton, who declared that he was satisfied with Brackenridge's
conduct.

By the time the expedition had crossed the mountains, the uprising
was already coming apart at the seams. David Bradford, who had
been excluded from the offer of amnesty, fled to Spanish Louisiana.
About two thousand of the best riflemen in the West also left the
country, including many a distiller, who loaded his pot still on a pack
horse or a keel boat and sought asylum in Kentucky where, hopefully,
a man could make "the creature" without giving the public debt a lift.

The punitive army moved forward in glorious autumn weather,
raiding chicken coops, consuming prodigious quantities of the commodity which lay at the heart of the controversy. Richard Howell,
governor of New Jersey and commander of the right wing, revived
the spirits of the Jersey troops by composing a marching song, "Dash
to the Mountains, Jersey Blue":

> To arms once more, our hero cries,
> Sedition lives and order dies;
> To peace and ease then did adieu
> And dash to the mountains, Jersey Blue.

Faded diaries, old letters and orderly books preserve something of
the gala atmosphere of the expedition. At Trenton a Miss Forman
and a Miss Milnor were most amiable. Newtown, Pennsylvania, was
ticketed as a poor place for hay. At Potts Grove a captain of the
cavalry troop got kicked in the shin by his horse. Among the Virginians, Meriwether Lewis enjoyed the martial excitement, wrote to
his mother in high spirits of the "mountains of beef and oceans of
Whiskey"; sent regards "to all the girls" and announced that he would
bring "an Insergiant Girl to se them next fall bearing the title of Mrs.
Lewis." If there was such a girl, he soon forgot her.

Yet where there is an army in being there are bound to be un-
pleasant occurrences. Men were lashed. Quartermasters stole government property. A soldier was ordered to put a Scotch-Irish rebel under
guard. In execution of the order, he ran said insurgent through with
his bayonet, of which the prisoner died. At Carlisle a dragoon's pistol
went off and hit a countryman in the groin; he too died. On November
13, long remembered in many a cabin and stump-clearing as "the dis-

mal night," the Jersey horse captured various citizens whom they described grimly as "the whiskey pole gentry," dragging them out of bed, tying them back to back. The troopers held their prisoners in a damp cellar for twenty-four hours without food or water, before marching them off at gun point to a collection center at Washington, Pennsylvania.

In late November, finding no one to fight, the army turned east again, leaving a volunteer force under General Morgan to conciliate and consolidate the position during the winter. Twenty "Yahoos" were carried back to Philadelphia and were paraded by the Philadelphia Horse through the streets of the city with placards marked "Insurrection" attached to their hats, in an odd federalist version of a Roman triumph. The cavalry was composed, as an admirer said, of "young men of the first property of the city," with beautiful mounts, uniforms of the finest blue broadcloth. They held their swords elevated in the right hand while the light flashed from their silver stirrups, martingales and jingling bridles. Stretched over half a mile they came, first two troopers abreast, then a pair of Yahoos, walking; then two more mounted men, and so on.

The army, meditating upon their fatigues and hardships, called for a substantial number of hangings. Samuel Hodgson, Commissary-general of the army, wrote to a Pittsburgh confidant, "We all lament that so few of the insurgents fell—such disorders can only be cured by copious bleedings. . . ." Philip Freneau, friend and literary colleague of Brackenridge, suggested in retrospect—ironically, of course —the benefits which would have accrued to the country "if Washing had drawn and quartered thirty or forty of the whiskey boys." Most of the captives escaped any punishment other than that of being held in jail without a trial for ten or twelve months. One died. Two were finally tried and sentenced to death. Eventually both were let off.

Gradually the bitterness receded. In August, 1794, General Anthony Wayne had crushed the Indians at the Battle of Fallen Timbers. A treaty was concluded with Spain in October, 1795, clearing the Mississippi for Western trade. The movement of the army into the Pennsylvania hinterland, meanwhile, brought with it a flood of cash which furnished the distillers with currency for paying their taxes. These events served to produce a better feeling toward the Union.

If the rising was a failure, so was the liquor tax. The military ad-

venture alone, without ordinary costs of collection, ran up a bill of
$1,500,000, or about one third of all the money that was realized
during the life of the revenue act. The excise was quietly repealed
during Jefferson's administration. Yet the watermelon armies and the
Whiskey Boys made a not inconsiderable contribution to our constitutional history. Through them, the year 1794 completed what 1787
had begun; for it established the reality of a federal union whose law
was not a suggestion but a command.

9

Mr. Jefferson's "Sovereignty of the Living Generation"

MERRILL D. PETERSON

• The 1976 Bicentennial celebrations provided the paradox of
conservative politicians eagerly attempting to honor a revolution. The spectacle might have shocked some of the Founding Fathers, not least among them Thomas Jefferson. We can
only speculate as to what his actual reaction would have been
had he stumbled upon, say, the Freedom Train or the recreation of the Battle of Long Island. Perhaps his writings provide some clues?

Jefferson's well-known endorsement of the need for rebellion and blood to nurture the "tree of liberty" has often been
viewed as incidental to his agrarian ideology. But Professor
Merrill D. Peterson of the University of Virginia, a leading
Jeffersonian scholar, argues here that the idea of a continuing
break with the past constituted a central part of Jefferson's
thought. The author of the Declaration of Independence was
a vigorous advocate of an ongoing revolution.

Yet Professor Peterson backs away from endorsing a radical
approach by suggesting that reform is the best means for "enlightened progress." Do you believe that the nation's third
President would have counseled moderation or encouraged
revolt to the dissidents of our own time?

The Bicentennial of the American Revolution ought to be a time for
restoring the dialogue between the spirit of the past and the spirit of
the future in our national life. We commemorate our origins because
our origins are intertwined with our destiny; memory is the reciprocal
of hope, and conservation and change are essential to each other.
"There is nothing real without both . . . ," as Alfred North Whitehead once said. "Mere conservation without change cannot con-

From *Virginia Quarterly Review* 52 (Summer 1976): 437–47. Reprinted by
permission of the publisher and the author.

serve . . . , mere change without conservation is a passage from nothing to nothing."

The dominant tense in America has been the future. The nation began in revolt not only against the British Empire but against the empire of the past. It began with a fundamental commitment to redeem man from history, with all its accumulated guilts and terrors, and to place him in possession of himself. Nature eclipsed history as the director of human affairs. A curious national tradition arose, one whose libertarian principles contravened the force of tradition itself. In "the American Creed," as Gunnar Myrdal once reminded us, "the principles *conserved* are liberal and some, indeed, are radical." So, paradoxically, successive generations of Americans freely legitimated change at the cutting-edge of the future without changing much of anything in the venerable core of national values and goals. They were radical in 1776, and so they may still be; but in celebrating them we are all conservatives.

From the beginning, of course, there have been different orientations, prospective and retrospective, reforming and preserving—a party of hope and a party of memory—and much of our history centers on the conflict between them. Thomas Jefferson stood at the forefront of change during the Revolutionary Era; through him the idea of progress entered into the American democratic ideal, and he became the paramount symbol uniting the nation's promise with its revolutionary birth. When he was seventy years of age, reviewing the great ideological conflict of his time for the benefit of John Adams, Mr. Jefferson saw it fundamentally as a conflict between the friends and the enemies of enlightened progress. "One of the questions you know on which our parties took different sides, was on the improvability of the human mind, in science, in ethics, in government, etc. Those who advocated reformation of institutions, *pari passu*, with the progress of science, maintained that no definite limits could be assigned to that progress. The enemies of reform, on the other hand, denied improvement, and advocated steady adherence to the principles, practices, and institutions of our fathers, which they represented as the consummation of wisdom, the acme of excellence, beyond which the human mind could never advance." It was this faith that lay behind the most radical idea in the Jeffersonian catalogue: "the sovereignty of the living generation."

II

Like most ideas this one germinated for some time before it came to birth. Jefferson was led to formulate it in September 1789 in the course of reflection on events of the preceding months inaugurating the French Revolution. As United States Minister to France, he observed these events closely; as a philosopher and friend of democratic revolution, he was more than a detached observer. In liberal circles at Paris he stood as the oracle of the revolutionary nation that inspired France. His advice was sought, and he gave it. He wished for France all the blessings of freedom and self-government, such as the Americans possessed, but cautioned that the country could not go from despotism to liberty all at once. Everywhere, during a residence of five years abroad, Jefferson saw the heavy hand of oppression. "The truth of Voltaire's observation offers itself perpetually," he wrote, "that every man here must be either the hammer or the anvil." Once while on a country walk he fell into conversation with a poor laboring woman met along the way. Her melancholy tale vividly enforced upon his mind the wretchedness produced by aristocratic privilege and the concentration of property in a few hands. "I am conscious that an equal division of property is impracticable," Jefferson reflected on this "little attendrissement." "But the consequences of this enormous inequality producing so much misery to the bulk of mankind, legislators cannot invent too many devices for subdividing property. . . . Whenever there is in any country, uncultivated lands and unemployed poor, it is clear that the laws of property have been so far extended as to violate natural right. The earth," he concluded, "is given in common stock for men to labor and live on." America, fortunately, was a long way from the European condition, yet it was not too early to introduce safeguards against falling into it.

With the French Revolution this sentiment took on the precision of an idea. It became for Jefferson the rationale for sweeping social and political reform, and he laid it out in a long letter addressed to James Madison. "The question whether one generation of men has a right to bind another, seems never to have been started either on this or our side of the water," he wrote. "Yet it is a question of such consequences as not only to merit decision, but [also to place it] among the fundamental principles of every government."

Setting out from the basic proposition *"that the earth belongs in usufruct to the living*: that the dead have neither powers nor rights over it," Jefferson calculated the natural life of a generation during its majority. He consulted the mortality tables of the great scientist Buffon and arrived at the term of nineteen years. He then gave three specific applications of the principle. First, as to property, above all landed property. Every generation had a natural right to labor on the earth. If one could "eat up the usufruct," or withhold it from those to come, "the lands would belong to the dead, and not to the living." Second, as to public debts. One generation could not be burdened with the debts of another. The enormous debts of the Bourbon monarchy had contributed to the French Revolution, just as those of Great Britain had earlier started the chain of events culminating in the American Revolution. Would it not be wise and just for France to declare in its new constitution that no debt could be contracted for payment beyond the term of nineteen years? Indeed, would not this furnish "a fine preamble" to the first American law appropriating the public revenue? Not only, Jefferson thought, would such a provision save the people from oppressive taxes; it would also "bridle the spirit of war" by reducing the power to borrow within natural limits. Third, and most importantly, Jefferson applied the principle to the constitution and laws of government. "No society can make a perpetual constitution, or even a perpetual law. The earth belongs always to the living generation. . . . The constitution and laws of their predecessors [are] extinguished . . . in their natural course with those who gave them being. . . . Every constitution then, and every law, naturally expires at the end of 19 years. If it be enforced longer, it is an act of force, and not of right."

Such was Jefferson's idea. He conceded to Madison that it might "at first blush . . . be laughed at as the dream of a theorist." But, on reflection, his brilliant friend would surely find it sound. It would "exclude at the threshold of our new government the contagious and ruinous errors of this quarter of the globe, which have armed despots with means, not sanctioned by nature, for binding in chains their fellow men." Once established, the doctrine would be seen as still another instance, like the Federal Constitution over which Madison had labored, of the triumph of reason over habit in the conduct of human affairs.

III

These American references, as has sometimes been observed, had the appearance of an afterthought in Jefferson's essay. The idea could scarcely have matured in America. It was formed by European realities, specifically those of France in 1789, and urgently addressed that situation. At the time Jefferson wrote, he was under the care of his physician, Dr. Richard Gem, an elderly Englishman practicing in Paris, a friend of the *philosophes*, an ardent champion of the revolution; and "the sovereignty of the living generation" seems to have been a favorite sentiment with him. The naked sentiment, certainly, was not unknown to eighteenth-century political speculation. Locke and Rousseau had made the point that all men have an equal right to the earth; Adam Smith had extended the reasoning to "successive generations of men"; and David Hume had taken up the argument in order to refute it. No one before Jefferson, however, had given form and dress to the notion. And while it is true that his theory expressed the speculative fervor—the rage against the past—more characteristic of the French Revolution than of the American, we cannot brush aside Jefferson's American references.

The essay, after all, was sent to Madison, not to Mirabeau, and he was urged to "force" the idea into discussion in American councils. It found its place readily enough within the confines of Jefferson's political philosophy. If men are by nature free and equal, no great leap of logic was necessary to argue that generations of men, in organized societies, are also free and equal. If the people are sovereign, if government rests on their consent, then that sovereignty must be a living presence, not something which, exercised once, is dead and gone forever after. Jefferson's aversion to the claims of inheritance, his reforms in Virginia to make the laws work for the diffusion of property, his abiding concern to keep alive "the spirit of revolution" in the people, his commitment to the progress of mankind—for all this, and more, "the sovereignty of the living generation" might appear as the grand organizing concept. Although the French Revolution gave birth to the idea, it ought to be seen as an illustration of how that revolution enlarged and clarified Jefferson's understanding of the meaning and the promise of the American Revolution.

Jefferson was back in the United States, about to become the country's first Secretary of State, when Madison offered his reflections on the theory. He did not laugh but gently suggested that for all its philosophical magnificence the doctrine was "not *in all respects* compatible with the course of human affairs," and proceeded to a refutation that might have devastated anyone but Jefferson. Madison had earlier, in *The Federalist*, taken issue with his friend's advocacy, in the *Notes on Virginia*, of frequent revision of the state constitution, since such continual change would "in a great measure, deprive the government of that veneration which time bestows on everything, and without which perhaps the wisest and freest government would not possess the requisite stability." Now Madison painted a frightful picture of the hazards of an interregnum every nineteen years. If the rights of property became "absolutely defunct" at the end of a fixed term, the most violent class conflict must ensue, property values would depreciate, and industry would be deprived of the encouragement offered by stable laws.

Although the earth might be viewed as a gift to the living, this could be true only of the earth in its *natural* state, said Madison, for the *"improvements* made by the dead form a debt against the living who take the benefit of them." Finally, Madison argued, there was no way the theory could be practically applied. Generations were not fixed mathematical points, as on Jefferson's model; they were, rather, like flowing waves, changing daily and hourly as new members were added to the society and old members taken from it. The only escape from the embarrassments of the generational theory lay in the doctrine of the *implied consent* of the living to the Constitution, the laws, the obligations descending from the dead. None of this, Madison assured his philosophical friend, was meant to impeach the bolder truths contained in his "great plan"; but it would be some time, Madison concluded with charming understatement, before such truths, "seen through the medium of philosophy, became visible to the naked eye of the ordinary politician."

As Jefferson himself turned his attention to the mundane affairs of the new government, he made no effort to "force" the doctrine into discussion. His great rival, Alexander Hamilton, hearing of it, thought that the doctrine aimed at the repudiation of debt and the destruction of property. But so far as it came into discussion in the ideological controversy of the 1790s, it was in connection with the French Revolution. The leading English polemicist against the revolution, Edmund Burke, appealed to the authority of ancient laws and institutions—to the spiritual partnership of the dead, the living, and the unborn—and denounced mischievous democratic ideas which broke the bonds between one generation and another and rendered men "little better than flies of a summer." Burke was answered by Thomas Paine, who helped to build the ideological bridge between the American and French revolutions. Paine and Jefferson had sometimes been together in Paris, and it is possible that "the sovereignty of the living generation" came into their conversation. At any rate, in *The Rights of Man* Paine employed the argument with withering scorn against Burke and on behalf of democratic revolution. "Every age and generation must be free to act for itself, *in all cases*, as the ages and generations which preceded it," Paine wrote. "The vanity and presumption of governing beyond the grave is the most ridiculous and insolent of all tyrannies." This great controversy reverberated through American politics, sharpened the opposing ideologies of Federalists and Republicans, and contributed to Jefferson's own "revolution of 1800," marked by his ascendancy to the presidency.

IV

Jefferson never attempted to institutionalize the theory, yet never abandoned it. Indeed, he often reasserted it, as in criticism of public financial policies that mortgaged future generations and, most notably, in championing reform of the Virginia Constitution of 1776. That constitution, too conservative for Jefferson in its time, became an anachronism in the nineteenth century. It was unjust. Two-thirds of the adults then living had died by 1816. "This corporeal globe, and everything upon it, belong to its present corporeal inhabitants during their generation," Jefferson insisted. "They alone have a right to declare what is the concern of themselves alone, and to declare the law of that direction." Every constitution should be revised at generational intervals. It was the only substitute for atrophy on one side or violent revolution on the other. For "laws and constitutions must go hand in hand with the progress of the human mind. . . . We might as well require a man still to wear the coat which fitted him when a boy," Jefferson declared, "as civilized society to remain ever under the regimen of their barbarous ancestors." The same spirit presided over the birth of the University of Virginia, today still remembered as "Mr. Jefferson's University." It was by the advance of knowledge from generation to generation that the freedom and happiness of mankind were advanced, "not *infinitely*," Jefferson said, "but *indefinitely*, and to a term which no man can fix or foresee."

Given the delicate balance between theory and practice which Jefferson maintained in his politics, he probably never intended rigorous application of the doctrine, meaning it, rather, as a moral directive to society. And in this sense it entered into the spirit of American democracy. There is a Jeffersonian ring in Alexis de Tocqueville's observation that in America "every man forgets his ancestors"—"each generation is a new people"—and the Burkian protest can be heard in Lord Macaulay's solemn warning, "Your constitution is all sail and no anchor."

The doctrine was repeatedly invoked in the nineteenth century to justify the overhaul of state constitutions, just as Jefferson had invoked it in Virginia. Frederick Jackson Turner set forth a celebrated theory of American history which turned on the idea of extended genesis, of continuous rebirth and renewal as the frontier moved across the continent. Henry George, the great social reformer, made Jefferson the patron saint of the Single Tax founded on the natural right of equal opportunity to land. New Deal reformers in the 1930s made the doctrine part of their creed for remodeling the federal government; and one of Jefferson's scriptures was engraved on the grand memorial erected to him in Washington. A directive toward democratic change, its appeal has generally been to liberals and radicals, yet even conservatives have found comfort in Jefferson's denunciation of free-spending governments which burden posterity with the debts of the dead.

In our day Rexford Tugwell's provocative book, *The Emerging Constitution* (1974), has again called attention to the theory of generational sovereignty. The theory is as old as the United States Constitution, but no one before Tugwell had the audacity to apply it to the nation's sacred covenant. The Constitution, he argues, is antiquated in concept, anachronistic in many of its provisions, and wholly unresponsive to the needs of modern society. It has no basis in the reason or will of the people; it lacks both vigor and credibility and is on the way to becoming a lifeless monument from the American past. Tugwell rejects as a shabby fiction the idea of "a living constitution," that is, one resting on implied consent and adapted to every occasion by legislative, administrative, above all judicial improvisation—rarely, by amendment. The conception of the Supreme Court as "a constituent assembly in continuous session," to use Woodrow Wilson's language, is seen as an impertinence in a democracy. Such a malleable, *ad hoc* constitution brings the nation perilously close to having no constitution at all. Like Jefferson, Tugwell maintains that the only alternative to the subversion of the process of free government is the periodic remaking of the fundamental law. "In a society as mobile and complex as ours," he writes, "the Constitution ought never to be more than one generation old." Without repeating Jefferson's mathematical calculations, Tugwell settles on virtually the same generational term, twenty years; and, going beyond Jefferson, he would void every constitution by its own clause after twenty-five years.

v

So there is still some kick in Jefferson's revolutionary idea. The instance of Tugwell calls up the larger question with which I began of the uses of the past in America. If the American Revolution was a revolt against the past—a leap into the future—ought not its bearings for us to be liberating rather than conserving, directed toward making the new rather than saving the old? The rationality of Tugwell's position is unassailable on Jefferson's terms, or perhaps on those of the Founding Fathers, who would doubtless be amazed to discover that their Constitution had endured to the nation's third century. Yet, in 1976, it is hard to imagine a more foolhardy undertaking than the formation of a new constitution of the United States; and one is tempted to reply to Tugwell as Madison replied to Jefferson. Whatever the value of Jefferson's assault on the vaunted "wisdom of ancestors"—the tyranny of the dead over the living—at the dawn of the age of democratic revolution, it loses a good deal in the gathering twilight. The party of memory has this to be said for it: the classic forms and principles it would conserve are the surest embodiment of authority, clarity, and coherence in a frenzied time, and without these enlightened progress is hopeless. The sense of tradition, of continuity with our origins, of creative dialogue with our past may offer the strongest basis of rationality we as a nation now possess. In today's fragmented and tormented society, where there is so little consensus of belief or even consciousness of first principles, the values and institutions received from the past provide us with the principal source of legitimacy. And so, if we affirm Jefferson, we can no longer deny Burke.

Yet the spirit, if not the letter, of Jefferson's bold proposition still speaks to us. A generation's sense of obligation to the past is valuable only if it serves a greater obligation to the future. As Whitehead said, "conservation without change cannot conserve." The same philosopher once wrote, "The art of free society consists in the maintenance of the symbolic code; and secondly in fearlessness of revision, to secure that the code serves the purposes which satisfy an enlightened reason. Those societies which cannot combine reverence to their symbols with freedom of revision, must ultimately decay either from anarchy or from the slow atrophy of a life stifled by useless shadows." This is the Jeffersonian directive. In the case of America, the symbolic code has its core in what Myrdal called "the American Creed" and traced back to the American Revolution. The challenge in this Bicentennial season is neither to exalt nor to resign the code but to re-examine, redefine, and reconstruct it so that it might answer the purposes of the future after it has answered those of the past. For unless the code serves change we are indeed faced with the prospect of atrophy or anarchy. The long heritage of freedom in this nation is not just a thing to save— to be fenced about and decorated like a dead man's grave—it is a thing to use. Jefferson understood this. "The earth belongs to the living, not to the dead." Each generation is responsible for working out its own vision of freedom, always on condition of fidelity to the ends of freedom itself. "Nothing is unchangeable," Jefferson intoned, "but the inherent and inalienable rights of man." This is both the anchor and the sail; and it is his most enduring legacy two hundred years after he wrote the nation's charter of liberty.

II   THE YOUNG REPUBLIC

IO

The Old Northwest

JAMES E. DAVIS

• An ongoing theme in American history has revolved around what is believed to have been the real participatory democracy that existed on the frontier. It was a democracy, so it is said, that eroded with the industrialization and urbanization of the landscape. From the romantic French settler J. Hector St. Jean de Crèvecoeur to Thomas Jefferson to Alexis de Toqueville this idea of an idyllic rural ideal was handed down. No one, however, elaborated it more fully than Frederick Jackson Turner, who gave the Presidential address at the 1893 convention of the American Historical Association in Chicago. It was the West, he said, which focused American energies; and it was the West—wild, isolated, and infinitely challenging— which formed that peculiarly adventurous democrat, the American. "Stand at the Cumberland Gap," Turner asserted, "and watch the procession of civilization marching single file." A century later one could have watched the same parade at the South Pass in the Rockies.

Much of the rhetoric and style of political life in the United States can be traced to the persistent appeal of the frontier concept. President Jimmy Carter's visits to Midwestern farms and to town meetings in New England are clearly attempts to appeal to the sentiment and/or the belief that the heart of American democracy is and always has been in the hamlets and rural areas.

This idealized portrait of early American life has been challenged by many historians since the end of World War II. Richard C. Wade has argued that it was the cities, not the farms, that were the spearheads of the frontier; others have questioned whether the entire vision of Jeffersonian democracy was a myth from the start. But the view that the frontier fostered a special kind of egalitarianism and democratic spirit is one that will not die. In the essay which follows, Professor James E. Davis brings out evidence that grass-roots democ-

racy was more than just a dream for early settlers. Whether
Davis's view of Old Northwest society as being characterized
by "creativity and egalitarianism" is accurate or just Jeffersonian mythology in a new form is up to the reader to decide.

They came to the lands north of the Ohio River from many places:
the valleys and highlands of the Upper South, the coastal plains and
inland regions of the Middle Atlantic states, and the boulder-strewn
hills of New England. Between the end of the American Revolution
and the admission of Illinois to the Union in 1818, settlers hacked
their way through dense forests, established farms and communities
along waterways, and pushed on to the broad expanses of prairie
country. Their reasons for migrating were as numerous as their origins. Perhaps the majority were enticed westward by hopes of economic gain. Some were motivated by curiosity and a sense of adventure; others by misfortune—economic disaster, death in the family, a
brush with the law, or persecutions accompanying the French Revolution and Napoleonic upheavals.

The lands were not empty when the newcomers arrived. The Indian population, although decreasing, was still powerful enough in the
1790s to inflict stinging defeats on federal forces in Ohio, and as late
as the War of 1812 the Indians and their British sponsors lashed into
the region with surprising strength. After the war the influence of
Great Britain diminished, and the Indians—their offensive power cur-
tailed—grudgingly yielded vast tracts of land to the Americans. The
newcomers also encountered French and French-Indian residents,
whose way of life was in eclipse. In short, those whose livelihood was
dependent upon furs, Indians, and isolated outposts yielded to those
who cleared the land, broke the prairie, and sank the taproot of rural
family life.

Usually disdainful of the French and the Indians, the American settlers sought to subdue the wilderness and re-create the best aspects of
their own cultures. In that attempt they were only partially successful.

From James E. Davis, "New Aspects of Men and New Forms of Society: The
Old Northwest, 1790–1820," Journal of the Illinois State Historical Society 69
(August 1976): 164–72.

The society that did evolve was a curious hybrid of outside ideas, aspirations, customs, and institutions, altered somewhat by elements of the French and Indian cultures and tempered by the sometimes harsh realities of the wilderness.

Two traits of the new settlers seem to have predominated: creativity and egalitarianism or republicanism. The purpose of this paper is to examine those traits and their likely causes, and to suggest, in turn, how life in the Old Northwest was influenced by them.

Republicanism in the late 1700s and early 1800s assumed several forms. One was a high, perhaps inflated, self-confidence that was reflected everywhere, particularly in the independent, even haughty and surly, attitudes of hired workers. Elias Pym Fordham, who came to the region in 1817, observed: "No white man or woman will bear being called a servant. . . . Hirelings must be spoken to with Civility and cheerfulness." Observing the republican West shortly after the War of 1812, Isaac Holmes warned, "Male and female servants, or, as they are there called 'helps,' must eat and drink with the family." From early Princeton, Indiana, it was reported that even servants brought from England to America were soon "on a happy equality, rising up last and lying down first, and eating freely at the same time and table. None here permit themselves to have a master, but negroes." A friend of Henry Bradshaw Fearon's, having the temerity to ask a pioneer woman for her master, received this bristling republican response, "In this country there is no mistresses nor masters; I guess I am a woman citizen." If it is true that republican spirit and democratic institutions have as their basis a self-confident population, then the opening years of the nineteenth century in the lands north of the Ohio augured well for an egalitarian society.

The accessibility of public officials further illustrates the prevalence of republicanism. Unlike the East, where magistrates, military officers, and politicians were held in awe, the Old Northwest was characterized by an easy familiarity between the public and authorities. One observer, perhaps somewhat carried away, wrote: "I wish I could give you a correct idea of the perfect equality that exists among these republicans. A Judge leaves the Court house, shakes hands with his fellow citizens and retires to his loghouse. The next day you will find him holding his own plough. The Lawyer has the title of Captain, and serves in his Military capacity under his neighbour, who is a farmer and a Colonel." Richard Flower wrote from his farm near Albion, Illinois: "I went into my field the other day, and began a conversation with my ploughman: his address and manner of speech, as well as his conversation surprised me. I found he was a colonel of militia, and a member of the legislature." The unpretentiousness of public officials was also observed by John Palmer, traveling near Cincinnati in 1817. After meeting a certain Judge Lowe, who was also a tavern-keeper, Palmer commented, "It no doubt seems singular to the English reader, to hear of judges and captains keeping taverns . . . but it is very common in this republican country." The accessibility of public officials and the familiarity with which they were treated appears to have bred, among their constituents, a healthy suspicion of government and politicians.

Yet the spirit of republicanism was liveliest when ordinary citizens plunged headlong into politics. It was widely believed that eligible voters should participate, or be willing to participate, in public affairs. In the early settlements, according to one historian: "Candidates were perpetually scouring the country . . . defending and accusing, defaming and clearing up, making licentious speeches, treating to corn whiskey, violating the Sabbath, and cursing the existing administration. . . . And every body expected at some time to be a candidate for something." Newcomers to the Old Northwest cast off habits of social deference, and for the first time in their lives scrambled after the numerous public positions that had to be filled if society was to function. In every village and courthouse, inexperienced people were thrust into roles of leadership. More important, the problems with which those political novices grappled were fundamental, dealing as they did with transportation, education, defense, and administration. Furthermore, the solutions arrived at in the early days of settlement established the tone of the community for decades to come.

The resolution of problems of frontier life illustrates the creativity of the pioneers in the Old Northwest. The Western waterways, filled with snags and subject to seasonal fluctuations, called for particularly creative solutions. By the 1820s, strange-looking, shallow-draft boats, powered by high-pressure, lightweight engines, were successfully navigating the Western waters.

Other problems generated equally creative, if not always completely effective, solutions. The difficulties encountered in breaking the unyielding prairie grass and constructing adequate fencing elicited from nimble minds a host of solutions. When settlement outstripped the effective reach of territorial or state government, popular *ad hoc* committees sprang into existence. New sicknesses, as well as old ones, prompted strange cures from quack and doctor alike. Richard Lee Mason, traveling through Indiana in 1819, commented on the strange food substitutions: "Yolk of egg, flour and water mixed is a good substitute for milk and is often used in coffee in this country. Rye is frequently substituted for coffee and sage tea in place of the Imperial." Such commonplace solutions to daily problems were only part of the unending experimentation that occurred at all levels of society and in all aspects of life. The numerous difficulties accompanying settlement produced an impressive amount of inventiveness and adaptability.

The economy of the Old Northwest, unlike that of the East, was not specialized. Few settlers were *full-time* judges, teachers, clergymen, legislators, or even farmers. Professional men performed manual tasks and suffered no loss of esteem as a result. One traveler in early Ohio noted: "The doctor returns from his rounds . . . feeds his pigs; and yet his skill as a physician is not doubted on that account. Nor is the sentence of the magistrate . . . esteemed less wise or impartial, even by the losing party of his wrangling disputants, because Cincinnatus-like, he is called from the plough tail to the bench of justice." Other settlers turned from one job to another and still another; such jacks-of-all-trades could be found in the Northwest long after Illinois achieved statehood. A Swedish traveler, Gustaf Unonious, wrote of that kind of mobility: "The speed with which people here change their life calling and the slight preparation generally needed to leave one calling for another are really surprising, especially to one that has been accustomed to our Swedish guild-ordinances. . . . A man who today is a mason may tomorrow be a doctor, the next day a cobbler, and still another day a sailor, druggist, waiter, or school master." Unonious may have exaggerated somewhat, but it is undeniably true that many early Illinoisans sampled a dozen occupations over the course of a lifetime—learning from each and transferring knowledge and skills from one activity to the next.

There are several reasons for the growth of republicanism and creativity in the Old Northwest. One was the diverse nature of those who settled the land. Each migratory group and each household arrived with its own ideas concerning the future of the new society. The resulting suspicions and disputes between Protestant and Catholic, Southerner and Northerner, and native and immigrant insured that there would be no deferential society in the Old Northwest. Family name, religious affiliation, and political influence probably counted for less in the unfolding society of the Old Northwest than in the more highly ordered and structured society of the East. The pluralism of the new society guaranteed that common problems would be attacked from a number of directions. And solutions were probably found more quickly than would have been the case if only one cultural group had settled the region.

The very act of migration also fostered republicanism and creativity. Migration was selective, beckoning to the fresh lands a disproportionately large number of young adult males and generally discouraging the old and females. Selective migration, it appears, also discouraged the very wealthy, the very poor, and the timid and trouble-laden. It is clear that society in the Old Northwest from 1790 to 1820 was no mere reproduction of Eastern society, efforts to the contrary notwithstanding. Rather, the selective nature of migration created vacuums, and those vacuums generated a republican rush for the political and social positions formerly held by those who stayed behind.

Those who even considered migrating were precisely those who were able, and perhaps eager, to see new possibilities and new ways of doing things. Timothy Flint, for example, asked, "What mind ever contemplated the project of moving from the old settlements over the Alleghany mountains . . . without forming pictures of new woods and streams, new animals and vegetables, new configurations of scenery, *new aspects of men and new forms of society?*" For many, the promise of the Old Northwest began not with actual arrival in the region but with creative and liberating dreams of "new aspects of men and new forms of society."

The trek westward removed the immigrants from scenes of defeat and frustration and gave them an exhilarating and immediate success, which encouraged them to seize further opportunities for advancement. A variety of people were thrown together and enriched each other by swapping bits of news, methods of travel, and farming techniques.

In short, the act of migration performed several functions: it selectively eliminated certain kinds of settlers, raised expectations, heightened confidence, and generated a creative mix of diverse people. As we have seen, settlers in the new lands scrambled for new positions, moved from occupation to occupation, and refused to have masters. Habitual deference collapsed, at least temporarily, and a number of years passed—perhaps a decade or two—before the fabric of society was tightly drawn. In the early days, it was virtually impossible for a settler to awe his fellows with his name, past social standing, or connections. Rather, people exerted themselves—they *willed* themselves—into new roles and thereby transformed themselves and their society.

The abundance and availability of good land were crucial to that transformation. That fact was not lost on Francis Hall, who traveled in the Old Northwest shortly after the War of 1812. Of the pioneer, he wrote, "With his axe on his shoulder, his family and stock in a light waggon, he plunges into forests, which have never heard the woodman's stroke, clears a space sufficient for his dwelling, and first year's consumption, and gradually converts the lonely wilderness into a flourishing farm." Farmers were relatively self-sufficient—making much of what they needed from materials at hand, and selling only

Physicians' advertisements from a Kaskaskia (Illinois) newspaper

DR. W. L. REYNOLDS,

Has removed to his new shop, on Charter street, where he can always be found. He has fresh and genuine *Cow Pock Matter,* and those who wish to avail themselves of its salutary effects, had better make early application. He continues to practice *Physic, Surgery and Midwifery* with the most unremitted attention. Those who have accounts of more than six months standing with him will please to call and settle, as his shop cannot be supplied without money.   Aug. 22

DOCTOR JOEL C. FRASER

Determining on a permanent residence at St. Charles, solicits the patronage of a general and liberal public as a practitioner of *Medicine* and *Surgery*—All calls in the line of his profession will be attended to with cheerfulness, and promptitude.

He has on hand some genuine *Vaccine or Cow-Pock Matter,* a safe and effectual preventive of the Small Pox. Those who wish to enjoy the advantage of the vaccine discovery, will please to call immediately. The poor will be inoculated GRATIS.   Sept. 17, 1817.

rarely to distant markets. (It appears that almost every farmer supple-
mented his income by providing overnight shelter for travelers.) That
many settlers were self-sufficient farmers was regarded with favor by
such agrarian critics as Johann David Schoepf: "These incessant emi-
grations, of which there will be no end so long as land is to be had for
little or nothing, hinder the taking up of manufactures. . . . It is
more befitting the *spirit* of this population, and that of all America, to
support themselves on their own land . . . than to live better continually employed for wages."

Writing of immigrants from England who settled near Olive-green
Creek in Ohio, William Tell Harris noted, "Though they have not
been here more than fourteen months, they have grown corn, potatoes,
pumpkins, cucumbers, greens, melons, and tobacco, sufficient to render them *independent* of their neighbours for support." Traveling in
Ohio in 1819, Richard Lee Mason wrote of "*Independent* people in
log cabins. They make their own clothes, sugar and salt, and paint
their own signs." Land was within the reach of the average citizen in
the Old Northwest and even the average alien. To a considerable degree the availability of land created, however briefly, something ap-
proaching an *economic* democracy in the Old Northwest; and that
condition in turn provided the security necessary for people to express
their republican tendencies and engage enthusiastically in political
democracy.

Although land was plentiful and cheap, labor was not. According to
William Faux, "Nothing is reckoned for land; land is nothing; labour
every thing. In England it was almost vice versa." Artisans, craftsmen,
and ordinary laborers were at a premium in the Old Northwest, and
they knew it. Their economic independence was greater than it had
been elsewhere and so, too, was their self-confidence. Until there were
large pools of surplus farm labor—which were not available before perhaps the late 1830s—laborers strutted about in good republican style,
confident in the knowledge that their services commanded premium
wages.

Business and professional success in the Old Northwest required
fewer skills, less capital, and less experience than were needed in the
East or the Sweden of Gustaf Unonious. The cobbler who grew weary
of mending boots and shoes could associate with a man practicing
medicine, observe him as he concocted and dispensed cures, pay him

a fee for a kit of pills and instruments, and then himself begin to practice medicine. Ease of changing jobs undoubtedly promoted republicanism and, according to Unonious, creativity as well. After noting, "A man who today is a mason may tomorrow be a doctor, the next day a cobbler," Unonious admitted that "distinct inconveniences arise from this situation; yet undeniably this unlimited freedom is exactly one of the important reasons why America has advanced with such tremendous speed. It has indeed given opportunity for many humbugs to flourish, but at the same time it has called forth many able men and has spurred them on to greater efforts." The virtual absence of restraining professional societies encouraged people to go from occupation to occupation, learning from each and transferring knowledge to each.

Republicanism and creativity were also fostered by generally inactive or ineffective state and federal governments. Government, it is true, did help to pave the way for settlement through diplomacy, warfare, purchase, and survey. But even with the consolidation of national power during the 1790s, the federal government was unable to enforce treaty provisions, subdue Indians north of the Ohio, or remove illegal squatters on public lands. More important, what we now consider the basic responsibilities of government—local defense, transportation, education, and protection from criminals—often rested primarily with *ad hoc* committees of local settlers. Just as diversity prevented one strain of culture from dominating all of the other strains, the absence of a strong and pervasive government insured that republican assertiveness and creativity would not be crushed or inhibited by exclusionary tests of religion, political correctness, or ideological purity. Francis Hall was well aware of that fact. Of the nation's expansion, he said, "Such is the growth, and such the projects of this transatlantic republic, great in extent of territory, in an active and well-informed ppopulation; but above all, in a *free government*, which not only leaves individual talent unfettered, but calls it into life by all the incitements of ambition most grateful to the human mind."

One observer, witnessing the influx of settlers into the region, was moved to write: "A sense of relative consequence is fostered by their growing possessions, and by perceiving towns, counties, offices and candidates springing up around them. One becomes a justice of the peace, another a county judge and another a member of the legislative assembly. Each one assumes some municipal function, pertaining to schools, the settlement of a minister, the making of roads, bridges, and public works. A sense of responsibility to public opinion, self respect, and a due estimation of character and correct deportment are the consequence."

Those arriving late in the settlement process often found that the best land—the town sites, bridge sites, mill sites, and simply the best soil—was either occupied or prohibitively expensive. They also found that entrenched interests controlled county and state political offices and social positions. Some of the late arrivals stayed on as hired help or tenant farmers; others, realizing that opportunity lay farther to the west, pushed on. In short, whether or not a settler in the Old Northwest became a creative republican depended, at least in part, upon the date of his arrival.

It is impossible to make a characterization that would apply to all the settlers who came to the Old Northwest. Yet today's historian would almost certainly agree with an 1818 visitor to the Old Northwest, who wrote, "The thinking man who wants to witness the expansion and development of a new people in a new land will here find a sweeping and an interesting field for his studies."

II

Indian Policy in the Jacksonian Era

RONALD N. SATZ

• As Frederick Jackson Turner, Bernard De Voto, Richard A. Bartlett, William H. Goetzmann, and dozens of other historians have noted, the expansion of the United States from its narrow base along the Eastern Seaboard to almost continental size has been a central fact of American development. The story of the confrontation and eventual domination of the vast and empty spaces by successive waves of pioneer Americans has become our national epic.

Much less attention has been focused on the fact that the settlement of the West ranks among the many examples of naked aggression offered by history. In simple terms, an entire people was removed, a people whose claims to the land often dated back hundreds of years before it was even seen by the first white man. Those Indians that did not die in battle, or from hunger, or from diseases introduced by the new "Americans" were pressed onto reservations that kept getting smaller and smaller, despite treaties and guarantees from the federal government.

That this history was largely ignored for a century and more is hardly surprising given the treachery and the shameful methods used to separate the Indians from what was once theirs. Scholars who did write on the subject were usually so convinced of their own racial and cultural superiority over the native people that their accounts are properly suspect.

The essay by Ronald N. Satz is part of a reappraisal by younger historians of the assumptions held by nineteenth-century policymakers concerning the removal of Indian tribes. Were the claims of these relatively nomadic Indians greater than those of the pioneers who wanted to cultivate the land and create a cornucopia of plenty in the midst of a wilderness? Or would you agree with twentieth-century historian Satz

(and nineteenth-century English traveler Frances Trollope)
that, as Satz puts it, "Indian removal epitomized everything
despicable in American character?"

There has long been a tendency among scholars to view the Indian removal policy of the Jacksonian era in dualistic terms—the forces of evil
supported removal while the forces of humanity opposed it. Recently,
Francis Paul Prucha, George A. Schultz, and Herman J. Viola have
attempted to show that enlightened thought supported Indian removal
as a means of rescuing the eastern Indians from the evil effects of close
contact with the advancing white frontier. Yet even these historians
admit that the actual removal process entailed numerous hardships for
the Indians.

This paper is an attempt to assess the goals, execution, and results
of the Indian removal policy in the 1830s and 1840s by focusing on
the application of that policy in the Old Northwest. The events surrounding the removal of the Five Civilized Tribes from the South
have long been, to use the words of Grant Foreman, "a chapter un-
surpassed in pathos and absorbing interest in American history." This
dramatic episode has, to some extent, obscured similar events taking
place farther north during the same period of time. The Old Northwest provides an interesting test case for an examination of the differences between the rhetoric and the reality of the removal policy. The
Indians in this region were not the beneficiaries of anything approach-
ing the tremendous outpouring of public sympathy for the Cherokees
and their neighbors in the Southeast. If the Cherokees faced a "Trail
of Tears" in spite of the great volume of petitions, letters, and resolutions presented to Congress in their behalf, what happened to the Indians in the Old Northwest who lacked such enthusiastic public
support?

An essential ingredient to an understanding of the Indian policy in
this period is the recognition that President Jackson and his successors
in the White House, the War Department, the Office of Indian Affairs, and Indian agents maintained that the removal policy would
bring at least four major benefits to the Indians. These included:

From *Michigan History* 60 (Spring, 1976): 71–93. Reprinted by permission
of the Michigan History Division, Lansing, Michigan.

1. fixed and permanent boundaries outside of the jurisdiction of American states or territories;
2. isolation from corrupt white elements such as gamblers, prostitutes, whiskey vendors, and the like;
3. self-government unfettered by state or territorial laws; and
4. opportunities for acquiring the essentials of "civilized" society—Christianity, private property, and knowledge of agriculture and the mechanical arts.

Such were the benefits that government officials claimed the removal policy would bring the Indians. As a test case of the application of this policy, let us focus our attention on events in the Old Northwest.

President Jackson asked Congress on December 8, 1829, to provide him with authority to negotiate treaties to transfer Indians living east of the Mississippi River to a western location. Jackson and his congressional supporters, in their great rush to push through such legislation, seemed unconcerned about the technical aspects of any great migration of eastern Indians to the trans-Mississippi West. Opponents of the scheme, however, raised several important questions: Would emigration be purely voluntary? Would treaty commissioners negotiate only with acknowledged tribal leaders or would land be purchased from individuals? How many Indians would go? What kind of preparations and resources would be necessary for them? What would be the specific boundaries between emigrant tribes? How would the indigenous tribes in the West react to the intrusion of new people? During the debates on the Removal Bill, Tennessean David Crockett warned that it was a dangerous precedent to appropriate money for the executive branch without specifically knowing how the president intended to use it. Crockett warned that if Congress turned a deaf ear to the rights of the Indians then "misery must be their fate."

Unfortunately for the Indians, Congress passed the Removal Act in May 1830, and, despite the opposition of the nascent Whig party, Indian removal became a generally accepted policy in the ensuing decades. Throughout this period, congressional interest focused on patronage, partisan politics, and retrenchment to the detriment of the administration of Indian affairs. While the Whigs found it expedient to condemn aspects of the removal policy when they were struggling to capture the White House, they found it desirable to continue the policy once in office. Henry R. Schoolcraft, an Indian agent in Michigan Territory, poignantly described a serious defect of American Indian policy when he noted that "the whole Indian race is not, in the political scales, worth one white man's vote." The result of this situation, as David Crockett had warned, was misery for the Indians.

Among those who witnessed the actual dispossession of the eastern tribes in the Jacksonian era were two foreign travelers who, while not being authorities on the American Indians, nevertheless clearly recognized the deceptions involved in the treaty-making process. French traveler Alexis de Tocqueville poignantly observed that American officials, "inspired by the most chaste affection for legal formalities," obtained Indian title "in a regular and, so to say, quite legal manner." Although bribery and threats often accompanied treaty making and the formal purchases of Indian land, the United States had legal confirmation of its acquisitions. Indeed treaty negotiators were able to "cheaply acquire whole provinces which the richest sovereigns in Europe could not afford to buy" by employing such tactics as bribery or intimidation. Another European visitor, English Captain Frederick Marryat, accurately reported that "the Indians . . . are *compelled* to sell—the purchase money being a mere subterfuge, by which it may *appear* as if the lands were not being wrested from them, although, in fact, it [*sic*] is."

President Jackson had early indicated that his primary interest was the removal of the southeastern tribes. Although congressmen from the Old Northwest advised him following the passage of the Removal Act that the time for securing removal treaties in their region was "auspicious," Old Hickory informed them that his immediate concern was to set into motion a great tide of southern Indian emigration. Events in Illinois in the spring of 1832, however, played into the hands of the supporters of Indian removal in the Old Northwest.

In the spring of 1832, a hungry band of a thousand Sac and Fox Indians and their allies left their new home in Iowa Territory and crossed the Mississippi River en route to their old capital on the Rock River. Under the leadership of the proud warrior Black Hawk, this band, which included women and children, entered Illinois in search of food and as a means of protesting against their treatment by white frontiersmen. Mass hysteria swept the Illinois frontier with the news that the Indians had crossed the river. Governor John Reynolds called up the state militia to repel the "invasion" despite the fact that Black

Hawk's band was clearly not a war party. The result was a short, bloody conflict brought on largely as a consequence of the actions of drunken state militia. The ruthless suppression of the so-called "Indian hostilities" in Illinois and neighboring Wisconsin in 1832, and the seizure of a large part of the trans-Mississippi domain of the Sac and Fox Indians as "indemnity" for the war, broke the spirit of other tribes in the Old Northwest. Under pressure from the War Department, the Winnebagos in Wisconsin soon signed a removal treaty ceding their land south of the Wisconsin River. One by one, other tribes succumbed to similar pressure.

As critics of the Removal Act of 1830 had feared, the War Department obtained many of these land cessions by bribery. Agents courted influential tribal leaders by offering them special rewards including money, merchandise, land reserves, and medals, among other things. Sometimes treaty commissioners selected chiefs to represent an entire tribe or group of bands. The Jackson administration, for example, secured the title to the land of the United Nation of Chippewa, Ottawa, and Potawatomi Indians in northeastern Illinois, southeastern Wisconsin, and southern Michigan by "playing Indian politics." Indeed, the very existence of the United Nation was the result of the government's insistence on dealing with these Indians as if they were a single unit. Yet neither the great majority of the Chippewas and Ottawas nor all of the Potawatomi bands recognized the authority of the so-called United Nation. The government's policy of dealing with the entity as the representative of all Chippewas, Ottawas and Potawatomis was a clever maneuver to oust these Indians from their lands. By working closely with mixed-blood leaders and by withholding Indian annuities, the War Department secured the desired land cessions from the United Nation in the early 1830s.

During the Jacksonian era, the War Department frequently used economic coercion as a means of securing Indian title in the Old Northwest. Since the 1790s, the department had invested funds appropriated by Congress for purchasing Indian land in state banks or stocks and had paid the Indians only the annual interest on the amount owed them under treaty stipulations. This annuity or trust fund system gave government bureaucrats virtual control over funds legally belonging to the Indians. Although Thomas Jefferson played an important role in establishing the precedent of withholding Indian annuities as a means of social control, this procedure became a standard policy after 1829.

Treaty commissioners, Indian agents, and other field officers of the War Department found that withholding annuities was a convenient means of inducing recalcitrant Indians to sign treaties and to emigrate. Commissary General of Subsistence George Gibson advised the Jackson administration, "Let the annuities be paid west of the Mississippi [River], and there is no reason to doubt that the scheme of emigration would meet with little future opposition." American officials maintained considerable influence over tribal politics by determining who would receive the annuities.

Another measure used to encourage Indians to make land cessions was the inclusion of provisions in removal treaties for the granting of land reserves to chiefs, mixed-bloods, or other influential members of the tribes. The motivation behind this practice was twofold. First, it allowed government officials to combat Indian and American opposition to the removal policy based on the fact that some Indians had demonstrated a willingness and capability of accepting the white man's "civilization." When Andrew Jackson encountered strong opposition to his efforts to remove the Cherokees and the other so-called Civilized Tribes from their Southern domain, he conceded that Indians willing to accept the concept of private property should be allowed to remain in the East on individual reserves and become citizens of the states in which they resided. Secondly and more importantly for the Old Northwest, the practice of providing reserves of land to certain Indians was an ingenious device for bribing chiefs or influential tribesmen into accepting land cession treaties and for appeasing white traders into whose hands their reserves were certain to fall.

Treaty commissioners in Indiana found it impossible to secure land cessions from the Miami and Potawatomi Indians without the approval of the Wabash Valley traders to whom they were heavily in debt. Land speculators and settlers regarded the Miami and Potawatomi reserved sections adjacent to the Wabash River and the route of the Wabash and Erie Canal as choice lands. Wabash Valley traders, Indian agents, and even United States Senator John Tipton ultimately secured most of these lands from the Indians and rented them to white settlers for high profits after the Panic of 1837. By 1840 treaties with the Miamis and Potawatomis of Indiana had provided for nearly two hundred thousand acres of individual reserves. The largest holders of these reserves were not Indians but Wabash Valley traders W. G. and G. W. Ewing and Senator Tipton. Thousands of acres of Indian land elsewhere in the Old Northwest also fell into the hands of speculators.

In spite of the fact that speculators and traders often pressured the Indians into relinquishing their reserves before the government even surveyed the ceded tribal land, little was done to protect the Indians from such swindlers. Indiana Whig Jonathan McCarty, a bitter political adversary of Senator Tipton, introduced a resolution in Congress in 1835 calling for an investigation of the handling of Indian reserves, but no action resulted. Jackson, and his successors in the White House, were anxious to tone down investigations of alleged frauds in Indian affairs in order to avoid possible political embarrassments. Even some of the staunchest opponents of the removal policy benefited directly from the sale of Indian lands. Daniel Webster, Edward Everett, Caleb Cushing and Ralph Waldo Emerson were among those who speculated in Indian lands in the Old Northwest.

In addition to granting land reserves to Indians, the War Department followed the practice of including provisions in removal treaties for the payment of Indian debts to traders as a means of promoting removal. Since the Indians relied heavily on traders for subsistence and advice in the Old Northwest, the inclusion of traders' debts was often crucial to successful treaty negotiations. Although the recognition of these debts helped to promote the signing of land cession treaties, the practice also meant that the Indians lost huge sums of money to men who frequently inflated the prices of the goods they sold or falsified their ledgers. Transactions at treaty negotiations relative to the sale of Indian land, the adjustment of traders' claims, and the like, were a complex business, yet many Indians, especially the full bloods, did not know the difference between one numerical figure and another.

The administration of Indian affairs in the mid-1830s was particularly vulnerable to criticism. The Panic of 1837 led many traders to exert political influence on treaty commissioners to have phoney Indian debts included in removal treaties. Commissioners Simon Cameron and James Murray awarded the politically influential American Fur Company over one hundred thousand dollars in alleged debt claims against the Winnebagos in Wisconsin in 1838 in return, according to rumor, for a large kickback. Only the military disbursing agent's refusal to pay the traders ultimately led to the exposure of the fraud. One eyewitness to this episode subsequently claimed that it was worse than the Crédit Mobilier scandal. An English visitor to Wisconsin several years after the incident reported that the acknowledgment of traders' claims during annuity payments was still a "potwallopping affair" in which the Indians left as empty-handed as when they had arrived. Both the Tyler and Polk administrations, in response to complaints from some congressmen, honest Indian agents, and concerned frontier residents, denounced the practice of acknowledging traders' debts in treaties. But the tremendous political influence of the traders, together with the War Department's emphasis on the speedy removal of Indians from areas desired by whites, led the government to follow the path of expediency. Traders continued to receive payments for their claims throughout the Jacksonian era.

If the techniques already mentioned failed to entice the Indians to emigrate, there was always brute force. The state of Indiana probably had one of the worst records in this respect. The Potawatomis ceded their last holdings in Indiana in 1836, but the treaty provisions allowed them two years to emigrate. Whites quickly began moving onto their land in order to establish preemption rights. As tension between the Indians and the whites grew, the Indiana militia rounded up the Potawatomis in 1838. When Chief Menominee, who had refused to sign the removal treaty, objected to the proceedings, the soldiers lassoed him, bound him hand and foot, and threw him into a wagon. The militia then hastily set into motion the Potawatomi exodus to the West—the "Trail of Death" along which about one hundred and fifty men, women, and children died as a result of exposure and the physical hardships of the journey. Several years later the Indiana militia also rounded up the Miami Indians in similar fashion to expedite their removal to the West.

By the end of Jackson's second term, the United States had ratified nearly seventy treaties under the provisions of the Removal Act and had acquired about one hundred million acres of Indian land for approximately sixty-eight million dollars and thirty-two million acres of land in the trans-Mississippi West. While the government had relocated forty-six thousand Indians by 1837, a little more than that number were still in the East under obligation to remove. According to the Office of Indian Affairs, only about nine thousand Indians, mostly in the Old Northwest and New York, were without treaty stipulations requiring their relocation, but there is evidence to indicate that the number of such Indians east of the Mississippi River at this time was much larger than the Indian Office reported. Indeed, there were probably more than nine thousand in Wisconsin Territory alone! The dearth of reliable population statistics for Indians during the Jacksonian era is a perplexing problem. By 1842, however, the United States had acquired the last area of any significant size still owned by the Indians in the Old Northwest. Only scattered remnants of the great tribes that had once controlled the region remained behind on reservations or individual holdings, chiefly in Michigan and Wisconsin.

The removal treaties of the Jacksonian era contained liberal provisions for emigrants and those remaining behind on reserves. They offered emigrants rations and transportation, protection en route to their new homes, medicine and physicians, reimbursement for abandoned property, funds for the erection of new buildings, mills, schools, teachers, farmers and mechanics, and maintenance for poor and orphaned children. The treaties read as if they were enlightened agreements. Yet there were several inherent defects in the treaty-making process. One of these was the assumption that the Indian leaders dealing with the government commissioners represented the entire tribe. Another was the assumption that the Indians clearly understood the provisions of the agreements. Still another was the fact that the Senate often amended or deleted treaty provisions without prior consultation with tribal leaders. Although treaty stipulations were provisional until ratified by the Senate, settlers rarely waited for formal action before they inundated Indian land. While Alexis de Tocqueville noted that "the most chaste affection for legal formalities" characterized American treaty making with the Indians, he also argued that "it is impossible to destroy men with more respect to the laws of humanity."

In spite of the favorable terms promised in removal treaties, most emigrants faced numerous hardships on their journeys to their new homes. A major reason for their misery was the system of providing them food and transportation by accepting the lowest bid from contractors. Many unscrupulous expectant capitalists furnished the Indians with scanty or cheap rations in order to make a sizeable profit from their contracts. The contractors were businessmen out to make money, and they were quite successful. Thomas Dowling, who received a contract in 1844 to remove six hundred Miami Indians from Indiana for nearly sixty thousand dollars, boasted to his brother that he would make enough profit to "rear the superstructure of an independence for myself, family, and relations."

In addition to the evils of the contract system, Indian emigrants also suffered from the government's perpetual concern for retrenchment. Although removal treaties provided for the medical care of emigrants, the War Department prohibited agents from purchasing medicine or surgical instruments until "actually required" during the economic hard times after 1837. Such instructions greatly hampered the effectiveness of the physicians accompanying migrating parties. To make matters worse, emigrants from the Old Northwest, many of them weakened by their constant battle with the elements of nature en route to the trans-Mississippi West, found themselves plagued with serious afflictions. Efforts to economize in removal expenditures by speeding up the movement of emigrants also led to much suffering. The War Department ordered in 1837 that only the sick or very young could travel west on horseback or by wagon at government expense. Even before this ruling, efforts to speed up the movement of migrating parties under orders from Washington officials proved detrimental to the Indians. An agent in charge of the removal of the Senecas from Ohio earlier in the 1830s, for example, wrote his superior that "I charge myself with cruelty in forcing these unfortunate people on at a time when a few days' delay might have prevented some deaths, and rendered the sickness of others more light, and have to regret this part of my duty."

Now let us examine the success of the removal policy in terms of the so-called benefits that government officials had argued it would bring to the Indians after their relocation. The first benefit was fixed and permanent boundaries outside the jurisdiction of American states and territories. Even before the Black Hawk War, the French travelers Alexis de Tocqueville and Gustave de Beaumont had voiced concern over the government's failure to establish a permanent Indian country for the northern Indians comparable to the one it was setting off west of Arkansas for the southern tribes. Sam Houston, a good Jacksonian Democrat, assured the travelers that Indian-white relations in the Old

Northwest were not as critical as in the South. He pointed out that permanent boundaries were unnecessary for the northern tribes since they would eventually be "pushed back" by the tide of white settlement. Following the Black Hawk War, Houston's contention proved correct.

The history of the relocation of the Winnebago Indians from Wisconsin illustrates the government's failure to systematically plan fixed boundaries for emigrants from the Old Northwest. When the War Department pressured the Winnebagos into signing a removal treaty at the cessation of the Black Hawk War, it left them with two alternative locations. One was the so-called "neutral ground" in Iowa between the Sac and Fox Indians and their Sioux enemies to the North. This location proved too precarious for the Winnebagos, who quickly made their way back to the second designated area that was within the territorial limits of Wisconsin, north of the Wisconsin River. When the Winnebagos moved into this area, they found themselves too tightly crowded together to live according to their old life styles. As a result, they frequently returned to the sites of their old villages south of the Wisconsin River.

In returning to their old homesites, the Winnebagos encountered other Indians as well as white settlers. While the War Department had induced the Winnebagos to leave southern Wisconsin in order to free them from white contact in that area, it had relocated tribes from New York there in order to free them from white contact in New York. Both the Winnebagos and the New York Indians relocated in Wisconsin soon became the victims of the great land boom that swept the territory in the 1830s as whites eagerly sought Indian land for settlement and timber.

By 1838 the Winnebagos had ceded all of their land in Wisconsin and had promised to move to the neutral ground in Iowa, but the "final" removal of the last band of these Indians in 1840 required the use of troops. For several years after their relocation, the Indian Office attempted to transfer them from Iowa to the Indian country west of Missouri. In 1841 the Tyler administration planned to have them join other northern tribes in a new Indian territory north of the present Iowa-Minnesota border and south of, roughly, the 46th parallel. This new location would appease residents of Iowa who were clamoring for the removal of the Winnebagos and settlers in Wisconsin who were anxious to expel the Winnebago stragglers and the New York Indians who had settled there. Such a northern location would also placate the citizens of Arkansas and Missouri who opposed any additional influx of Indians on their western borders. The War Department favored this plan because it would provide a safe corridor for white expansion to the Pacific through Iowa and would place the Indians of the Old Northwest far south of the Canadian border thus luring them away from British-Canadian influence.

In spite of the War Department's plans, large numbers of Winnebagos drifted back to Wisconsin during the 1840s. Efforts to relocate them in present-day Minnesota between the Sioux and their Chippewa enemies led again to Winnebago defiance. Despite the use of military force to compel them to go to their "proper homes," the Winnebagos were greatly dispersed in Wisconsin, Iowa, and Minnesota at the end of the decade, to the annoyance of white settlers in those areas. The condition of these Indians clearly indicates that the War Department was lax in undertaking long-range planning for a permanent home for the tribes of the Old Northwest. The government continually reshuffled these Indians in order to make room for northeastern tribes and the growing pressures of white settlement. Whenever the white population pattern warranted it, the War Department merely redesignated new locations for the Indians. Nor did the government pay much attention to the needs of emigrants. Menominee Chief Oshkosh, in complaining about Winnebago intrusions on Menominee land in Wisconsin in 1850, cited several reasons why the Winnebagos continually left their new locations and returned to Wisconsin; these included the poor soil in their new country, the scarcity of game there, and, most importantly, their dread of their fierce Sioux neighbors.

The agony of the Winnebagos was not unique. Many other tribes faced the prospect of removing to an allegedly permanent location more than once. Continued white hostility following the Black Hawk War led the United Nation of Chippewas, Ottawas, and Potawatomis, for example, to give up their claims to northern Illinois, southeastern Wisconsin and several scattered reserves in southern Michigan in 1833 for a tract of land bordering the Missouri River in southwestern Iowa and northwestern Missouri. The new Potawatomi lands included the Platte Country, the region in present-day northwest Missouri watered by the Little Platte and Nodaway rivers. This area was not included in the original boundaries of Missouri in 1820. The inclusion of the Platte Country in the land designated for the Potawatomis demonstrates once again the poor planning of the War Department. In 1832 Missouri Governor John Miller had called for the annexation of this region and Missouri Senators Lewis F. Linn and Thomas Hart Benton joined him in arguing that the area was necessary for the political and economic growth of their state. Although over one hundred Potawatomis had signed the original treaty, the War Department, in its effort to appease Missourians, secured an amended treaty, signed by only seven Indians, that substituted a similar amount of land in Iowa for the Platte Country.

While the government was seeking to modify the original treaty to placate Missouri, Potawatomis who had signed that document moved to the Platte Country. The number of tribesmen there grew as small bands from Indiana continued to travel West in accordance with the provisions of the original treaty. Many Potawatomis came to view the government's new proposed location for them in Iowa as being too close to the Sioux. The Jackson administration reluctantly permitted them to settle temporarily in the Platte Country until they could find suitable sites for new villages in southeastern Iowa. There were still approximately sixteen hundred Potawatomis in the Platte Country in March 1837 when President Martin Van Buren proclaimed the area part of the state of Missouri. The War Department soon ejected them from there and resettled them in southwestern Iowa and Kansas. Government officials consolidated the Potawatomis into one reservation in northcentral Kansas in 1846 and subsequently relocated them in Oklahoma during the 1860s.

The experiences of the Winnebago and Potawatomi Indians clearly indicate that the new boundaries for emigrants from the Old Northwest were far from permanent. Treaty commissioners merely reshuffled the tribes around as frontiersmen, speculators, and state officials pressured the War Department to open more Indian land to white settlement. Federal officials failed to undertake long-range planning for the establishment of permanent boundaries for the emigrant tribes from this region. The sole effort in this direction before 1848, the Tyler administration's attempt to create a northern Indian territory, failed because the War Department had neglected the needs and the desires of the Indians.

At the end of the Jacksonian era, Indian Commissioner William Medill reported that the Polk administration had begun to mark off a northern Indian "colony" on the headwaters of the Mississippi River for "the Chippewas of Lake Superior and the upper Mississippi, the Winnebagoes, the Menomonies, such of the Sioux, if any, as may choose to remain in that region, and all other northern Indians east of the Mississippi (except those in the State of New York), who have yet to be removed west of that river." Together with the removal of Indians from the "very desirable" land north of the Kansas River to a southern "colony" west of Arkansas and Missouri, Medill hoped that the concentration of the northern Indians on the headwaters of the Mississippi River would provide "a wide and safe passage" for American emigrants to the Far West. Medill's report of November 30, 1848, was a tacit admission of the government's failure to provide Indian emigrants from the Old Northwest with fixed and permanent boundaries as guaranteed by the Removal Act of 1830. Throughout this period, the exigencies of the moment determined the boundaries that American officials provided for the Indians.

The second alleged benefit of removal was isolation from corrupt white elements such as gamblers, prostitutes, whiskey peddlers, and the like. The government's lack of planning for the permanent relocation of the tribes of the Old Northwest meant that these Indians were continually in the path of the westward tide of white settlement. Although Congress passed a Trade and Intercourse Act in 1834 to protect the Indians from land hungry whites, as well as whiskey peddlers and similar groups, nothing, including Indian treaty rights, stopped the advance of white settlement. Liquor was readily available to most tribes. In 1844 Thomas McKenney, an expert on Indian affairs, reported that the Menominees in Wisconsin, who had undergone several relocations, were "utterly abandoned to the vice of intoxication." Efforts to strengthen the Trade and Intercourse Laws in 1847 failed once again to halt the liquor traffic. Frontier citizens, especially the traders and their powerful political allies, blatantly refused to cooperate in enforcing the laws.

Tribal self-government unfettered by state or territorial laws was the third benefit that removal was supposed to bring the Indians. Yet the Trade and Intercourse Acts of 1834 and 1847 placed the Indians at the mercy of the white man's conception of justice. The legislation clearly provided that American laws would take precedence over Indian laws and customs in all cases involving both groups. Since the local judicial officers in the white communities adjoining Indian settlements reflected the dominant attitudes of their respective communities and often had ties with local businessmen and traders, they were not always effective administrators of the federal laws designed to protect the Indians from whiskey peddlers or other avaricious whites. The presence of federal Indian agents and military detechments near Indian settlements, moreover, meant that the Indians were not completely sovereign. Indian agents and the commanding officers of frontier posts often played "Indian politics." They found it much easier to deal with a central tribal authority rather than a series of chiefs or headmen and encouraged the recognition of one individual as the principal tribal leader. One vehicle used to accomplish this purpose was the allocation of Indian annuities. By determining who would receive the annuities, the War Department manipulated tribal politics. The result of such efforts was the emasculation of tribal self-government.

The fourth alleged benefit of removal was "civilization." American officials involved in the formulation and execution of Indian policy argued that the Indians lacked the essentials of civilized society—Christianity, private property, and knowledge of agriculture and the mechanical arts. Indian removal, they maintained, would provide ample opportunities for the uplifting of the Indians. Yet the removal policy did not bring great benefits, in terms of the white man's "civilization," to a significant number of Indians.

The constant reshuffling of tribes to new "permanent" locations failed to promote Indian interest in the white man's "civilization." How could the Winnebagos who had suffered tremendous social and psychological strains as a result of their continuous uprooting and relocation be expected to have interest in, or make significant advances in, the adoption of Christianity or any of the other so-called prerequisites of "civilized" society? Other Indians had similar reactions.

The events surrounding the acquisition of Chippewa and Ottawa lands in Michigan demonstrate some of the reasons for the failure of government efforts to promote its "civilization" program among the Indians of the Old Northwest. In 1836 the Chippewas and Ottawas had ceded their lands with the understanding that the government would allot them permanent reservations in northern Michigan and provide blacksmiths, farmers, and teachers to help them learn white trades and farming techniques. The land cession treaty provided federal funds to accomplish the "civilization" of these Indians, but the entire project was doomed before it began.

When the Senate considered the ratification of the treaty, it amended the document so that the reserves in northern Michigan would only be temporary residences. The Indians were understandably disturbed by this unilateral alteration of the treaty, and they were reluctant to move to temporary reserves in order to clear the land and to take up farming. Commissioner of Indian Affairs Carey Allen Harris, moreover, urged that government funds for these Indians be kept to a minimum until they settled at a permanent location.

Because their "permanent" boundaries always seemed to be temporary ones, the Indians of the Old Northwest found it more convenient to live off their annuities than to labor in their fields. As Chippewa Indian George Copway lamented, "no sooner have the Indians gone on and made improvements, and our children began to like to go to the school houses which have been erected, than we hear the cry of the United States government, 'We want your lands'; and, in going from one place to another, the Indian looses [sic] all that he had previously learned." As a result of this situation, the Indians paid more attention to the fur traders than to the school teachers. The tribes in this region relied heavily on the traders for food and goods. Government officials tended to see this dependence on the traders as a sign of idleness or weakness of character. Their ethnocentricism blinded them to the fact that farming had long been women's work among these tribes. The fur trade, wild grain, and fish were traditionally much more important to the livelihood of these Indians than American agricultural products.

Other probelms inherent in the "civilization program" included the personnel employed to "civilize" the Indians. Such appointments offered patronage-hungry politicians a means of rewarding their supporters. Consequently, the teachers hired to work with the Indians did not always bring altruistic motives to their jobs. Some of them were even "indolent and shif[t]less." The employment of missionaries as civilizing agents caused special problems. Interdenominational rivalries greatly impeded their work. Some Indians demonstrated open hostility to missionaries because they associated them with efforts to remove their people from their ancient homes. Presbyterian minister Peter

13

The Mormons: From Poverty and Persecution to Prosperity and Power

RODMAN W. PAUL

• The Church of Jesus Christ of Latter Day Saints is one of
the few religious institutions that is indigenous to the United
States. It was founded in Palmyra, New York by Joseph
Smith, who subsequently led a small band of followers from
New York to Kirtland, Ohio; then to Independence, Missouri; then to Nauvoo, Illinois. At every point the Mormons
encountered hostility and prejudice, in part because their doctrines directly challenged important points of accepted Christian theology and in part because they held to an unorthodox
style of wedded life whereby a man could have more than one
wife at the same time. Polygamy did not go down well with
the citizenry of the nineteenth-century American frontier. Joseph Smith himself became a martyr to his cause, and his remaining followers, led by Brigham Young, possibly escaped a
similar fate only by embarking on a dangerous and lonely
journey to a spot which was then quite literally in the middle
of nowhere—the site of present-day Salt Lake City.

The saga of the Mormons has been told many times—both
by followers of Joseph Smith and Brigham Young and by
persons who were convinced that Smith was a fool or a charla-
tan or both. Professor Rodman W. Paul's essay provides a
more balanced view, one that takes account of both the
strengths and the weaknesses of the unusual and highly successful Mormon Church.

In the month of February 1846, when conditions for travel were as
unpropitious as possible, the Mormons began moving out of their
newly built city of Nauvoo, Illinois, in order to cross the ice-strewn

Reprinted by permission from *American Heritage* 28 (June 1977): 74–83. ©
1977 by American Heritage Publishing Co., Inc.

Mississippi, on the first leg of a long and uncertain journey. A forced abandoning of barely completed homes, this time with the loss of much property and the necessity for travel in the dead of winter, was no new experience for the adherents of the Church of Jesus Christ of Latter-day Saints. Twice before, in Ohio and Missouri, the violence of their non-Mormon neighbors had forced the "Saints" to give up newly established colonies, but Nauvoo was the worst disaster yet, for in 1844 an Illinois lynching mob had murdered Joseph Smith, founder of the Mormon Church, the man who claimed to have talked with God and angels, the man who claimed to have found and translated the golden tablets on which the Book of Mormon was engraved, the man who had directed—some would say dictated—every social, economic, political, and religious aspect of Mormon daily life.

As her family's laden wagons struggled down to the shore of the ice-bound Mississippi, the awesome dangers of the venture were all too clear to Sarah D. Rich, who later recorded her emotions in an appealingly misspelled manuscript:

> To start out on such a jeorney in the winter as it ware and in our state of poverty it would seam like walking into the jaws of death. But we had faith in our heavenly father and we put our trust in him, feeling that we ware his chosen people and had imbraced his gospel and insted of sorrow we felt to rejoice that the day of deliverence had come.

A "chosen people," the elect of God, the only true believers—such phrases characterized the Mormons as they saw themselves. The confident faith that inspired such thinking was at once a force that held the Mormons together and an irritant that antagonized those who were not Mormons ("Gentiles," as the Saints called them). Despite, or perhaps because of, the Mormons' remarkable success in creating a vigorously independent and thriving city at Nauvoo, the assaults of the Gentiles had made life in Illinois too dangerous and costly to be endured. Smith's principal successor, Brigham Young, had taken the lead in determining that the Mormons must begin a massive folk migration that would carry them far beyond contact with non-Mormons. The plan finally decided upon was to cross the vast emptiness of the Great Plains to some as yet uncertain point just beyond the Rockies. It would be a huge undertaking that would require several years, for ultimately over fifteen thousand people and whatever belongings they had salvaged in their enforced winter exodus had to be moved more than a thousand miles and resettled in a desert.

To any dispassionate observer, a folk-migration begun in the worst time of year and with shortages of wagons, teams, and food must have seemed truly a case of "walking into the jaws of death," as Mrs. Rich expressed it. By all logic, this should have been the moment for Mormonism to break up. With their prophet and original organizer murdered, their homes lost, and signs of dissidence among them, the Mormons in this dreary winter of 1846 should have been ready to follow many another new sect into disintegration and ineffectuality.

But what in fact is the status of the Mormons today, more than 130 years after their trek to the land of Zion in the Salt Lake Valley of Utah? They are one of the fastest-growing and most prosperous denominations in the country. They claim nearly 2,500,000 adherents within the United States and another million overseas, and, thanks to energetic proselytizing at home and abroad, their numbers increase almost daily. So does their influence. The Mormons, who were unsophisticated, poorly educated rural folk in 1846, have joined the general American trend by turning away from the countryside to dwell in suburbs' and cities, and away from farming and simple crafts to the professions, commerce, finance, and industry.

Today more than half of the American Mormons live outside Utah and its immediate neighbors, and they are as likely to be found directing major businesses and real-estate operations in Los Angeles, Detroit, or New York as working in Salt Lake City. Nor do they confine themselves to private business. They have contributed senators, congressmen, governors, and presidential candidates. In local affairs they have won membership on school boards, city councils, and citizens' advisory groups. Their attitudes are precisely those one would expect of an affluent, confident middle class blessed with homes of visible confort. While there are liberals among them, most, especially among the leaders, are political conservatives. Unlike their forefathers of three generations ago, they no longer favor social or economic experimentation, be it in town building, irrigation systems, or multiple wives. They still have a remarkable cohesiveness, but much of their force is directed inward now, toward strengthening the church by conserving its membership, rather than outward toward meeting widely felt social or economic needs.

How do we account for this extraordinary change in the Mormons' numbers, fortunes, and attitudes? Can an analysis of their history supply explanations that will satisfy Mormons and non-Mormons alike? The significance of the Saints makes an attempt well worth the effort, for in the nineteenth and early twentieth centuries the Mormons were the most important single colonizing agency in settling the huge Western region between the Rocky Mountains and the Sierra Nevada-Cascades, and today they seem on their way to becoming leaders in the nation as a whole.

The story begins with the unity that came to the Mormons as the result of sharing an unusual faith, a faith that automatically set its believers apart from the general population. Most Protestant splinter groups merely reinterpreted the accepted King James Bible and rearranged some existing pattern of church government, but Mormonism went far beyond that, for it asserted that there had been modern revelations from God to an actual, known nineteenth-century human being, Joseph Smith of western New York State.

Smith was the son of debt-ridden, ill-educated parents who had drifted out of New England to make a new (and ultimately unsuccessful) beginning at Palmyra, New York, a town situated between the head of the Finger Lakes and Lake Ontario. This was part of the "burned-over" district, so called because during Joseph Smith's youth wave after wave of emotional religious revivals—the fires of God—swept through the region.

Like his neighbors, Smith matured in an atmosphere of poverty and slight education, but he was notable for a high native intelligence. At some point in the 1820s, according to Smith's own account, an angel in "a loose robe of most exquisite whiteness" appeared in Smith's bedroom and informed him of the existence of a sacred book, the Book of Mormon, that was "written upon gold plates" and buried on a hill "convenient to the village of Manchester, Ontario County, New York." After a four-year delay during which he had to purify himself, Smith believed himself divinely commissioned to translate the text of the golden tablets from an ancient language into 275,000 words of more-or-less King James Version English. The huge manuscript was then set into print in 1830 on a local newspaper press and published as *The Book of Mormon: An Account Written by the Hand of Mormon,*

Upon Plates Taken from the Plates of Nephi, by Joseph Smith, Junior, "Author and Proprietor."

Faith in the authenticity of that book was essential to membership in what officially became known as the Church of Jesus Christ of Latter-day Saints. To accept Mormonism one had to believe *literally* that an angel revealed to Smith this hitherto unknown sacred book, comparable to the Bible, and, further, that thereafter God repeatedly communicated with Joseph Smith, whose revelations of God's will were both numerous and explicit, ranging from general rules for the government of the church to highly specific instructions to named individuals. Those who were capable of literal belief in so revolutionary a set of religious assumptions inevitably set themselves apart from the skeptical or derisive majority of Americans, and thus became what the Mormons themselves called a "peculiar people." Becoming a "peculiar people" in turn led to persecution and to the martyrdom of their prophet, Joseph Smith. Paradoxically, the assaults upon them had a unifying effect: nothing so unites a group as the sense of standing together against a hostile world.

But their ability to hold together was facilitated also by something that was as unique as the modern revelation upon which the Mormon faith was founded. Joseph Smith had created the only true theocracy that America has ever seen. One dictionary defines theocracy as a "system of government by priests claiming a divine commission." In the Mormon Church, from Smith's time to the present day, there have never been professional priests. Instead, every adult white male of good character is a priest and by hard work can rise to successively higher rank and responsibility in the church's very definite hierarchy.

The individual male earns his living in a regular secular job and must manage to do his own work while meeting the church's very heavy demands upon his time. The only exceptions are at the pinnacle of the Mormon hierarchy, where the sheer weight of responsibilities makes it necessary for the individual to give up his secular calling in order to devote full time to the church's demands. Save at the very top, where a "living allowance" is provided, no one gets paid for doing the church's work; on the contrary, all Mormons are expected to support this elaborate organization by paying a genuine tithe—a real 10 per cent of their income.

Women and blacks may not become priests. The women are expected to work hard as a kind of ladies' auxiliary, but they must achieve glorification and satisfaction in the church through their husbands' service to the church and through the bearing of children. Annie Clark Tanner, who was born in rural Utah in 1864 and raised as the daughter of Wife Number Two in a devout polygamous family, summed up the underlying philosophy in two sentences:

THE DOMESTIC BLISS OF BRIGHAM YOUNG

While their religion differed from orthodox Protestantism in many respects, the most "peculiar institution" of the Mormons was polygamy, which they insisted was ordained by the Scriptures. Orthodoxy disagreed, and until 1890, when the church officially renounced the practice, polygamy was a constant source of pious outrage and derision. . . . Mark Twain was a good deal more gentle in his own remarks on the subject. He had stopped off in Salt Lake City on his way West in 1861, and in *Roughing It*, published in 1872, he fantasized about certain practical difficulties in the daily life of Brigham Young:

"None of our party got an opportunity to take dinner with Mr. Young, but a Gentile by the name of Johnson professed to have enjoyed a sociable breakfast in the Lion House. He gave a preposterous account of the 'calling of the roll,' and other preliminaries, and the carnage that ensued when the buckwheat cakes came in. But he embellished rather too much.

He said that Mr. Young told him several smart sayings of certain of his 'two-year-olds,' observing with some pride that for many years he had been the heaviest contributor in that line to one of the Eastern magazines; and then he wanted to show Mr. Johnson one of the pets that had said the last good thing, but he could not find the child. He searched the faces of the children in detail, but could not decide which one it was. Finally he gave it up. . . .

" 'I thought I would know the little cub again but I don't.'

"Mr. Johnson said further, that Mr. Young observed that life was a sad, sad thing—'because the joy of every new marriage a man contracted was so apt to be blighted by the inopportune funeral of a less recent bride.' And Mr. Johnson said that while he and Mr. Young were pleasantly conversing in private, one of the Mrs. Youngs came in and demanded a breast-pin, remarking that she had found out that he had been giving a breast-pin to No. 6, and

"The Priesthood is a spiritual power which purports to give man superior wisdom. Because of this superiority in power and authority, a wife was subservient to her husband." If such an attitude sounds absurd today, in the nineteenth century it was not very remote from views widely accepted among the general American population.

Before she was twenty, Annie Clark herself became Wife Number Two of a polygamous husband, thus beginning what proved to be a

she, for one, did not propose to let this partiality go on without making a satisfactory amount of trouble about it. Mr. Young reminded her that there was a stranger present. Mrs. Young said that if the state of things inside the house was not agreeable to the stranger, he could find room outside. Mr. Young promised the breast-pin, and she went away. But in a minute or two another Mrs. Young came in and demanded a breast-pin. Mr. Young began a remonstrance, but Mrs. Young cut him short. She said No. 6 had got one, and No. 11 was promised one, and it was 'no use for him to try to impose on her—she hoped she knew her rights.' He gave his promise, and she went. And presently three Mrs. Youngs entered in a body and opened on their husband a tempest of tears, abuse, and entreaty. They had heard all about No. 6, No. 11, and No. 14. Three more breast-pins were promised. They were hardly gone when nine more Mrs. Youngs filed into the presence, and a new tempest burst forth and raged round about the prophet and his guest. Nine breast-pins were promised, and the weird sisters filed out again. And in came eleven more, weeping and wailing and gnashing their teeth. Eleven promised breast-pins purchased peace once more.

" 'That is a specimen,' said Mr. Young. 'You see how it is. You see what a life I lead. A man *can't* be wise all the time. . . . My friend, take an old man's advice, and *don't* encumber yourself with a large family —mind, I tell you, don't do it. In a small family, and in a small family only, you will find that comfort and that peace of mind which are the best at last of the blessings this world is able to afford us, and for the lack of which no accumulation of wealth, and no acquisition of fame, power, and greatness can ever compensate us. Take my word for it, ten or eleven wives is all you need—never go over it.' "

singularly unhappy, unstable, yet long-continued marital relationship (ten children). Her own and her mother's experiences led her to comment on the obvious connection between her church's attitude toward women and its stubborn defense of its most publicized institution, polygamy. "Polygamy," Mrs. Tanner said, "is predicated on the assumption that man is superior to woman," and that man must be given "privileged rights in domestic affairs."

The church's stand on blacks has become even more anachronistic than its attitudes toward women. Blacks are encouraged to join, but unlike other males, they must not expect to enter the priesthood. According to Mormon belief, their color means that they bear a lifelong curse as the descendants of one of the sons of Adam and Eve, Cain, who in a fit of jealousy slew his brother Abel. For this bloody deed, Cain and his descendants were cursed with black skins—the "mark of Cain." Someday, Mormon theory runs, the curse will be lifted, but until that time participation in the priesthood is forbidden to blacks, although not to some other nonwhites, such as Polynesians. For modern Mormon liberals, the church's flat prohibition—and the blunt implication of racial inferiority—has become a heavy cross.

From the beginning the Mormon Church has thus been an organization that is staffed by unpaid white male nonprofessionals, and is supported by remarkably generous giving by all loyal Mormons. The church is organized into successively higher levels of authority; beginning at the level of the local congregation, which is called a "ward" and is presided over by a layman called a "bishop," and rising up through a larger geographical entity called a "stake," above which are the central authorities of the church, who have operated out of Salt Lake City ever since the Mormons have been in Utah. Twice a year there is a huge meeting in Salt Lake City to which the faithful are earnestly urged to come. It is at those semiannual meetings that the faithful are told what their leaders have decided.

How are officials chosen for these different levels? Joseph Smith declared that his church was to be not so much a theocracy but rather what he termed a "theo-democracy." In practice this has meant that the leaders of the church select some promising Mormon for a post, and then ask the people of the particular group he will lead to ratify the choice by a show of hands in meeting. The approval so given is known as the "sustaining vote." Normally it is forthcoming, since the voting group knows that the nomination represents their leaders' wishes and, as Mrs. Tanner remarked, "obedience was the basis of our religion." From Joseph Smith's time to the present this elaborate church structure has provided a definite place and role for every active Mormon. The energies, the enthusiasms, and money of each member are enlisted.

The church has dominated not only the religious life of its members but also their social life, frequently their political life, and at times their economic activities. After the Mormons moved to Utah, the church created and controlled the only government Utah had until 1850. When Congress established a territorial form of government in that year, Brigham Young became the first governor, and the church remained a *de facto* force in government at all levels. Nor did the church's influence in government cease after the federal government displaced Brigham Young as territorial governor in 1857.

This theocracy could operate the more easily because from the beginning the Mormons had shown a remarkable spirit of communitarian cooperation. Because the early Mormons were too poor and too limited in education and experience to undertake big projects as individuals, they learned to work together under the leadership of their church. By pooling their labor under church direction, and employing only the simplest tools and equipment, they planned and built towns, irrigation canals, roads, and factories—without accumulating a large capital debt.

Joseph Smith initiated these arrangements and developed a cadre of effective leaders who served as his immediate subordinates. For his administrative accomplishments he deserves more credit than he has usually received. At his death in 1844 Joseph Smith was succeeded by one of the outstanding organizers of the nineteenth century, Brigham Young, who ruled the church until his own death in 1877. If the circumstances of his life had worked out differently, Brigham Young might have become a captain of industry—an Andrew Carnegie or John D. Rockefeller or perhaps a railroad builder.

Young's beginnings in rural Vermont and New York State were as humble as Joseph Smith's. He once declared that he had had only eleven days of formal schooling. Yet in adult life, when he stood at the head of the Mormon Church, he impressed his visitors. In 1860, Sir Richard Burton, the famous British world traveler, found him "at

once affable and impressive, simple and courteous: his want of preten-
sion contrasts favorably with certain pseudo-prophets that I have
seen. . . . He impresses a stranger with a certain sense of power. . . .
He can use all the weapons of ridicule to direful effect" and can repri-
mand his followers "in purposely violent language." Albert D. Rich-
ardson, the journalist, added his own evaluation in 1867:

> With an affable and dignified manner he manifests the unmis-
> takable egotism of one having authority. In little ebullitions of
> earnestness he speaks right at people, using his dexter forefinger
> with emphasis, to point a moral. He treats the brethren with
> warmth, throwing his arm caressingly about them and asking
> carefully after the wives and babies.
>
> Provincialisms of his Vermont boyhood and his western man-
> hood still cling to him. He says "leetle," "beyond" and "disre-
> member." An irrepressible conflict between his nominatives and
> verbs, crops out in expressions like "they was."

This able, energetic, earthy man became the absolute ruler and the
revered, genuinely loved father figure of all Mormons everywhere. He
used the church hierarchy as the instrument through which he ruled,
and from among the church leaders he selected the captains and lieutenants he needed to carry out his purposes. But Young himself was a
master of detail who kept in touch with everything. In his letters to
his sons he constantly exhorted his progeny to observe, improve,
work, and be useful. He held himself to those same exacting standards. Whenever he traveled, which he did frequently, he always knew
a great deal about not only each town he visited but also many of the
individuals who lived there. To a hard-working rural Mormon, it
meant everything that the ruler of the church knew that Sister Eliza
had had an unusually hard time after the birth of her sixth child, or
that Brother Isaiah had been the principal carpenter in rebuilding the
local church after it had suffered storm damage.

His visits to local communities were rustic versions of a royal progress. All of the townsmen put on their best clothes, buildings were decorated, the street strewn with flowers, the brass band played, and the
school children sang:

> Come join the army, the army of our Lord,
> Brigham is our leader, we'll rally at his word,
> Sharp will be the conflict with the powers of sin,
> But with such a leader we are sure to win.

Young could be ruthless and crude, but he had many qualities more notable than his most publicized achievement, which was the admittedly impressive catalog of his wives—ultimately he married twenty-seven women. The most reliable statisticians credit Young with fifty-six or fifty-seven children by sixteen of those wives. Even with the separate apartments that he maintained for them, Young's ability to keep so many wives from quarreling and so many children from overwhelming him would in itself prove that he must have been a remarkable, not to say masterful, diplomat.

During the thirty years between the Mormons' arrival in Utah in 1847 and 1877, Young directed the founding of 350 towns in the Southwest. A modern historian has remarked that the two most important forces in settling the intermountain West were the Union Pacific Railroad and the Mormon Church—two large, well-organized, and centrally directed institutions. In such a harsh geographic setting, the job could not possibly have been done by exclusive reliance upon the efforts of unorganized individuals.

How the process worked was illustrated by the founding of the town of Springville, southeast of Salt Lake. Although two Mormon militiamen discovered the site early in 1849, Brigham Young decreed that settlement must await the arrival of Bishop Aaron Johnson, who was to lead a wagon train across the plains to Utah during the summer of 1850. Johnson, who like so many of the early Mormons was of New England ancestry (Connecticut-born), was just the kind of proven leader to whom Brigham Young habitually turned when a difficult new task was at hand.

A Mormon since 1836, only six years after Joseph Smith had founded the denomination, Johnson had risen to successively higher responsibilities during the Mormons' town-building in Ohio, Missouri, and Illinois and during their exodus from Nauvoo. When the bearded bishop finally brought his train of 135 wagons safely to Salt Lake City, Brigham Young came to greet the newcomers and arbitrarily "cut out" the first eight wagons, announcing to their drivers that they were to go with Johnson to found Springville. From his own family Johnson, in turn, selected two of his wives and three of his sons to accompany him with this advance detachment.

The chosen site was a lovely one. Tall wild grasses covered a strip of virgin land that had the massive Wasatch Range of the Rockies at its back, and the glittering waters of Utah Lake before it, while Hobble Creek, flowing out from the mountain canyons, gave assurance of water for irrigation.

Under Johnson's leadership, the necessary tasks were quickly assigned. Some were to harvest the wild grasses with scythes; others were to take axes and teams up into the mountains to bring out logs; while still others were to lay out a fortified settlement that would cover an acre and a half, big enough to shelter both settlers and domestic livestock from the possibility of Indian attack and the certainty of winter storms. Typical of the Mormons, one of the early buildings was a schoolhouse and another a structure large enough for dances and social gatherings, and presently for amateur theatricals, for the Mormons never let their New England heritage lead them into discouraging harmless pleasures and sociability.

There were difficult early years at Springville when poor crops reduced the pioneers to eating thistle roots, pig weed, red root, and sego bulbs, but by the time Johnson died in 1877, worn out from too many years of multivarious duties, the town had long been a decided success. Johnson had been bishop, judge, brigadier general of local militia, philanthropist to all in need, and "head of all the public affairs," as his son expressed it. Family tradition has it that his children numbered fifty-five and his wives either eleven or thirteen. (A slight uncertainty, where the numbers are so high, can easily be forgiven.)

Most of the towns that Young caused to be founded were in arid regions that required irrigation systems and the careful use of limited supplies of water, timber, and good land, needs which the Mormons fulfilled in their own, almost revolutionary manner. For the United States as a whole this was an age of unrestrained laissez faire, in which the primary standard of judgment was private profit rather than community need, but the Mormons immediately placed social values ahead of individual desires. Towns were planned according to the old New England pattern: the residences and their attendant kitchen gardens were clustered in the middle of the town, so that the people would be close to neighbors, the school, and the church building, while the irrigable crop lands were out in the more open country beyond the settlement, and the pasture lands were still farther away. Water was declared by Brigham Young to be the property of *all* the people rather than private property, and was to be distributed through an irrigation system built under church leadership and by the labor of the people who would be using it. Use of the water was tied to the land that needed it and was regulated by the local people, so that water monopoly was impossible. When disputes about water arose, they were usually taken to the local bishop of the church ward for his mediation or arbitration, instead of spending time and money to file suit in the courts.

In declaring water to be the property of the whole community, and in working out this simple pattern for use, Young and his people were discarding several centuries of Anglo-American precedents developed under the common law for use in a humid climate. Elsewhere in the West a great deal of expensive litigation could have been avoided if lawyers and legislators had been more willing to throw away Blackstone's *Commentaries* and follow the example set by the unsophisticated but pragmatic Mormons.

In Brigham Young's eyes, building towns and irrigation systems was not enough. The Mormons had always wanted to make themselves economically self-sufficient, so that they would not be at the mercy of the nation's non-Mormon majority when they needed supplies. Once they had become settled in Utah and had survived the difficult first years, they began a remarkable if unsuccessful drive to create all kinds of industries and services. Factories, mills, an iron foundry, express and teamster services, local railroads, cooperative stores, woolen mills, cotton growing, and a sugar-beet industry were examples of ventures that Young persuaded the faithful to finance through drafts upon the local congregations to supply money, labor, draft animals, and raw materials. Unfortunately, these subsidized ventures were, at best, high-cost enterprises producing for a limited market, and after the transcontinental railroad was completed in 1869, cheaper, better-finished goods flooded in from the Middle West and East to wipe out such of the Mormon experiments as had not already failed of their own unsoundness.

The sum total of all these efforts suggests how and why the Mormons were able to hold together and indeed to grow steadily in numbers and resources through the difficult and crucial years of the 1850s, 1860s, and 1870s. They were united by accepting an unusual faith; they were led by a remarkable man who headed a theocracy that penetrated every aspect of daily life and could normally count upon obedient responses to its directives; and they were addicted to cooperative, communitarian ways of meeting all challenges. But in addition to these forces from within, they were strengthened in their loyalty to the church by the periodic attacks made upon them by the United States government, which in turn was responding to the hostile public opinion constantly being whipped up by reformers, newspaper editors, politicians, and women's organizations. In 1857 President James Buchanan, who was soon to vacillate over coercing the seceding Southern states, did not hesitate to send the United States Army into Utah under the command of the future Confederate general Albert Sidney Johnston to compel the Mormons to accept federal rule and federal law. Inevitably, a morbidly illogical act of retaliation took place: the "Mountain Meadows Massacre" of September, 1857, in which more than one hundred members of a Gentile emigrant train passing through Utah were slaughtered, almost certainly by Mormons in alliance with friendly Indians. This event, which Mormon historian Juanita Brooks has called "one of the most despicable mass murders of history," was an aberration, a paranoid reaction that might have been expected of a harassed and persecuted people whose local leaders had been driven to the equivalent of a wartime hysteria by the "invasion" of federal troops. In any case, the massacre did nothing to alleviate tensions between the Mormons and the national government.

In the 1860s and 1870s Congress passed laws to eliminate polygamy and to take the trial of cases of alleged plural marriage out of the hands of the Mormon judges and juries, who invariably failed to convict. With the Edmunds Act of 1882 and the Edmunds-Tucker Act of 1887, Congress began an even more vigorous attack on the Mormon Church and polygamy. Arrest and imprisonment of polygamous Mormon leaders, confiscation of church property, federal control of voting, and invasion by United States marshalls gradually reduced the Mormons' physical ability to resist the imposition upon them of standards of behavior that would be in harmony with the majority of the United States.

Still, polygamy, so long a part of Mormon culture, was difficult to excise; it continued to be practiced, though on a much reduced scale, and the church fought the Edmunds-Tucker Act all the way to the United States Supreme Court. Finally, in 1890, the Court upheld the constitutionality of the act, and the Mormons were beaten. In September of that year, Wilford Woodruff, then president of the church, issued an official declaration:

> Inasmuch as laws have been enacted by Congress forbidding plural marriages, which laws have been pronounced constitutional by the court of last resort, I hereby declare my intention to submit to those laws, and to use my influence with the members of the Church over which I preside to have them do likewise.

The declaration was unanimously declared "official and binding" by a vote during the October general conference, and the doctrine of plural marriage was no longer officially part of Mormon dogma.

While Woodruff's declaration did not necessarily bring an immediate end to existing polygamous relationships, nevertheless it gave promise that the church would no longer promote the institution, and with polygamy out of the way insofar as politics were concerned, Congress permitted Utah to draft a constitution and become a state in 1896.

What has happened since then is extraordinarily interesting. Having once resolved to surrender on the key issue of polygamy, the Mormon leadership decided further to reduce distrust and dislike by deliberately conforming to the rest of the United States in many other aspects of life. This meant accepting the patterns of thought of Victorian middle-class America, including laissez-faire economics and a hostility to anything that suggested socialism—despite decades of Mormon church socialism. The Mormons' economic cooperatives were allowed to pass into private ownership, to be operated as profit-seeking enterprises, sometimes as the private property of the local or general leaders of the church.

While the private profit motive grew at the expense of the old zeal for communitarian enterprises, Mormons of all levels of income continued to tithe and to devote extraordinary amounts of time to the work of the church. The church continued to be the center of their emotional and social lives. And since the church was so central to the thinking of all practicing Mormons, and since it had always given political leadership in the past, so did it continue to exercise a heavy influence on politics in the new era.

Politically the Mormons had been organized in a party of their own—the so-called Peoples' Party—prior to making peace with the national government. Now the leaders decided that the Mormons would have more influence in Washington if they joined the national parties, dividing more or less equally between the Republicans and Democrats, so that the Mormons would have a solid bloc of votes in both camps. The faithful were solemnly instructed so to do—although in practice the leadership itself tended to find the atmosphere of the Republican party more congenial than that of the Democratic party.

This was only natural, for starting with Nauvoo and the first decade in Utah, there had been a tendency for the men at the head of the Mormon Church to become well-to-do property owners and businessmen. As Horace Greeley, the famous journalist, somewhat acidly remarked after meeting Brigham Young's principal associates in 1859, "their Mormonism has not impoverished them." By the late nineteenth century this group of prosperous leaders had grown both in wealth and in influence. For them conformity to the mores of Victorian America was no problem once the divisive issue of polygamy was no longer present. In politics their natural allies were the Old Guard Republicans in Washington and in the individual states. In labor relations a comparable affiliation with well-to-do middle-class America also occurred. Since many more of the Mormon leaders of that day belonged to the owner or manager class than to the ranks of the workers, it is understandable why they joined Middle Western and Eastern employers in denouncing labor's attempts to organize.

This tendency to affiliate with the conservative, ruling, entrepreneurial elements of American society was strengthened by at least two factors. One was the relatively provincial setting of most Mormon communities at the turn of the century, even after the arrival of local railroads. The present-day dispersion of Mormons to big cities in non-Mormon regions is a phenomenon that has developed only since the Great Depression and the Second World War. Most Mormons of seventy or eighty years ago still lived in small towns and modest-sized cities that had little communication with the big national and regional centers where, in the age of Theodore Roosevelt and Robert La Follette, liberals and progressives were arguing fiercely over new ideas about social justice and using the power of the state to curb monopoly and economic abuse.

The other factor was a practice established by Brigham Young, who perferred that at his death his successors should be chosen on the basis of seniority. By following this practice, the Mormons have acquired the oldest rulers of any organization known to modern man. To cite recent experience, David O. McKay, who was president of the church for nineteen years, died in 1970 at the age of ninety-six. His successor, Joseph Fielding Smith, was ninety-three when he took over McKay's duties and ninety-five when he died. Smith's successor, Harold B. Lee, was a comparatively youthful seventy-three, yet survived only eighteen months in office. The present head, Spencer W. Kimball, is eighty-two. No matter how great the good will of such men, it is asking too much to expect them to comprehend the attitudes of the great majority of Americans who are young enough to be their children, grand-children, or even great-grandchildren.

It is almost unnecessary to add that in the general drive to make peace with middle-class America, the old tendency to Mormon separatism has been replaced by an earnest patriotism. Does this mean that the modern Mormons have been fully absorbed into American society? That basic question has deeply concerned a new group of Mormon intellectuals who have become increasingly significant during the past decade. In 1966 this group founded *Dialogue*, a serious journal in which to thrash out the problems they faced in attempting to harmonize the faith, teachings, and practices Joseph Smith had revealed to their forefathers in the 1830s and 1840s, with the harshly insistent conditions of the 1960s and 1970s. The very first issue of this new journal started with an admirable editorial preface that declared:

> Today . . . most Mormons live outside Utah. . . . Today it is not unusual to see Mormon Congressmen in Washington, Mormon business executives in Chicago, Mormon professors at Harvard, or Mormon space scientists at Houston. Mormons are participating freely in the social, economic, and cultural currents of change sweeping twentieth-century America.

Then, with no transition, the editorial suddenly added this assertion:

> But Mormons do remain apart from greater American society. Their experience, heritage, and tradition of years in isolation remain an integral part of Mormon belief; Mormon doctrine reinforces individual withdrawal and defiance of conformity in the face of modern convention. This new era of life in the secular world, far from the cloisters of a Rocky Mountain Zion, has

created a host of dilemmas for the individual who seeks to reconcile faith and reason.

All Americans face in some degree the problem of reconciling ancestral faith with contemporary thought and practice. But for the Mormons the problem is more difficult because Mormonism is such a complete way of life. Even though Mormons participate vigorously in the PTA, the Chamber of Commerce, local politics, business, and the professions, they still spend much of their lives in self-contained Mormon groups. From childhood until old age they meet, talk, play, and pray in their own groups. They have their own charities, projects, entertainments. They have elaborate youth programs at high schools and colleges, as part of their campaign to hold their young people in the church (as well as gain new members) during the years when most denominations lose a high percentage of their young men and women.

Where most Americans must find their individual and often lonely ways through this confusing modern era, the Mormons can live in a warmly supportive group atmosphere, if they wish. To break with so all-embracing a pattern is a wrenching, distorting experience. For just that reason independent thinking and modern doubts have come only slowly to most Mormons. It is far easier to conform to the church's omnipresent guidance than to challenge it. At the same time, change is coming to the world with extraordinary speed. The continued subordination of women and blacks, at a time when outside opinion has turned so drastically against discrimination, illustrates the weight of cultural lag within the Mormon community. Will the Mormons be able to work out adjustments to contemporary pressures, without sacrificing the essence of their distinctive and close-knit culture? For the moment, the answer must be in doubt, but in view of the Mormons' record of meeting challenges in the past, it is by no means certain that they will fail.

ficient to drive the Southern states out of the Union. Professor Don E. Fehrenbacher offers a reasoned analysis of the shifting view of Lincoln and points out that there are solid reasons why the shift is back toward a more adulatory view of the wartime President.

If the United States had a patron saint it would no doubt be Abraham Lincoln; and if one undertook to explain Lincoln's extraordinary hold on the national consciousness, it would be difficult to find a better starting-point than these lines from an undistinguished poem written in 1865:

> One of the people! Born to be
> Their curious epitome;
> To share yet rise above
> Their shifting hate and love.

A man of the people and yet something much more, sharing popular passions and yet rising above them—here was the very ideal of a democratic leader, who in his person could somehow mute the natural antagonism between strong leadership and vigorous democracy. Amy Lowell, picking up the same theme half a century later, called Lincoln "an embodiment of the highest form of the typical American." This paradox of the uncommon common man, splendidly heroic and at the same time appealingly representative, was by no means easy to sustain. The Lincoln tradition, as a consequence, came to embrace two distinct and seemingly incompatible legends—the awkward, amiable, robust, rail-splitting, story-telling, frontier folklore hero; and the towering figure of the Great Emancipator and Savior of the Union, a man of sorrows, Christlike in his character and fate.

Biographers have struggled earnestly with this conspicuous dualism, but even when the excesses of reminiscence and myth are trimmed away, Lincoln remains a puzzling mixture of often conflicting qualities—drollness and melancholy, warmth and reserve, skepticism and piety, humbleness and self-assurance. Furthermore, he is doubly hard to get at because he did not readily reveal his inner self. He left us no

Reprinted from *Civil War History* 20, no. 4: Copyright © 1974 by the Kent State University Press.

diary or memoirs, and his closest friends called him "secretive" and "shut-mouthed." Billy Herndon in one of his modest moods declared, "Lincoln is unknown and possibly always will be." Plainly, there is good reason for scholarly caution in any effort to take the measure of such a man.

No less plain is the intimate connection between the Lincoln legend and the myth of America. The ambiguities in his popular image and the whisper of enigma in his portraits have probably broadened the appeal of this homespun Westerner, self-made man, essential democrat, and national martyr. Almost anyone can find a way to identify with Lincoln, perhaps because "like Shakespeare . . . he seemed to run through the whole gamut of human nature." Whatever the complex of reasons, successive generations of his countrymen have accepted Abraham Lincoln as the consummate American—the representative genius of the nation. One consequence is that he tends to serve as a mirror for Americans, who, when they write about him, frequently divulge a good deal about themselves.

Of course the recurring election of Lincoln as *Representative American* has never been unanimous. There was vehement dissent at first from many unreconstructed rebels, and later from iconoclasts like Edgar Lee Masters and cavaliers of the Lost Cause like Lyon Gardiner Tyler. In the mainstream of national life, however, it became increasingly fashionable for individuals and organizations to square themselves with Lincoln and enlist him in their enterprises. Often this required misquotation or misrepresentation or outright invention; but lobbyists and legislators, industrialists and labor leaders, reformers and bosses, Populists, Progressives, Prohibitionists, and Presidents all wanted him on their side. New Deal Democrats tried to steal him from the Republicans, and the American Communist party bracketed him with Lenin. Lincoln, in the words of David Donald, had come to be "everybody's grandfather."

Most remarkable of all was the growing recognition of Lincoln's greatness in the eleven states of the Confederacy, ten of which had never given him a single vote for President. This may have been a necessary symbolic aspect of sectional reconciliation. Returning to the Union meant coming to terms with the man who had saved the Union. No one took the step more unequivocally than Henry W. Grady, prophet of the New South, who told a New York audience in

1886 that Lincoln had been "the first typical American, the first who comprehended within himself all the strength and gentleness, all the majesty and grace of this Republic." When Southerners talked to Southerners about it, they were usually more restrained. Nevertheless, by the early twentieth century, the Lincoln tradition was becoming a blend of blue and gray, as illustrated in *The Perfect Tribute*, a story from the pen of an Alabama woman about a dying Confederate soldier's admiration for the Gettysburg Address.

Bonds of sympathy between Lincoln and the South had not been difficult to find. He was, after all, a native Southerner—implacable as an enemy, but magnanimous in victory and compassionate by nature. In his hands, nearly everyone agreed, the ordeal of Reconstruction would have been less severe. Even Jefferson Davis concluded that his death had been "a great misfortune to the South."

In addition, Lincoln seemed to pass the supreme test. He could be assimilated to the racial doctrines and institutional arrangements associated with the era of segregation. The historical record, though not entirely consistent, indicated that his opposition to slavery had never included advocacy of racial equality. With a little editing here and some extra emphasis there, Lincoln came out "right" on the Negro question. This was a judgment more often understood than elaborated in Southern writing and oratory, but certain self-appointed guardians of white supremacy were sometimes painfully explicit in claiming Lincoln as one of their own. He had been willing, they said, to guarantee slavery forever in the states where it already existed. He had issued the Emancipation Proclamation with great reluctance. He had opposed the extension of slavery only in order to reserve the Western territories exclusively for white men. He had denied favoring political and social equality for Negroes, had endorsed separation of the races, and had persistently recommended colonization of Negroes abroad. This was the Lincoln eulogized by James K. Vardaman of Mississippi, perhaps the most notorious political racist in American history, and by the sensational Negrophobic novelist, Thomas Dixon. In his most famous work, *The Clansman*, Dixon had Lincoln as President parody himself during a discussion of colonization:

> We can never attain the ideal Union our fathers dreamed, with millions of an alien, inferior race among us, whose assimilation is neither possible nor desirable. The Nation cannot now exist half

white and half black, any more than it could exist half slave and half free.

When one remembers that all this time millions of black Americans were still paying homage to the Great Emancipator, dualism begins to seem pervasive in the Lincoln tradition. Racist elements, to be sure, were never very successful in promoting the image of Lincoln as a dedicated white supremacist, but support from an unlikely quarter would eventually give the idea not only new life but respectability in the centers of professional scholarship.

During the first half of the twentieth century, Lincoln studies became a functional part of the literature of the Civil War, in which the problem of race was present but not paramount. Titles of the 1940s indicate the general bent of interest: *Lincoln and His Party in the Secession Crisis; Lincoln and the Patronage; Lincoln's War Cabinet; Lincoln and the Radicals; Lincoln and the War Governors; Lincoln and the South.* There was, it should be observed, no *Lincoln and the Negro.* That would come, appropriately, in the 1960s.

The sweep of the modern civil rights movement, beginning with the Supreme Court's anti-segregation decision in 1954, inspired a new departure in American historical writing. Never has the psychological need for a usable past been more evident. Black history flourished and so did abolitionist history, but the most prestigious field of endeavor was white-over-black history. Attention shifted, for example, from slavery as a cause of the Civil War to slavery as one major form of racial oppression. With this change of emphasis, the antebellum years began to look different. A number of monographs appearing in the 1960s, such as Leon F. Litwack's *North of Slavery*, demonstrated the nationwide prevalence of white-superiority doctrines and white-supremacy practices. Many Republicans and even some abolitionists, when they talked about the Negro, had sounded curiously like the slaveholders whom they were so fiercely denouncing. In fact, it appeared that the North and the South, while bitterly at odds on the issue of slavery, were relatively close to one another in their attitudes toward race. And Lincoln, according to Litwack, "accurately and consistently reflected the thoughts and prejudices of most Americans."

The racial consensus of the Civil War era made it easy enough to understand why black Americans failed to win the equality implicit in emancipation, but certain other historical problems became more difficult as a consequence. For instance, if most Northerners in 1860 were indeed racists who viewed the Negro with repugnance as an inferior order of creation, then why did so many of them have such strong feelings about slavery? And why did racist Southerners fear and distrust racist Republicans with an intensity sufficient to destroy the Union? And does not the achievement of emancipation by a people so morally crippled with racism seem almost miraculous—like a one-armed man swimming the English Channel? No amount of talk about overwrought emotions or ulterior purposes or unintended consequences will fully account for what appears to be a major historical paradox, with Lincoln as the central figure.

When the civil rights struggle got under way in the 1950s, both sides tried to enlist Lincoln's support, but the primary tendency at first was to regard desegregation as a belated resumption of the good work begun with the Emancipation Proclamation. Many leading historians agreed that during the Presidential years there had been a "steady evolution of Lincoln's attitude toward Negro rights." The changes carried him a long way from the narrow environmental influences of his youth and made him, in the words of Richard N. Current, more relevant and inspiring than ever "as a symbol of man's ability to outgrow his prejudices."

This was the liberal interpretation of Lincoln's record on racial matters. It came under attack from several directions, but especially from the ranks of intellectual radicalism and black militancy, both academic and otherwise. New Left historians, many of them activists in the battle for racial justice, could find little to admire in Abraham Lincoln. Compared with abolitionists like William Lloyd Garrison and Wendell Phillips, he seemed unheroic, opportunistic, and somewhat insensitive to the suffering of black people in bondage. He was "the prototype of the political man in power, with views so moderate as to require the pressure of radicals to stimulate action." His pre-war opposition to slavery, embracing the Republican policy of nonextension and the hope of ultimate extinction, reflected a "comfortable belief in the benevolence of history." It amounted to a "formula which promised in time to do everything while for the present risking nothing."

Election to the Presidency, in the radical view, produced no great transformation of his character. "Lincoln grew during the war—but he didn't grow much," wrote Lerone Bennett, Jr., a senior editor of

Ebony. "On every issue relating to the black man . . . he was the very essence of the white supremacist with good intentions." He moved but slowly and reluctantly toward abolishing slavery, and his famous Proclamation not only lacked "moral grandeur," but had been drafted "in such a way that it freed few, if any, slaves." His reputation as the Great Emancipator is therefore "pure myth." Most important of all, Lincoln probably believed in the inferiority of the Negro and certainly favored separation of the races. He was, in Bennett's words, "a tragically flawed figure who shared the racial prejudices of most of his white contemporaries."

This, then, was the radical interpretation of Lincoln's record on racial matters, and what strikes one immediately is its similarity to the views of professional racists like Vardaman and Dixon. The portrait of A. Lincoln, Great White Supremacist, has been the work, it seems, of a strange collaboration.

No less interesting is the amount of animus directed at a man who died over a hundred years ago. In the case of black militants, hostility to Lincoln has no doubt been part of the process of cutting loose from white America. Thus, there is little history but much purpose in the statement of Malcolm X: "He probably did more to trick Negroes than any other man in history."

For white radicals, too, rejection of Lincoln signified repudiation of the whole American cultural tradition, from the first massacre of Indians to the Vietnam War. In what might be called the "malign consensus" school of United States history, Lincoln remained the Representative American, but the America that he represented was a dark, ugly country, stained with injustice and cruelty. Plainly, there is much more at stake here than the reputation of a single historical figure.

James K. Vardaman, it is said, used to carry with him one particular Lincoln quotation that he would whip out and read at the slightest opportunity. This excerpt from the debate with Douglas in 1858 at Charleston, Illinois, is now fast becoming the most quoted passage in all of Lincoln's writings, outstripping even the Gettysburg Address and the Second Inaugural. Pick up any recent historical study of American race relations and somewhere in its pages you are likely to find the following words:

> I will say then that I am not, nor ever have been in favor of bringing about in any way the social and political equality of the

white and black races,—that I am not nor ever have been in favor of making voters or jurors of negroes, nor of qualifying them
to hold office, nor to intermarry with white people; and I will
say in addition to this that there is a physical difference between
the white and black races which I believe will for ever forbid
the two races living together on terms of social and political
equality. And inasmuch as they cannot so live, while they do remain together there must be the position of superior and inferior, and I as much as any other man am in favor of having the
superior position assigned to the white race.

It is, of course, a quotation that bristles with relevancy. Problems that
once preoccupied Lincoln's biographers, such as his part in bringing
on the Civil War and the quality of his wartime leadership, have been
more or less pushed aside by a question of newer fashion and greater
urgency. It is well phrased in the Preface to a collection of documents
titled *Lincoln on Black and White* (1971): "Was Lincoln a racist?
More important, how did Lincoln's racial views affect the course of
our history."

Anyone who sets out conscientiously to answer such a query will
soon find himself deep in complexity and confronting some of the fundamental problems of historical investigation. In one category are various questions about the historian's relation to the past: Is his task
properly one of careful reconstruction, or are there more important
purposes to be served? Does his responsibility include rendering moral
judgments? If so, using what standards—those of his own time or those
of the period under study? Then there are all the complications encountered in any effort to read the mind of a man, especially a politician, from the surviving record of his words and actions. For instance,
what he openly affirmed as a youth may have been silently discarded
in maturity; what he believed on a certain subject may be less significant than the intensity of his belief; and what he said on a certain occasion may have been largely determined by the immediate historical
context, including the composition of his audience.

Terminological difficulties may also arise in the study of history,
and such is the case with the word "racist," which serves us badly as a
concept because of its denunciatory tone and indiscriminate use. Con-
ducive neither to objectivity nor to precision, the word has been employed so broadly that it is now being subdivided. Thus we are invited
to distinguish between ideological racism and institutional racism, be-

tween scientific racism and folk racism, between active racism and inactive racism, between racism and racial prejudice, between racism and racialism, between hierarchical racism and romantic racialism. In its strictest sense, racism is a doctrine, but by extension it has also come to signify an attitude, a mode of behavior, and a social system. The *doctrine*, a work of intellectuals, is a rationalized theory of inherent Negro inferiority. In a given person, however, it can be anything from a casual belief to a philosophy of life. As an *attitude*, racism is virtually synonymous with prejudice—an habitual feeling of repugnance, and perhaps of enmity, toward members of another race. It can be anything from a mild tendency to a fierce obsession. Racism as a *mode of behavior* is prejudice activated in some way—a display of racial hostility that can be anything from mere avoidance of the other race to participation in a lynching. Racism as a *social system* means that law and custom combine to hold one race in subordination to another through institutional arrangements like slavery, segregation, discrimination, and disfranchisement. Individuals can help support such a system with anything from tacit acquiescence to strenuous public service in its defense. These multiple and graduated meanings of the word "racism" are important to remember in exploring the historical convergence of Abraham Lincoln and the American Negro.

"One must see him first," says Bennett, "against the background of his times. Born into a poor white family in the slave state of Kentucky and raised in the anti-black environments of southern Indiana and Illinois, Lincoln was exposed from the very beginning to racism." This is a familiar line of reasoning and credible enough on the surface. Any racial views encountered during his youth were likely to be unfavorable to the Negro. But more important is the question of how *often* he encountered such views and how *thoroughly* he absorbed them. Besides, the assumption that his racial attitudes were shaped more or less permanently by his early social environment does not take into account the fact that youth may rebel against established opinion. Lincoln did in a sense reject his father's world, leaving it behind him forever soon after reaching the age of twenty-one. Certainly his personal knowledge of black people was very limited. After catching a few glimpses of slavery as a small boy in Kentucky, he had little contact with Negroes while growing up in backwoods Indiana or as a young man in New Salem, Illinois. Those first twenty-eight years of his life take up just three pages in Benjamin Quarles's book, *Lincoln and the Negro.*

If Lincoln entered manhood with strong feelings about race already implanted in his breast, one might expect to find indications of it in his earlier letters and speeches. For instance, on a steamboat carrying him home from a visit to Kentucky in 1841, there were a dozen slaves in chains. They had been, literally, sold down the river to a new master, and yet they seemed the most cheerful persons on board. Here was inspiration for some racist remarks in the "Sambo" vein, but Lincoln, describing the scene to a friend, chose instead to philosophize about the dubious effect of "condition upon human happiness." That is, he pictured Negroes behaving, as George M. Fredrickson puts it, "in a way that could be understood in terms of a common humanity and not as the result of peculiar racial characteristics." Although one scholar may insist that Lincoln's racial beliefs were "matters of deep conviction," and another may talk about "the deep-rooted attitudes and ideas of a lifetime," there is scarcely any record of his thoughts on race until he was past forty years of age. Long before then, of course, he had taken a stand against slavery, and it was the struggle over slavery that eventually compelled him to consider publicly the problem of race.

There is no escape from the dilemma that "relevance" makes the past worth studying and at the same time distorts it. We tend to see antebellum race and slavery in the wrong perspective. Race itself was not then the critical public issue that it has become for us. Only widespread emancipation could make it so, and until the outbreak of the Civil War, that contingency seemed extremely remote. Our own preoccupation with race probably leads us to overestimate the importance of racial feeling in the antislavery movement. In fact, there is a current disposition to assume that if a Republican did not have strong pro-Negro motives, he must have acted for strong anti-Negro reasons, such as a desire to keep the Western territories lily-white.

Actually, much of the motivation for antislavery agitation was only indirectly connected with the Negro. For example, the prime target often seemed to be, not so much slavery as the "slave power," arrogant, belligerent, and overrepresented in all branches of the Federal government. In Lincoln's case, no one can doubt his profound, though perhaps intermittent, sympathy for the slave. Yet he also hated slavery in a more abstract way as an evil principle and as a stain on the national honor, incompatible with the mission of America.

It is a mistake to assume that Lincoln's actions in relation to the Negro were determined or even strongly influenced by his racial outlook. He based his antislavery philosophy, after all, squarely upon perception of the slave as a man, not as a Negro. According to the Declaration of Independence, he declared, all men, including black men, are created equal, at least to the extent that none has a right to enslave another. This became a point at issue in the famous debates with Stephen A. Douglas, who vehemently denied that the Declaration had anything to do with the African race. Lincoln, in turn, accused his rival of trying to "dehumanize" the Negro. But he had constructed an argument against slavery which, carried to its logical conclusion, seemed to spell complete racial equality. So Douglas insisted, anyhow, while Lincoln protested: "I do not understand that because I do not want a negro woman for a slave I must necessarily want her for a wife."

Opponents of slavery everywhere had to contend with the charge that they advocated Negro equality. In the Democratic press, Republicans almost invariably became "Black Republicans," and political survival more often than not appeared to depend upon repudiation of the epithet. Thus the race question was most prominent in the antebellum period as a rhetorical and largely spurious feature of the slavery controversy.

Lincoln's first general remarks about racial equality on record were made in 1854, when the repeal of the Missouri Compromise drew him back to the center of Illinois politics. What to do, ideally, with Southern slaves, he pondered in a speech at Peoria. "Free them, and make them politically and socially our equals? My own feelings will not admit of this; and if mine would, we well know that those of the great mass of white people will not." More often that year, however, he talked about the humanity of the Negro in denouncing the extension of slavery. Then came the election of 1856 and Frémont's defeat, which Lincoln analyzed with some bitterness: "We were constantly charged with seeking an amalgamation of the white and black races; and thousands turned from us, not believing the charge . . . but *fearing* to face it themselves." It was at this point, significantly, that he became more aggressive and explicit in disavowing racial equality. He began using census figures to show that miscegenation was a by-product of slavery. He spoke of the "natural disgust" with which most white people viewed "the idea of indiscriminate amalgamation of the white and black races." And, under heavy pounding from Douglas during the senatorial campaign of 1858, he answered again and again in the manner of the notorious Charleston passage quoted above. Indeed, his strongest feeling about race appears to have been his vexation with those who kept bringing the subject up. "Negro equality! Fudge!!" he scribbled on a piece of paper. "How long, in the government of a God great enough to make and maintain this Universe, shall there continue knaves to vend and fools to gulp, so low a piece of demagoguism as this?"

Most of Lincoln's recorded generalizations about race were public statements made in the late 1850s as part of his running oratorical battle with Douglas. Furthermore, nearly all of those statements were essentially disclaimers rather than affirmations. They indicated, for political reasons, the *maximum* that he was willing to deny the Negro and the *minimum* that he claimed for the Negro. They were concessions on points not at issue, designed to fortify him on the point that *was* at issue—namely, the extension of slavery. If he had responded differently at Charleston and elsewhere, the Lincoln of history simply would not exist. And words uttered in a context of such pressure may be less than reliable as indications of a man's lifetime attitude.

At least it seems possible that Lincoln's remarks in middle age on the subject of race were shaped more by his political realism than by impressions stamped on his mind in childhood. The principal intellectual influence, as Frederickson has demonstrated, was Henry Clay, Lincoln's political hero, whom he studied anew for a eulogy delivered in 1852. Clay, in his attitude toward slavery, represented a link with the Founding Fathers. A slaveholder himself who nevertheless believed that the institution was a "curse," he began and ended his career working for a program of gradual emancipation in Kentucky. He helped found and steadily supported the American Colonization Society. In his racial views, moreover, Clay emphasized the Negro's humanity and reserved judgment on the question of innate black inferiority. Lincoln not only adopted Clay's tentative, moderate outlook but extensively paraphrased and sometimes parroted his words.

Considering, then, the peculiar context of his most significant remarks on the subject of race, and considering also his dependence on Clay, it seems unwise to assert flatly, as some scholars do, that Lincoln embraced the doctrine of racism. Not that it would be astonishing to find that he did so. The assumption of inherent white superiority was almost universal and rested upon observation as well as prejudice. Comparison of European civilization and African "savagery" made it extremely difficult to believe in the natural equality of white and black races. Yet Lincoln's strongest statements, even if taken at face value and out of context, prove to be tentative and equivocal. He conceded that the Negro *might not* be his equal, or he said that the Negro *was not* his equal *in certain respects*. As an example, he named *color*, which certainly has a biological implication. But we cannot be certain that he was not merely expressing an aesthetic judgment or noting the social disadvantages of being black. He never used the word "inherent," or any of its equivalents, in discussing the alleged inferiority of the Negro, and it is not unlikely that he regarded such inferiority as resulting primarily from social oppression. In 1862, he compared blacks whose minds had been "clouded by slavery" with free Negroes "capable of thinking as white men." His last recorded disclaimer appears in a letter written as President-elect to a New York editor. He did not, it declared, "hold the black man to be the equal of the white, unqualifiedly." The final word throws away most of the declaration and scarcely suits a true ideological racist. Here there is a doubleness in the man as in the legend. It appears that he may have both absorbed and doubted, both shared and risen above, the racial doctrines of his time.

Lincoln, who had four sons and no other children, was presumably never asked the ultimate racist question. He did indicate a disinclination to take a Negro woman for his wife, agreeing with most of his white contemporaries in their aversion to miscegenation. Otherwise, there is little evidence of racism as an attitude or racism as a mode of behavior in his relations with Negroes. Frederick Douglass, sometimes a severe critic of his policies, said emphatically: "In all my interviews with Mr. Lincoln I was impressed with his entire freedom from popular prejudice against the colored race." During the war years in Washington, the social status of Negroes underwent a minor revolution, exemplified in the arrival of a black diplomat from the newly-recognized republic of Haiti. Lincoln, according to Current, "opened the White House to colored visitors as no President had done before, and he received them in a spirit which no President has matched since." Douglass and others appreciated not only his friendliness but his restaint. There was no effusiveness, no condescension. "He treated Negroes," says Quarles, "as they wanted to be treated—as human beings."

On the other hand, Lincoln in the 1850s did plainly endorse the existing system of white supremacy, except for slavery. He defended it, however, on grounds of expediency rather than principle, and on grounds of the incompatibility rather than the inequality of the races. Assuming that one race or the other must be on top, he admitted preferring that the superior position be *assigned* to the white race. Thups there was little association of institutioal racism with ideological racism in his thinking.

Although Lincoln was by no means insensitive to the deprivation suffered by free Negroes, he saw little hope of improving their condition and in any case regarded slavery as a far greater wrong. Moreover, it appeared that any serious attack on institutional racism would raise the cry of "Negro equality," and thereby damage the antislavery cause.

But then, if he hated slavery so much, why did Lincoln not become an abolitionist? There are several obvious reasons: fear for the safety of the Union, political prudence, constitutional scruples, a personal distaste for extremism, and perplexity over what to do with freed slaves. In addition, it must be emphasized that Lincoln, as Lord Charnwood observed, "accepted the institutions to which he was born, and he enjoyed them." Social reform was a fairly new phenomenon in antebellum America. Only a relatively small number of persons had adopted it as a lifestyle, and Lincoln cannot be counted among them. This author of the greatest reform in American history was simply not a reformer by nature. He even acquiesced in the retention of slavery, provided that it should not be allowed to expand. For him, the paramount importance of the Republican anti-extension program lay in its symbolic meaning as a commitment to the principle of ultimate extinction. Some later generation, he thought, would then convert the principle into practice. What this amounted to, in a sense, was antislavery tokenism, but it also proved to be a formula for the achievement of political power, and with it, the opportunity to issue a proclamation of emancipation.

Of course, it has been said that Lincoln deserves little credit for emancipation—that he came to it tardily and reluctantly, under Radical duress. "Blacks have no reason to feel grateful to Abraham Lincoln," writes Julius Lester in *Look Out, Whitey! Black Power's Goin' Get Your Mama!* "How come it took him two whole years to free the slaves? His pen was sitting on his desk the whole time. All he had to do was get up one morning and say, 'Doggonnit! I think I'm gon' free the slaves today.' " But *which* morning? That turned out to be the real question.

Lincoln, it should be remembered, was under strong pressure from *both* sides on the issue of emancipation, and so the Radical clamor alone will not explain his ultimate decision. Nevertheless, when the war began, many Americans quickly realized that the fate of slavery might be in the balance. Veteran abolitionists rejoiced that history was at last marching to their beat, and Lincoln did not fail to read what he called "the signs of the times." Emancipation itself, as he virtually acknowledged, came out of the logic of events, not his personal volition, but the time and manner of its coming were largely his choice.

There had been enough Republicans to win the presidential election, but there were not enough to win the war. They needed help from Northern Democrats and border-state loyalists, who were willing to fight for the Union, but not for abolition. A premature effort at emancipation might alienate enough support to make victory impossible. It would then be self-defeating, because there could be no emancipation without victory. Lincoln's remarkable achievement, whether he fully intended it or not, was to proclaim emancipation in such a way as to minimize disaffection. He did so by allowing enough time for the prospect to become domesticated in the public mind, and by adhering scrupulously to the fiction that this momentous step was strictly a military measure. Much of the confusion about the Emancipation Proclamation results from taking too seriously Lincoln's verbal bowings and scrapings to the conservatives, while all the time he was backing steadily away from them.

The best illustration is his famous reply of August 22, 1862, to the harsh criticism of Horace Greeley, in which he said that his "paramount object" was to save the Union. "What I do about slavery, and the colored race," he declared, "I do because I believe it helps to save the Union; and what I forbear, I forbear because I do *not* believe it would help to save the Union." The most striking thing about the entire document is its dissimulation. Although Lincoln gave the impression that options were still open, he had in fact already made up his mind, had committed himself to a number of persons, had drafted the Proclamation. Why, then, write such a letter? Because it was not a statement of policy but instead a brilliant piece of propaganda in which Lincoln, as Benjamin P. Thomas says, "used Greeley's outburst to prepare the people for what was coming."

There were constitutional as well as political reasons, of course, for casting the Proclamation in military language and also for limiting its scope to those states and parts of states still in rebellion. In a sense, as historians fond of paradox are forever pointing out, it did not immediately liberate any slaves at all. And the Declaration of Independence, it might be added, did not immediately liberate a single colony from British rule. The people of Lincoln's time apparently had little doubt about the significance of the Proclamation. Jefferson Davis did not regard it as a mere scrap of paper, and neither did that most famous of former slaves, Frederick Douglass. He called it "the greatest event in our nation's history."

In the long sweep of that history, emancipation had come on, not sluggishly, but with a rush and a roar—over a period of scarcely eighteen months. Given more time to reflect on its racial implications, white America might have recoiled from the act. Lincoln himself had never been anything but a pessimist about the consequences of emancipation. Knowing full well the prejudices of his countrymen, he doubted that blacks and whites could ever live together amicably and on terms of equality. Over a century later, it is still too early to say that he was wrong.

With stark realism, Lincoln told a delegation of free Negroes in August 1862: "On this broad continent, not a single man of your race is made the equal of a single man of ours. Go where you are treated the best, and the ban is still upon you." And while blacks suffered from discrimination, whites suffered from the discord caused by the presence of blacks. "It is better for us both, therefore, to be separated," he said.

But Lincoln apparently never visualized a segregated America. For him, separation meant colonization, which, as a disciple of Henry Clay, he had been advocating at least since 1852. Perhaps the strangest feature of Lincoln's presidential career was the zeal with which he tried to promote voluntary emigration of free Negroes to Africa or Latin America. He recommended it in his first two annual messages, urged it upon Washington's black leadership, and endorsed it in his Preliminary Emancipation Proclamation. He had foreign capitals circulated in a search for likely places of settlement. Furthermore, with funds supplied by Congress, he launched colonization enterprises in Haiti and Panama, both of which proved abortive.

What surprises one the most about these almost frantic activities is their petty scale. Lincoln implored the delegation of Washington Negroes to find him a hundred, or fifty, or even twenty-five families willing to emigrate. The Haitian project, if completely successful, would have accommodated just five thousand persons—about the number of Negroes born every two weeks in the United States. It would have required an enormous effort even to hold the black population stable at four and one-half million, let alone reduce it appreciably. Back in 1854, Lincoln had admitted the impracticability of colonization as anything but a long-range program. Why, then, did he betray such feverish haste to make a token beginning in 1862?

One interesting answer emerges from the chronology. Most of the colonization flurry took place during the second half of 1862. After that, Lincoln's interest waned, although, according to the dubious testimony of Benjamin F. Butler, it revived near the end of the war. After issuing the Emancipation Proclamation on January 1, 1863, Lincoln never made another public appeal for colonization. It appears that his spirited activity in the preceding six months may have been part of the process of conditioning the public mind for the day of jubilee. The promise of colonization had always been in part a means of quieting fears about the racial consequences of manumission. Offered as the ultimate solution to the problem of the black population, it could also serve as a psychological safety valve for the problem of white racism. This combination of purposes had inspired a number of Republican leaders to take up the cause of colonization in the late 1850s. One of them, the brother of his future postmaster-general, had told Lincoln then that the movement would ward off the attacks made upon us about Negro equality."

In his second annual message of December 1, 1862, Lincoln said, "I cannot make it better known than it already is, that I strongly favor colonization," Then he continued in a passage that has received far less attention: "And yet I wish to say there is an objection urged against free colored persons remaining in the country, which is largely imaginary, if not sometimes malicious." He went on to discuss and minimize the fear that freedmen would displace white laborers, after which he wrote:

> But it is dreaded that the freed people will swarm forth, and cover the whole land? Are they not already in the land? Will liberation make them any more numerous? Equally distributed among the whites of the whole country, and there would be but one colored to seven whites. Could the one, in any way, greatly disturb the seven? There are many communities now, having more than one free colored person, to seven whites; and this, without any apparent consciousness of evil from it.

Here, along with his last public endorsement of colonization, was an eloquent plea for racial accommodation at home. The one might remain his ideal ultimate solution, but the other, he knew, offered the only hope in the immediate future.

Yet, if his plans for Reconstruction are an accurate indication, Lincoln at the time of his death had given too little consideration to the problem of racial adjustment and to the needs of four million freedman. How much that would have changed if he had not been killed, has been the subject of lively controversy. Certainly his policies by 1865 no longer reflected all the views expressed in 1858, when he had repudiated both Negro citizenship and Negro suffrage. Now, by fiat of his administration in defiance of the Dred Scott Decision, blacks were citizens of the United States, and he had begun in a gentle way to press for limited black enfranchisement. He had overcome his initial doubts about enlisting Negroes as fighting soldiers, was impressed by their overall performance, and thought they had earned the right to vote.

Lincoln once told Charles Sumner that on the issue of emancipation they were only four to six weeks apart. The relative earliness of his first favorable remarks about Negro enfranchisement suggests that he had again read the "signs of the times." It is not difficult to believe that after the war he would have continued closer to the Sumners than to the conservatives whom he had placated but never followed for long. And one can scarcely doubt that his postwar administration would have been more responsive to Negro aspirations than Andrew Johnson's proved to be.

But for several reasons Lincoln's role was likely to be more subdued than we might expect from the Great Emancipator. First, during peace-time, with his powers and responsibilities as Commander-in-Chief greatly reduced, he probably would have yielded more leadership to Congress in the old Whig tradition. Second, at the time of his death, he still regarded race relations as primarily a local matter, just as he had maintained during the debates with Douglas: "I do not understand there is any place where an alteration of the social and political rela-tions of the Negro and white man can be made except in the State Legislature." Third, Negroes as Negroes were nearly always connota-tive in Lincoln's thinking. Their welfare, though by no means a mat-ter of indifference to him, had never been, and was not likely to be-come, his "paramount object." They were, in the words of Frederick Douglass, "only his stepchildren."

Finally, in his attitude toward the wrongs of the free Negro, Lin-coln had none of the moral conviction that inspired his opposition to slavery. He never seems to have suspected that systematic racial dis-crimination might be, like slavery, a strain on the national honor and a crime against mankind. Whether that is the measure of his greatness must be left to each one's personal taste. Of Copernicus we might say: What a genius! He revolutionized our understanding of the solar sys-tem. Or: What an ignoramus! He did not understand the rest of the universe at all.

18

The Southern Rebellion
and the Sioux Uprising

GERALD S. HENIG

• *The most heated controversies among historians arise not over what happened but rather why it happened. How much importance should authors grant to cultural factors? How much to economic forces? How much weight should be given to the personal recollections of participants in important events?*

Historians often evade questions of causality, except in an immediate sense. Instead of taking an explicit stand on the significance of economic forces in shaping the direction of events, we are more likely to concentrate on the specific occurrence in question and avoid placing it in too large a context. Nonetheless, the broader questions remain implicit in any historical account, whether the writer chooses to address them openly or not.

In 1862, after federal troops had been pulled out of the West for service against the Confederacy, most of the Plains Indians rose up against the whites. For the next five years, intermittent clashes kept the whole area in a state of alarm. In the account below of the bloody Sioux uprising in Minnesota, Gerald S. Henig places primary importance on the national context in which the rebellion began. He suggests that the most important cause of the uprising might be found not so much in the actions of the individuals who were there but rather in an external event—the Civil War—that on the surface bore only a slight relation to the Indian question. Professor Henig indicates by way of conclusion that not only would the uprising have taken a different character in the absence of the North-South conflict but it might also not have occurred at all.

Obviously, no single, final cause can ever be found for any human event. But in the case of the Sioux uprising the usual difficulties in determining causality are considerably multiplied by the lack of source material. As Henig concedes, any conclusions remain extremely tentative in the absence of documents giving the contemporary Indian view of the conflict.

In terms of lives lost, property destroyed, and tragic consequences for both Indians and whites, the Sioux (or Dakota) Uprising in Minnesota in the summer of 1862 has few, if any, parallels in American history. Those who have investigated the war, whether soon after or in later times, probably would find common ground with John G. Nicolay, one of President Lincoln's private secretaries. In Minnesota at the time on a treaty-making assignment, he noted that from "the days of King Philip to the time of Black Hawk, there has hardly been an outbreak so treacherous, so sudden, so bitter, and so bloody, as that which filled the State of Minnesota with sorrow and lamentation. . . ."

Aside from its severity, the Sioux rebellion has another distinction as well. Although the 1,500 or so Indians most involved would be defeated and dispersed by the early fall of 1862, the incident was destined to be the first of many that would plague the frontier until the final Indian surrender at Wounded Knee, South Dakota, in 1890. Thus the outbreak in Minnesota was the initial and most destructive campaign waged by the Plains Indians during this period. Perhaps this helps to explain why there has always been a keen interest in the motivation behind the uprising.

The over-all causes of the conflict are well known, and some of them will only be briefly discussed. Most of them stem from the constant demands for Indian lands made by westward-moving settlers and consequent treaties to "legalize" the land take-overs. The government negotiated a series of treaties with the Sioux which, including those signed in 1858, resulted in the loss of practically all of their Minnesota lands except for a ten-mile-wide reservation on the south side of the Minnesota River from west of New Ulm to Big Stone Lake. This area did not include a good hunting ground; so the Sioux, a nomadic and proud people, now found themselves largely dependent for food and

Reprinted from *Minnesota History*, 45 (Fall 1976): 107–10. Copyright © by the Minnesota Historical Society. Used with permission.

money on the form of annuities provided by the government under the terms of the various treaties. While some Sioux were converted to Christianity and engaged in farming as they were encouraged to do, most of them refused to conform, insisting that the treaties were unfair, that white settlers were encroaching upon their lands and abusing them and their women, and that the government's agents were making no attempt to protect them. In short, the Sioux remained "suspicious and anxious," and by the early 1860s the "frontier had become extremely combustible." As seen elsewhere in this issue, the explosion at last occurred on August 17, 1862, with the killing of five settlers at Acton, and early on August 18 with the attack led by Little Crow on the Lower Sioux Agency.

Why did the Sioux become anxious for war? Did they truly believe they could emerge victorious? And if so, what led them to that conclusion? Admittedly, these are difficult questions to answer, if for no other reason than that the Sioux left few written records. But as with other "inarticulate" nonwhite groups in American history, evidence bearing on their views and actions does exist in the form of letters, reports, and reminiscences of whites who in some way had direct contact with them. In the case of the Sioux, for example, this would include settlers in the area, reservation employees and their families, missionaries, government agents, captives of the Indians, soldiers, newspaper reporters, and the like. And there are a few long-after Indian accounts. If used with caution, the testimony from these various quarters could prove to be highly significant. Some of it, in fact, suggests an avenue of thought which has not been adequately considered by historians—namely, that the Civil War then raging between the North and the South played a decisive role in convincing the Sioux that the time was ripe for their own war against the Union. Indeed, as one perceptive observer of the uprising later put it: "The outbreak will not be fully accounted for until we have linked it with the Southern rebellion."

From the very beginning, the Sioux were well aware of the armed conflict taking place below the Mason-Dixon line. As news of the war reached the reservations, either through the newspapers (which many of the mixed-bloods and some of the Indians could read), or by word of mouth, it "would be taken up and passed on to be circulated among the lodges." According to Jannette E. De Camp Sweet, whose first husband had charge of the lumber mill at the Lower Agency, the Sioux came almost daily to her house "with their bags of corn to be ground, and would linger about the doors and windows asking questions and receiving answers about everything usually discussed . . . but they seemed more especially interested in the conflict between our disrupted states." For that matter, Little Crow himself "watched the war between the North and the South with the deepest solicitude. His runners were always early at the office waiting arrival of the mail, and, after gathering the news concerning the war, hastened to their chief."

During the summer of 1862 the war in the eastern theater was going badly for the Union. News of General George B. McClellan's abortive Peninsular Campaign apparently did not escape the attention of the Sioux. "We understood that the South was getting the best of the fight," Big Eagle later recalled in his famous account of the uprising, "and it was said that the North would be whipped." Stephen R. Riggs, a Presbyterian missionary, confirmed this point. Writing several years after the outbreak, he noted that when "a battle occurred between our forces and the rebels, in which the latter had the advantage in any respect, our Indians were sure to learn the fact, and, oftentimes, with exaggerations."

Consequently, many Sioux feared that the government would become bankrupt and unable to grant future annuities to them. The fact that their payments were already past due in 1862 seemed to add a degree of validity to their fears. Other members of the tribe, however, anticipated even more disastrous consequences, as revealed by questions they posed to the missionaries: "Whether it was true that the South had burned all our large cities, New York, Boston, Philadelphia? Whether the Great Father had been killed or taken prisoner, our armies destroyed, and the enemy coming to make slaves of all of us?"

Under these circumstances, it is not surprising that the Sioux began to whisper "that now would be a good time to go to war with the whites and get back the lands." For those who still harbored doubt concerning the wisdom of such action, much of it was probably dispelled when Congress on July 17 authorized a draft of 300,000 nine-month militia men, with quotas assigned to the states. Determined to fill Minnesota's quota, state authorities encouraged all able-bodied men to enlist, including those residing on the reservations. As a result, the

Indian agent for the Sioux, Thomas J. Galbraith, recruited a company of soldiers called the Renville Rangers, many of whom were mixed-bloods. In the eyes of the Indians, it now seemed clear that the Union was "in the last throes of dissolution."

Even Little Crow's confidence in the government was shaken, despite the fact that he had visited Washington and other Eastern cities and had some understanding of the power of the whites. Their "early defeats, losses in battle, and the enlisting of men at the Agency," in the opinion of Dr. Asa W. Daniels, the physician at the Lower Sioux Agency, "encouraged hopes of success in an uprising." Whatever may have prompted the enigmatic chief to lead his men into battle will probably remain a matter of some conjecture, but one thing is certain: By mid-August 1862, more and more Sioux were beginning to believe that the authority of the Union could be challenged.

Of even greater import, however, was the growing conviction among a number of warriors that such a challenge would be met with very little, if any, opposition. After all, not only had the able-bodied men on the reservations been enlisted for service in the Union army, but throughout the state "nearly all the white men capable of bearing arms had gone south." The Sioux were well aware of these conditions. During the past year, when they hunted in various parts of Minnesota, they saw nothing but old men, women, and children, and "all that were fit to be soldiers had gone to the wars."

Much of the state was indeed left virtually undefended. Charles S. Bryant, a St. Paul attorney who became familiar with the uprising through his work in settling the claims for property damages committed by the Indians, maintained that the entire organized force for the defense of the Minnesota frontier at times did not exceed 200 men, leading the Sioux to believe that the whites were weak and that the government's attention was directed solely toward the struggle in the South. Other informed contemporaries, including government officials, newspaper reporters, and victims of the outbreak, arrived at similar conclusions. Outspoken Jane Grey Swisshelm of the *St. Cloud Democrat*, acting as a correspondent for the *New York Tribune*, was particularly outraged, blaming the Lincoln Administration for the uprising, since it refused to use slaves in the armed services and thus drained the "North Star State of her hardy frontier defenders." Before long the President would reverse his policy and employ blacks in the army, but for the moment Minnesota was left exposed, and the Sioux decided that "now was the time to strike. . . . They could make their way down to Saint Paul, and repossess themselves of the good land of their fathers, for which they had been so poorly remunerated."

Obviously, the Sioux had enough provocation to arrive at such a decision on their own. But this did not deter some from thinking that the Indians had external help—that they were instigated by outsiders, probably Confederate agents. Horace Greeley of the *New York Tribune,* for example, believed that this was the case. A week after the outbreak, Greeley insisted that:

> The Sioux have doubtless been stimulated if not bribed to plunder and slaughter their White neighbors by White and Red villains sent among them for this purpose by the Secessionists. . . . They will have effected a temporary diversion in favor of the Confederacy, and that is all *their* concern.

High-ranking government officials, moreover, held the same opinion as Greeley. The United States Consul General in Canada, Joshua Giddings, reported that Confederate agents were very active in northwestern Minnesota, operating through Canadian Indians and fur traders. Secretary of the Interior Caleb B. Smith, "after a careful examination of all the data which the Indian Bureau had been able to obtain," also believed that "southern emissaries" were responsible for inciting the Sioux. And finally, Lincoln himself, in his annual message on December 1, 1862, told Congress he had information "that a simultaneous attack was to be made upon the white settlements by all the tribes between the Mississippi river and the Rocky mountains."

Yet, if there was concrete information of Confederate agents engaged in conspiratorial activities among the Sioux, it never surfaced. For that matter, those who were actually on the scene, either as victims of the outbreak or in battle against the Indians, denied the existence of secessionist emissaries. It is more than likely, therefore, that these unsubstantiated accusations probably reflected the Union's weariness with its own war in the South and its willingness to heap all that was evil on the shoulders of the Confederacy.

On the other hand, there is solid evidence suggesting that the Sioux were incited by white men, many of whom belonged to what was called the "old moccasin Democracy" of the territory and state. With the Republican victory in 1860, these men were ousted from their positions as government employees and traders on the reservations. Eventually they comprised the "Copperhead element" in the area, expressing sympathy for the Southern cause and, according to several eyewitnesses, neglecting no opportunity to tell stories which would "poison the minds of the Indians and inflame them against the present agent and the government." To make matters worse, Union defeats on the battlefield tended to lend credence to their tales that the Great Father "was whipped" and that the Indians would receive no further annuities.

Attempts by newly appointed government officials to disprove these fabrications met with little success. The Confederate sympathizers, who had known the Indians far longer than their recently installed Republican opponents, were evidently more adept in working "upon the fears and hopes of the dissatisfied and restive Sioux." As one victim of the outbreak (who had been held captive for several weeks) later wrote: "I was assured by many of the wisest among the Indians that it was what the traders told them more than anything else that caused the uprising." In any case, subsequent events carried a tragically ironic twist. Apparently the pro-Southern traders and other former reservation employees had "carried it a little too far." When the Sioux engaged in their war against the whites, they made no distinction between Unionists and Copperheads.

Disloyal whites were not the only ones to have their plans backfire. The Sioux themselves would experience a similar fate. They had hoped to gain the support of the Confederacy; in fact, Little Crow was reported to have made plans to sell the Minnesota Valley to the Southern states. The Confederacy, however, failed to respond. The Sioux also anticipated possible aid from the British. Many among them were aware that the Civil War had seriously disrupted Anglo-American relations. Furthermore, the Indians believed that in gratitude for the help they had given Great Britain in the War of 1812, the British would now return the favor. But nothing materialized. Nevertheless, after the Sioux were defeated, Little Crow, who escaped capture, ultimately made his way to Canada with a small band. There he demanded supplies from the British authorities, but received nothing but mere handouts of food. The chief later returned to Minnesota and, in July, 1863, was shot to death near Hutchinson by two settlers who were out hunting.

Thus, from beginning to end, the Sioux outbreak of 1862 was a tragic and brutal episode in the history of Indian-white relations in America. Like similar conflicts, its underlying causes were complex and deeply rooted in the past. Yet, would it have occurred if the national situation had been different? Perhaps missionary Stephen R. Riggs, who had spent several decades with the Sioux, was right when he declared: "If there had been no Southern war, there would have been no Dakota uprising and no Minnesota massacres!"

19

The Politics of Reconstruction in the North

RICHARD N. CURRENT

• *The phrase "radical reconstruction" appears in almost every text book in American history. It is difficult, however, to point to any permanent changes that resulted from Reconstruction policies. The Civil War led to the Thirteenth Amendment, which abolished slavery, and to the Fourteenth, which granted citizenship to anyone born or naturalized in the United States and which required states to proceed with "due process of law" before depriving any citizen of life, liberty, or property. These Constitutional amendments passed through Congress before Reconstruction in the South began. For almost a decade from 1867, military forces occupied the Southern states and influenced the region's politics. But in crucial areas, such as social mobility, education, and occupational opportunities, little was done to help the former slave. No major political or military figures of the Confederacy suffered anything more than temporary imprisonment and suspension of political rights for a few years. The structure of Southern society remained relatively intact, and the descendants of pre-Civil War leaders emerged as the key personages in the post-Reconstruction South.*

We know much less about what happened in the North in the dozen years following the end of the Civil War, and misconceptions have followed from this neglect. One of the most serious is the tendency to view northern Republicans in oversimplified terms—either as radicals or as moderates. The article by Professor Richard N. Current demonstrates that more complex forces were operating within the party. The leaders, he says, were dominated not by ideology but by practical vote-getting concerns. Accordingly, the key to Republican success lay not in a coherent political program but rather in a shifting—indeed often self-contradictory—stand that reflected the conflicting sentiments of the electorate.

Implicit in this picture, as in most accounts of American history, is a pluralist view of society. Professor Current accepts the standard position of social scientists that the United States is composed not of a few well-defined classes but rather of a hodgepodge of disparate interest groups out of which political and social compromises can be reached.

At the end of the Civil War the Republican or "Union" party dominated Wisconsin politics. Republicans held the governorship and all the other state administrative posts, the three positions on the state supreme court, a large majority of the places in each house of the legislature, five of six congressional seats, and both United States senatorships. For eight years more the party continued to keep itself in power, though with a fluctuating share of the total vote. Then, in 1873, the Republicans faltered, losing the control of the state government that they had held since 1857.

The Republicans' almost unbroken record of success during the Reconstruction years was by no means automatic. It depended on the care with which the leaders maximized the party's strengths and minimized its weaknesses. Its greatest strengths were its appeals to patriotism (or sectionalism), idealism, and materialism. The leaders could identify the party with noble causes, with the war aims of union and freedom: and so long as their fellow partisans controlled Congress and the Presidency they could also promise the more solid benefits of the federal patronage and the federal pork barrel. To some extent, the party's weaknesses derived from its very strengths. Antislavery idealism, insofar as it carried over to the postwar movement for Negro rights, ran against the much stronger force of racism. The reform spirit, which animated the antislavery drive, also gave rise to demands for sumptuary laws against drinking and Sabbath-breaking, laws that would turn away foreign-born voters, who looked upon such legislation as a product of continuing nativism. Moreover, the reforming impulse directed itself against monopolies, against corporations in general and railroads in

Reprinted by permission of the State Historical Society of Wisconsin, from *The History of Wisconsin. Volume II: The Civil War Era, 1848–1873* (Madison, 1976), pp. 563-97.

particular, and as a result of the Republicans' effectiveness in promoting federal aid to private enterprise, especially through the financing of "internal improvements," the party exposed itself to charges of favoritism toward big business.

The leaders had to deal carefully, then, with the shifting crosscurrents of sectionalism, idealism, materialism, racism, nativism, and antimonopolism. Only by so doing could the politicians hold the party together and keep it on top. Holding it together required some effort, since the party was and had been from the beginning a congeries of rather disparate elements. It had originated in 1854 as a coalition consisting mainly of Whigs but containing also Free Soilers and other dissident Democrats. As it grew it incorporated all except a few of the Know Nothings; and at the same time, by disavowing Know-Nothing aims and muting temperance and Sabbatarian cries, it managed to attract a number of immigrants, at least among some of the Protestant groups. Before the war it overcame centrifugal tendencies by emphasizing the one principle that all its various followers held in common, the principle of free soil, or opposition to the extension of slavery into the territories. During the war the party drew the support of additional Democrats, some as converts, others as fellow travelers, and it made use of centripetal force even stronger than free-soilism, the force of a shared determination to win the war. Once the war had been won the slavery had been abolished, however, the leaders, if they were to remain in power, needed to find new issues that would unite the party, while continuing to avoid those that might divide it.

One possibility was to keep the war memories alive, and thus maintain the identification of the Republican party with patriotism and the opposition with treason. This could be done, in part, by making an issue of the veterans, backing them in peace as in war, and thus cultivating their support along with the support of their relatives and friends and of self-consciously loyal citizens in general.

Lucius Fairchild, the first three-term governor of Wisconsin (1866–1872), early saw the possibility. Himself a veteran who had lost his left arm at Gettysburg, Fairchild campaigned in 1865 as the Soldier's Friend. He got endorsements from his old comrades and promised generous benefits, including preference in political appointments, to all Wisconsin soldiers and especially to the disabled. In his first Inaugural the governor, his empty sleeve conspicuous, spoke of the nobility of sacrifice in the nation's cause. He referred to secession as treason and called for the hanging of Jefferson Davis as a traitor. In 1866 the Grand Army of the Republic's Madison department, a veterans' organization that Fairchild had helped to form, demanded that all leaders of the late Confederacy be condignly punished and that they be completely debarred from politics.

Once a colonel, now governor, Fairchild continued to view himself as still, at least potentially, a commander of troops against the traitorous foe. Again and again he referred to the veterans' "fears of another civil war" in case of a Democratic victory. "I confess to some little feeling of this kind," he wrote confidentially, in 1866, "and to a strong wish to prepare, so far as I am able as the governor of this state, to meet all enemies on their own terms." Publicly he insisted that only the maintenance of the Republicans in power would prevent a renewal of rebellion. Year after year he and his followers continued to identify the Republican party with the Union army, as they did at an 1866 rally in Madison, where youthful party workers flaunted banners reading: "We vote as we fought, against traitors," and "Where the traitor's bullet failed his ballot shall not conquer."

If most of the men who had served the Union in war could be counted upon to support the Republican party in peace, most of those who had evaded service could be expected to assist the Democrats. So, while encouraging the veterans to vote, the Republicans could further help themselves by taking the ballot away from men who, when drafted, had failed to report or who, after induction, had deserted. This would be as constitutional as it would be just, the state Attorney General advised the legislature in 1866, confirming the opinion his predecessor had given the previous year. Accordingly, laws of 1866 and 1867 disfranchised draft dodgers and deserters, provided for the publication of a list of their names, and required the posting of three copies of the list at every polling place. A "blue pamphlet" containing some twelve thousand names was printed. Inclusion of a man's name was to be taken as *prima facie* evidence of his guilt and hence of his ineligibility to vote. Democrats protested that the laws violated the ancient Anglo-Saxon principle of no punishment without prior conviction, and the critics were by no means appeased when, in 1868, an amendment made it possible for a listed man to get his name removed by proving his innocence to the satisfaction of the Attorney General. Even before the official pamphlet had been published, Governor Fairchild was already preparing partial lists to be used against Democrats in the congressional elections of 1866. For a few years the pamphlet was of some value to the Republicans. Despite the zeal of Fairchild and certain of his fellow partisans, however, the disfranchising laws soon became dead letters.

For Republicans, the question of taking the vote away from deserters was much less controversial than the question of giving it to blacks, whatever their war records. At the end of the war the issue of suffrage for Wisconsin Negroes was touchy indeed, despite their infinitesimal number and their willing service in the Union army. Wisconsin's blacks had done their part and, understandably, they thought this entitled them to the ballot. "The record of the last four years is still before us," a convention of the "colored citizens" of Wisconsin resolved on October 9, 1865; "white men and colored have fought side by side. . . . Our deeds upon the battle fields have been sealed in blood, and render us worthy all the privileges that we ask of the voters."

The next month the voters could decide on Negro suffrage in a referendum—the third such referendum to be held in accordance with the constitution of 1848. In the 1849 election a suffrage bill had been favored by 5,265 ballots and opposed by only 4,075, but a total of more than 31,000 votes was polled in the election itself. Fewer than a third of the voters had bothered to express themselves on the bill. Though it had received more affirmative than negative votes, it had not received in its favor a majority of all the votes cast at the election, and even its proponents therefore considered it as lost. In 1857 another suffrage bill was voted down, 41,345 to 28,235. Then, in 1865, the legislature passed yet another bill, in response to a petition from 102 blacks.

At their state convention that September in Madison the Republicans faced the question whether to endorse the suffrage proposal and make it a party issue in the fall election. A leading party organ, the *Wisconsin State Journal* of Madison, was urging the adoption of a platform of principles around which "genuine and earnest Union men" could rally, was reporting that a large majority approved the suffrage bill, and was citing in its favor the highest party authority, that of

President Andrew Johnson, who had said that "each State should be left to regulate the question of suffrage for itself." Yet, in fact, Johnson was unwilling for Wisconsin or other Northern states to be left to regulate the question in favor of the blacks. His agent in Wisconsin was Senator James R. Doolittle, a former Democrat, the Senate's foremost wartime advocate of the "colonization" abroad of freed slaves, and an unctuous but effective orator. "All attempts to make this new issue of Negro suffrage a plank in the platform of the party," Doolittle told Governor Fairchild, "is simply suicide." Presiding at the Madison convention, Doolittle managed to exclude from the platform any reference to Negro suffrage in Wisconsin.

Some Republicans—formerly antislavery radicals, now the "friends of equal rights"—denounced the "pernicious influence" of Doolittle and threatened to break away from the "Union" party. They called a second convention, to meet in Janesville and represent the "liberty-loving" people of the state. In Janesville the radicals found themselves a decided minority of the Union party, however, and they concluded their rump session by endorsing the candidates who had been nominated in Madison.

During the 1865 campaign the Democrats, who had an explicit anti-suffrage plank in their platform, called upon Fairchild to debate the question with their gubernatorial candidate, Harrison C. Hobart, a former assemblyman and Civil War hero. Some of the Republican newspapers frankly advocated equal voting rights, and so did the radical politicians, prominent among them Sherman Booth and Byron Paine, the one the hero of the Joshua Glover slave rescue of 1854 and the other the attorney who had defended Booth and persuaded the state supreme court to defy federal authority and declare the Fugitive Slave Act of 1850 unconstitutional. But Fairchild hid behind his party's noncommittal platform and refused to speak out. His advisers cautioned him that Negro suffrage was distasteful to many party members, and particularly to war veterans. "Nothing would please the copperheads more than to induce or compel you in some way to define your position in writing," one of his friends counseled. "The 'Nigger' is the only card they have left." By his silence, however, Fairchild risked losing the support of radical voters. So, late in the campaign, he wrote letters to Booth and other radical politicians telling them that he personally favored Negro suffrage and wished them to quote him whenever they met with like-minded Republicans.

When the returns were in, the strategy of Fairchild seemed to have worked. He won by 10,000 votes and Negro suffrage lost by almost 9,000. The suffrage bill did much better in the Republican than in the Democratic counties, but nowhere did it do so well as Fairchild himself. Of the thirty-eight counties he carried, only twenty-four had a majority for the bill. Of the remaining nineteen counties, which his opponent carried, not one gave a majority for it. His fears regarding the veterans' antipathy to it appear to have been justified, if the separately counted soldier vote is taken as an indicator. By November 1865, only about 1,500 Wisconsin soldiers were still voting in the field. They went more than three to one, 1,169 to 330, against the bill while going for Fairchild in about the same proportion. The "suffrage question, if made an issue, would have carried us under," Doolittle assured him after the election.

Despite the suffrage proposition's defeat, the radical Republicans were soon to have their way, and blacks were to be voting at the next election in Wisconsin. At the recent election a Milwaukeean named Ezekiel Gillespie had gone to the polls, along with Sherman Booth, and had offered his ballot even though he was unregistered, the board of registry having turned him away as a person of "mixed African blood." The election inspectors refused his ballot. Gillespie, with the aid of his lawyer, Byron Paine, then sued the inspectors, who offered a demurrer before the county court which promptly moved the case on appeal to the state supreme court.

In *Gillespie v. Palmer et al.* (1866) Paine undertook to prove that Gillespie already had the right to vote in 1865 because the Negro suffrage measure had actually been approved at the 1849 election, in the very first referendum under the state constitution. The constitutional phrase "a majority of all votes cast at such election," Paine argued, must mean simply a majority of the votes cast on the specific issue. Otherwise, the measure could never be passed—even if all the voters should mark their ballots in its favor. These ballots could not add up to a "majority of all votes cast" at the election, for "all votes" would be the sum of those cast for the proposition plus those cast on both sides for governor plus those for lieutenant governor and so on. Surely the framers of the constitution had not intended any such thing, nor had they meant to require more votes for passing a suffrage bill than for ratifying a suffrage amendment, which would require approval by merely "a majority of the voters voting thereon."

The three judges, all Republicans, accepted Paine's reasoning, literal and strained though much of it was. They ruled that, despite the consensus to the contrary, which had prevailed for nearly seventeen years, Negroes had had the right to vote in Wisconsin since 1849, when a majority of voters casting ballots on the proposition—but only one-sixth of those voting in the election—had assented to a suffrage bill.

The court's decision created "quite a commotion" in Milwaukee. Some Democrats threatened that any Negro attempting to vote in the upcoming local election would be mobbed. The blacks were not intimidated, and though there was the "rare sight of negroes voting," the election of April 3, 1866, was one of the quietest the city had ever experienced: "Not a single fight occurred at any of the polls." Some of the black voters were immediately summoned, for the first time, for jury duty. In the Madison election the Negro turnout was large. There was even a black candidate for mayor, William H. Noland, and he received 306 votes to 691 for his opponent, Elisha W. Keyes, the postmaster and boss of the "Madison Regency." But Noland, a leader of the Madison black community, got no votes from his fellow blacks. All his votes came from Democrats, who had announced his candidacy against his will and as a joke. In a dignified election-day statement he declared he was a "Union man," that is, a Republican, and was himself voting the "straight Union ticket." "If any Democrat wishes to compliment me let him go and do likewise." In both Madison and Milwaukee nearly all the Negroes apparently voted straight Republican, except in some Milwaukee wards where the Republicans put up no slates.

For Wisconsin Republicans, the Negro vote proved an asset only in marginal instances. It made the difference between defeat and victory, for example, in one of the closely contested Madison wards in 1866. But the Negro vote was too small to affect the outcome of most elections. Calculating the consequences of the possible defection of Andrew Johnson's adherents, Republican politicians concluded, in May 1866, that the loss would be "more than balanced by the enfranchised colored vote." This conclusion depended, however, more on the smallness of the anticipated loss than on the largeness of the anticipated gain. After all, there were only a few hundred black adult males in the state.

On balance, Negro suffrage at home was more a liability than an asset to Wisconsin Republicans. Their black support confirmed the charge of "niggerism" and helped the Democrats turn the widespread Negrophobia to their account. Democratic newspapers never tired of recounting supposed Negro "outrages" and describing Republican candidates as "Negro lovers." The Oshkosh *City Times* implied that Congressman Philetus Sawyer, for one, would stoop to almost anything for the "vote of a nigger" and accused him of neglecting whites to patronize blacks. If the party division had been closer, if the Republicans had been weaker, the added burden of race prejudice might have been too much for the party to bear.

While bearing that burden, the party leaders also had to deal with the potentially disruptive issue of the postwar reconstruction of the South. In Wisconsin, as in other states, the Republican party had adopted the name "Union" so as to encourage the affiliation of Democrats who backed the war effort. At the national convention of 1864 the Republicans had sealed the coalition by choosing the War Democrat Johnson as Lincoln's running mate. After Lincoln's assassination and Johnson's accession, the coalition could remain intact only so long as the Democrat in the White House could keep the loyalty of the Republicans in Congress and throughout the country.

At the outset Johnson seemed to be in a position to exert an especially strong hold on the Union party in Wisconsin. His assistant postmaster general—whom he was to elevate to the head of the Post Office Department in July, 1866—was Alexander W. Randall, a two-term governor of the state. Randall's friend Elisha W. Keyes was postmaster as well as mayor of Madison. Through his friendship with Randall he had a large share in the disposal of jobs in the more than 1,000 Wisconsin post offices. Associated with Keyes was Horace Rublee, chairman of the Republican (Union) state committee and co-owner and co-editor of the *Wisconsin State Journal*. Together, Keyes and Rublee ran the most powerful Republican machine in the state.

When Johnson took over, Keyes urged the people to "rally around" the new President as he tried to reunite the nation.

Johnson soon had on his side not only the Republican bosses of Wisconsin but also the state's senior senator, James R. Doolittle. At the time of Lincoln's death Doolittle had been cooperating with Lincoln in his effort to reconstruct and readmit Louisiana on fairly quick and easy terms. Doolittle differed with his Senate colleague from Wisconsin, Timothy O. Howe, who was dissatisfied with Lincoln's policy and wished Lincoln "w'd tell the rebels" that the President could "only grant pardons" and that Congress alone could admit states. At first Doolittle feared that Johnson, as President, would deal too harshly with the defeated Southerners, but Doolittle soon convinced himself that Johnson's policy would be essentially the same as Lincoln's. Before long he felt that he and Johnson, along with Senator Preston King of New York, constituted a "trio whose hearts & heads" sympathized "more closely and more deeply than any other trio in America." (King shortly thereafter committed suicide, leaving Doolittle and Johnson as twin spirits.)

The Wisconsin party's first big postwar test of unity and of support for the Johnson administration occurred at the state convention of September, 1865. As chairman of the platform committee, Doolittle was ready with a set of resolutions applauding Johnson's program for speedily restoring the Southern states. He got his resolutions adopted after seeing the delegates turn down, by an overwhelming voice vote, an amendment calling for Negro suffrage in the South—a plank he thought would have driven "thousands of War Democrats" out of the party. To Johnson he boasted of his success, and the *Wisconsin State Journal* gave its approval to his stand on restoration; but other party organs dissented, as did Senator Howe, and some of the radicals condemned Doolittle as a rebel sympathizer. Thus, despite the seeming consensus he had contrived, the Republican party already was developing strains.

After the 1865 election Johnson's Assistant Postmaster General, Randall, predicted to a Wisconsin correspondent, "There is coming a 'big row' shortly which will and is clearing out the whole radical portion of our party and probably leading the Democratic element of the party to 'seek new alliances.' " A "big row" was indeed on the way, and some former Democrats were to desert the Wisconsin organization, but the radicals were by no means to be cleared out. The party itself was to be radicalized. Randall and the rest of Johnson's friends, not his opponents, would have to look for new alliances.

When, during the winter of 1865–1866, Johnson and the congressional Republicans quarreled over reconstruction policy, only two members of the Wisconsin delegation took the side of the President. These two were Senator Doolittle and Congressman Charles A. Eldredge, the state's lone Democrat. Senator Howe and the other five congressmen supported the Republican program to postpone the seating of senators and representatives from the South, to extend the life and powers of the Freedmen's Bureau, and to confer civil rights upon Southern blacks.

At first the Madison Regency tried to stay out of the fight. Keyes kept still and occupied himself with his duties as mayor of Madison. Rublee's *Wisconsin State Journal*, without taking a stand, gave equal space to the opposing speeches of Doolittle and Howe. But neutrality was no longer possible for Wisconsin Republicans after Johnson vetoed the Freedmen's Bureau bill and then the civil rights bill, thus ending all hopes for a compromise. The Republicans in the legislature, thoroughly aroused, telegraphed instructions to the state's senators in Washington to vote for overriding the second veto. When Doolittle disregarded the instructions, the legislature formally requested him to resign. Now even the Madison Regency split. Keyes, after failing to "squelch" or even "tone down" the resignation demand, assured Doolittle that the country would "yet see the folly" of pursuing a course different from Doolittle's. Keyes called a "Union meeting" and there spoke out in favor of Johnson's policy. Horace Rublee, however, warned Doolittle that the great majority of Wisconsin Republicans were deeply alarmed by the President's course. The *Wisconsin State Journal* criticized the vetoes and endorsed Howe's position.

Wisconsin politicians brought about something of a party realignment as they prepared for a trial of strength between Johnson's adherents and his opponents in the campaign of 1866. As two of his top lieutenants in the land, Senator Doolittle and Postmaster General Randall [Randall became Postmaster General in 1866.—ed.] played leading roles in the National Union movement, through which its sponsors intended to bring together a great middle grouping of Republican and Democratic voters and thus elect to Congress a majority favorable to the President. But Randall and Doolittle failed to rouse much Republican support for the movement even in their home state. Keyes himself lay low for the time being. Cooperating with the two Johnson leaders was Alexander Mitchell, banker, railroad magnate, and one of Milwaukee's richest men, who had acted with the Republicans during the war but was now about to leave them and join the Democrats. "It requires no sacrifice from Democrats to support Johnson," another Republican-for-Johnson heard from a man in Appleton, "but, with Repub's, they must brace against [the] bulk of previous political associations." Indeed, Democrats flocked to the President's standard with an enthusiasm that to Doolittle was gratifying and yet embarrassing, especially when he was flattered by Marcus M. Pomeroy, editor of the La Crosse *Democrat* and lately the most vicious anti-Lincoln Copperhead in the state if not in the entire country. For a time there were two parties claiming the magic name of "Union"—the National Union and the Republican Union. Soon the former became practically indistinguishable from the regular Democratic organization, and the latter reconstituted and retitled itself as simply the good old Republican party.

During the 1866 campaign, however, party lines and party loyalties remained uncertain and confusing enough that Randall and Doolittle found it hard to make effective use of presidential patronage. Randall was quoted as saying that only those sustaining the President should eat his bread and butter—which led Johnson's foes to dub his followers the Bread and Butter party. The problem was to know who could be depended upon to sustain the President. Alexander Mitchell advised Doolittle that their side would "gain little additional political strength by removing A. & appointing B." unless B. should actually prove a better Johnson man. "I do not see that the new appointees . . . are likely to be any better administration men than the old—if as good." Another difficulty lay in the jealousy between Republican and Democratic friends of the President. Democratic leaders feared that Doolittle and Randall, "because of old party associations," were "more likely to bestow the patronage at their disposal" upon Republicans than upon Democrats. Nevertheless, the patronage dispensers made a number of changes in Wisconsin. What effect these had, other than to exacerbate the anti-Johnson feeling of many Republicans, it would be hard to say.

The bitterness of the campaign solidified the Republican party, bringing tightly together all its factions except the tiny group of die-hard Johnsonites. The proposed Fourteenth Amendment became a test not only of Republicanism but also of patriotism, of true Union-ism. According to the Milwaukee *Sentinel*, which had lost its govern-ment printing contract because of its anti-Johnson stand, the "Rebels" were giving no sign that they had ceased to be "deadly enemies of the Union." The were refusing to ratify the amendment and they were adopting black codes which, for "atrocity," found "no equal in the annals of Russian serfdom." Condoning and encouraging the recal-citrant Southerners were Johnson and Doolittle. From one voter, who signed himself "Four Fifths of Wisconsin," Doolittle received this bit of advice: "You have turned *Traitor* to your State and gone over to Johnson and the *rebels*. . . . Come home and put a *ball* through your *rotten* head."

Such bitterness made for a sizable Republican turnout on election day. As the 1866 returns showed, the party had gained more from con-versions than it had lost from defections. The five Republican congress-men were reelected, along with the one Democrat, and the Republican majority in the state legislature was increased from forty-seven to fifty-nine. Addressing the legislature early in 1867, Governor Fairchild took the result as a mandate for ratification of the Fourteenth Amend-ment: "Most of you are here to-day, because your constituents knew that you deemed this amendment just and necessary." Both houses promptly ratified it.

Wisconsin Republicans maintained their unity in supporting the pas-sage of the reconstruction acts of 1867, the impeachment of Johnson, the presidential candidacy of Ulysses S. Grant, and the ratification of the Fifteenth Amendment. They ceased to consider Johnson's friend Doolittle even nominally a party member, and they did not count him among the seven Republican senators who broke ranks at the impeach-ment trial, though they blamed him, along with each of the seven, for the one not-guilty vote that proved decisive in bringing about the ac-quittal. When his senatorial term ended in 1869, they replaced him with Matthew H. Carpenter, a postwar convert from his earlier Democratic faith who had confirmed his Republicanism with his oratorical attacks on Doolittle during the 1866 campaign. Keyes having come out, after a two-year silence, for Grant and then for Carpenter, the new senator used his influence with the new President to get Keyes continued as Madison postmaster. Soon Keyes became the state Republican boss. With such a skillful organizer in command, with Carpenter and Howe cooperating in the Senate, with a harmonious delegation in the House, and with a sympathetic and obliging occupant of the presidency, the Wisconsin party operated as a highly efficient and fairly cohesive organization, despite the continued tension of personal rivalries within it.

A number of Wisconsinites, or ex-Wisconsinites, were also active as Republican politicians in one or another of the Southern states. These men were mostly former Wisconsin soldiers who had remained in or returned to the South, viewing it as a land of economic opportunity, a new frontier. Some of the newcomers from Wisconsin, like some of those from other Northern states, went into politics when the reconstruction acts gave the vote to the freedmen and made possible the rise of the Republican party in the South. The Republicans from the North soon came to be denounced as "carpetbaggers."

Among the carpetbaggers from Wisconsin, the most prominent was Harrison Reed, once a newspaper publisher in Milwaukee and in Madison and one of the founders of Neenah. Reed served as governor of Florida from 1868 to 1872, a fellow Wisconsinite as lieutenant-governor, and still another, a brother of Alexander W. Randall, as chief justice of the Florida supreme court. John S. Harris, a former Milwaukee businessman, was elected to the United States Senate from Louisiana. At least two men from Wisconsin represented Southern constituencies in the national House of Representatives, the one being sent from Alabama, the other from Tennessee. Wisconsinites also held office as Lieutenant-Governor of Alabama, state treasurer of Texas, and public land and immigration commissioner of Arkansas. Wisconsin men were mayors of Nashville, Chattanooga, and other Southern cities. They filled jobs as local officials and sat in state legislatures throughout the South. Among the lesser jobholders the most conspicuous Wisconsinite was Albert T. Morgan, once a farm boy in the vicinity of Fox Lake, who, in Mississippi, became a delegate to the state constitutional convention, a member of the state senate, and the sheriff of Yazoo

County. Morgan outraged conservative white Mississippians by marrying a mulatto woman and by shooting to death a political rival who tried to take over the sheriff's office.

Though doing handsomely for Grant in the Presidential election of 1868, the Republicans did much less well for their gubernatorial and legislative candidates in the state elections of 1867 and 1869. The party's majorities in the legislature shrank to ten in the assembly and only one in the senate. From the returns some of the Republican leaders drew the lesson that the bloody shirt and radical reconstruction no longer were adequate as campaign appeals. "Reconstruction is gone," Governor Fairchild opined. He thought the party ought to put less emphasis on abstract principles and more emphasis on material interests. "A material programme founded on proposed advantages to the people," a friend had advised, would be "ten times as strong as any other, and would set all other parties aside and make a new party for itself, if necessary."

There was a material program that had long been immensely popular in Wisconsin, so popular that none of the state's politicians had ever dared oppose it, though they might disagree as to how and where it ought to be applied. That was, of course, the old Whig program of federal aid for internal improvements. As successors of the Whigs, the Republicans had endorsed such aid in their national platforms. Hence in Wisconsin the Republicans had a more persuasive claim than the Democrats to being true devotees of the policy.

Much along that line remained to be done for the state after the war. There were harbors to be dredged and deepened at all the lake ports. There were canals to be dug and, most important, the ambitious Fox–Wisconsin waterway, connecting Lake Michigan and the Mississippi River, to be completed. Though the southern part of the state was already crisscrossed by rail lines, there were still railroads to be built in the north. Wisconsinites were practically unanimous in believing they must have better and cheaper transportation, by land and water, if they were to market profitably their two most valuable products—wheat and lumber—and if they were to develop the state's economy as a whole. Few doubted that they must have federal assistance if they were to achieve these aims.

Wisconsin Republicans used the state's need for internal improvements to justify their demands for a radical reconstruction of the South. If the Southern states should be restored quickly and with little change, warned Senator Howe in 1866, the Southern representatives could join with Northern Democrats to block the kind of economic legislation that Wisconsinites desired. The *Wisconsin State Journal* presented figures to show that, under Johnson's plan of restoration, the South would offset the Northwest in congressional power. As a matter of fact, the Northwest often ran into conflict with the Northeast, whose representatives generally had much less enthusiasm for improvement expenditures than for tariff protection. Whatever their differences on economic policy, however, the Northwestern and Northeastern Republicans had a common interest in opposing the early readmission of Southern Democrats, who could be expected to resist the appropriations and the tariffs alike.

From 1865 on, Wisconsin's Republican congressmen kept busy introducing and pressing requests for surveys, land grants, and construction money in furtherance of plans for building railroads and canals and improving rivers and harbors. In the annual pork barrel, the river and harbor appropriation bill, the Wisconsin delegates usually got most of what they wanted, in exchange for their support of tariff measures. In the 1868 bill, however, they received only enough for the repair and maintenance of works already under way, the Northeastern Republicans taking the position that extravagance would be politically unwise in an election year. The Wisconsin Democrats then tried to claim for themselves the improvements cause. They contended that, once their party was in power in Washington, Congress would spend less on reconstructing the South and more on improving the North. They made the most of the fact that their presidential candidate, Horatio Seymour of New York, was a director of the Green Bay and Mississippi Canal Company, the company that had charge of the Fox–Wisconsin waterway. Seymour's election, they said, would mean a President who would take a personal interest in the development of the state.

All along, Governor Fairchild had advocated internal improvements in addition to veteran benefits. In 1869, when he was seeking a third term without the backing of the state machine, he made improvements the paramount issue and himself their foremost champion. He hoped to attract the support of railroad promoters, pine-land speculators, and others in northwestern Wisconsin by keeping alive the St. Croix land grant, which was intended for the construction of a line from the Mississippi River to Lake Superior, and which was about to expire. At the same time he expected to win over the farmers along the Fox–Wisconsin route by providing a new stimulus to that project. "Give 'em *hell* on *Improvements,* and you're all right in this section," a well-wisher advised him. He met with the governors of Iowa and Minnesota to arrange for bringing their combined pressure upon Congress, obtained a promise of $5,000 from his own legislature to pay for lobbying, visited Washington to use his persuasive powers on congressmen, addressed a Portage gathering of enthusiasts from Wisconsin and neighboring states, and indeed talked about improvements at every opportunity. That year Wisconsin again got a fairly generous share of the river and harbor appropriations, and Fairchild secured his re-election without the assistance of Boss Keyes.

By 1870 the advocates of a Fox–Wisconsin canal were convinced it would never be completed unless the federal government not only provided much more money but also assumed responsibility for the project. The twofold task of securing federal funds and arranging for a government purchase fell mainly upon Congressman Philetus Sawyer of Oshkosh. His fellow townsmen long had dreamed of converting Oshkosh into a great inland seaport through the completion of the canal, and he himself had worked hard to get appropriations for that and for other Wisconsin improvements ever since going to Congress in 1865. As an influential member of the House committee on commerce, Sawyer took personal charge of the 1870 river and harbor bill, and he also helped in the passage of a measure authorizing the government to buy the Fox–Wisconsin works and rights from the Green Bay and Mississippi Canal Company. Oshkosh Democrats asserted that, as a friend of the Chicago and North Western Railway, Sawyer secretly aimed to thwart the canal enterprise and, in the purchase bill, had consented to terms he knew the company would reject. Late in the campaign, by pre-arrangement, the company itself refuted the Democrats by announcing its acceptance of the government's terms. On election day the voters returned Sawyer to Congress with his largest majority yet.

"I am as usual getting up the River & Harbor bill, and that dont damage our prospects any," Sawyer wrote to Fairchild in 1872. So long as Sawyer remained in the House of Representatives, until 1875, he continued to see that his state and district got an undue share of federal largess. To what extent this contributed to Wisconsin's economic growth, it is hard to say. Much of the government's money seemed simply to disappear in the shifting sands of the rivers to be "improved," and the dream of a great ship canal was never to be realized. There can be no doubt, however, that the federal expenditures contributed mightily to the success of Wisconsin's Republican party.

By 1872 the party had recovered most of its former strength. After a setback in 1870 it had made gains in 1871, increasing its majorities in both houses of the legislature and bringing to the governorship another Republican, the wealthy businessman and former congressman Cadwallader C. Washburn, who won the office over Doolittle, who was by 1871 an out-and-out Democrat once more. The Wisconsin Democracy, despite its acquisition of Doolittle and Mitchell and other onetime Johnson Republican leaders, seemingly remained an almost hopeless minority party. As a contemporary observed, it was "like an ox in a blizzard turning his tail to the storm"; it "kept up its organization, fought on the defensive as well as it could and faced the inevitable," that is, defeat. Yet it possessed one tremendous potential advantage, one that could transform defeat into victory if the circumstances were right. In the past the Democratic party had been the favorite with most of the immigrants. It now needed only to regain its previous share of the ethnic vote.

To both parties in Wisconsin, this vote was crucial, since the state contained such a large foreign-born population. The Roman Catholics— German, Irish, Dutch, Belgian, French-Canadian—remained with few exceptions faithful to the Democratic party, but the Republican party had attracted most of the British and the Norwegians and some of the Protestant Germans. To keep its supremacy after the war, the party had to maintain if not increase its proportion of the foreign vote.

In 1866 the Republicans tried to curry favor with the Irish by cheering them on in the Fenian movement. The Fenians claimed more than 6,000 Wisconsin members, who contributed money and men for a proposed invasion of Canada. President Johnson, enforcing the neutrality laws, sent troops to stop the invasion and arrest its leaders. Wisconsin Republicans denounced Johnson for his interference, and

Democratic newspapers ridiculed his critics for their pretended "love for the Irish." To show the Republicans' insincerity, the Democratic Appleton *Crescent* raised the pointed question: "Why did not the Howe-Sawyerites repeal the damnable *Neutrality laws* before they adjourned?" Apparently the Republicans beguiled few Irishmen for very long. Irish precincts, such as the townships of Erin in Washington County and Erin Prairie in St. Croix County, continued to give the Republicans at most eight or ten votes out of 200 or more.

To the extent that they were associated with Negro suffrage in Wisconsin and radical reconstruction in the South, the Republicans repelled rather than attracted Catholic immigrants, Germans in particular. The most overwhelming majorities against the 1865 suffrage proposal came from the heavily German counties north and northwest of Milwaukee, while the largest majorities in its favor came from southeastern counties with the highest proportion of settlers with a New York or New England background. The semi-official organ of the Wisconsin hierarchy, the German-language Milwaukee *Seebote*, continually deplored the congressional program of reconstruction. The procurator of the Milwaukee seminary for priests, writing to a missionary and funding society in Munich, said that Republican congressmen, "perhaps the most depraved" in the country's history, were beginning to be "ashamed of their constant attacks on President Johnson," but they still were proceeding to "torment the South in an unnatural manner." Native Protestant spokesmen, however, endorsed the radicals and their policy. The Presbyterian and Congregational Conference of 1866 approved of granting civil rights to freedmen. The Methodist Conference of 1868 declared that the same moral issues were involved in reconstruction as in the rebellion.

While antagonizing German Catholics, the Republicans could continue to hold the support of many German Protestants—freethinkers, evangelicals, and some Lutherans—so long as the party refrained from taking up the causes of Sabbatarianism or temperance. Most of the German immigrants, whatever their religion, continued to enjoy and to insist upon their traditional "German Sunday" with its after-church drinking, dancing, and general *Gemuetlichkeit*. But pious sectarians of old American stock viewed such merrymaking as a profanation of the Sabbath. The same Puritan ethic that prescribed emancipation and equal rights prescribed also temperance and a quiet Sunday—to be enforced by the government if necessary. During the war and immediately after it, the puritanical reformers concentrated their attention on saving the Union and freeing and elevating the slaves. For the time being the state's strict liquor-control act, repealed in the early 1850s, was not revived. The prewar Sunday-closing law remained on the books but went unenforced.

Before long, however, the voices of moral reform began to be heard again, and risky though the drink issue was, the Republicans eventually took it up. In 1872 Governor Washburn recommended that the legislature consider the subject of liquor control, and in response a Rock County representative, Alexander Graham, introduced a thoroughgoing bill. This would require a $2,000 bond from liquor licensees, would make them liable for damages caused directly or indirectly by intoxicated customers, and would impose heavy penalties on those convicted of drunkenness. When the legislature passed and the governor signed the Graham law, Germans understandably blamed the Republican party. German leaders, among them the brewers Valentin Blatz and Joseph Schlitz, formed the Wisconsin Association for the Protection of Personal Liberty, accused the Republicans of having converted Wisconsin into a police state, and called upon liberty-loving citizens to vote for candidates pledging to repeal the liquor act.

The party loyalty of German Republicans, already strained by the Graham law, was further weakened as a result of the party split that developed from the Liberal Republican opposition to President Grant. Previously, in 1870, Wisconsin party leaders had turned the Franco-Prussian War to their own advantage; they had taken care that German voters should be "led to see that in the Franco-German War the Republicans have stood by the Germans & Fatherland while the Democrats have gone almost body & soul for the French." Now, in 1872, the anti-Grant Republicans were trying to deflect the German vote to the Liberal cause by showing that the Grant administration had, in fact, helped the French and hurt the Prussians. In the Senate, Carl Schurz of Missouri joined Charles Sumner of Massachusetts in charging that the Administration, in a flagrant breach of neutrality, had sold government arms to E. Remington & Sons for resale to France. Schurz, formerly a Wisconsinite, still had a following among Wisconsin Germans. Senator Carpenter did his best to refute the charge. As a leading member of an investigating committee, he wrote what Sumner called a "whitewashing report."

In Wisconsin the Liberal Republican movement was largely a Teutonic phenomenon. Milwaukee Germans organized on March 19, 1872, the first Liberal Republican club in the state. Germans rallied to the cause in such numbers that some leaders were a little embarrassed, and one spokesman made a point of denying that it was essentially a German affair. The most influential German-language paper of the Republicans, the Milwaukee *Herold*, switched from the regular party to the Liberal faction. To counter the Liberal appeal, the Grant Republicans subsidized a previously neutral German-language paper in Madison and another in Milwaukee, and they nominated German candidates for Congress in the two districts (out of the new total of eight) where the Democrats presented the greatest threat.

In the 1872 election the Liberal Republicans and the Democrats faced one serious handicap. Their presidential candidate, Horace Greeley of New York, had a long record as a radical Republican and a moral reformer. Personally, he was a teetotaler—a contemptible "water-bibber," as Wisconsin Germans saw him. He had little charm for either disaffected Republicans or regular Democrats—like the one in Dane County who found it hard to "digest the Greeley dose, which with all its sugar coating" was "very nauseous" to him. On election day thousands of apathetic Liberals and Democrats stayed at home. Grant carried Wisconsin, 104,992 to 86,477, though with a smaller majority than in 1868. Six of the eight Republicans running for Congress were victorious, as were a majority of those running for the state legislature. The party had staved off the disaster that had threatened as a consequence of the liquor law and German defections.

But temperance remained an explosive issue, and the Republicans did nothing to defuse it. In the 1873 legislature they tightened instead of relaxing or repealing the Graham law. As if this were not enough, the acting mayor of Madison began to enforce the old law against selling or giving away liquor on Sundays. To protest the "abridgement of their natural freedom," antitemperance leaders called a convention in Milwaukee and sought the support of all liberty-loving citizens, "without discrimination as to birth-place, party, or religious belief." Most of the delegates were Germans (they argued over the question whether the proceedings should be in German or in English), and prominent among them were saloonkeepers, brewers, and distillers. These interests would be able, as Governor Washburn feared, to provide the Republicans' opponents with ample finances, with all the "sinews of war," in the state election of 1873.

When putting together the ticket for that election, the Republicans gave German voters additional reason for taking offense. The Republican leaders had intended, as usual, to name a German for the important position of state treasurer and a Norwegian for the much less prestigious job of state immigration commissioner. But the Norwegians vehemently objected, insisting on the treasurer's post for one of their own, Ole C. Johnson. To appease the Norwegians, the bosses put Johnson in the place of Henry Baetz, the incumbent treasurer and the party's most influential German politician. They left Baetz off the ticket altogether and placed a comparatively obscure German at the tail end of it.

Thus, as the fateful election of 1873 approached, the Republicans confronted the prospect of losing the votes of Germans who considered themselves the victims of discrimination on ethnic grounds. But the Republicans also faced the danger of a much more massive defection on the part of farmers and businessmen, of whatever nationality, who were discontented for economic reasons. Resentment against big corporations, monopolies, and especially railroads had been festering for several years, and now the resentment was coming to a head.

The railroad companies were becoming the biggest and most monopolistic of corporations, the Chicago and North Western and the Milwaukee and St. Paul acquiring ownership or domination of every line of any importance in the state. Alexander Mitchell, president of the M. & St. P., also controlled, through ownership or lease, nearly all the grain elevators in Milwaukee. Thus the one man held in his grasp the entire Milwaukee wheat trade. On September 15, 1873, just as the political campaign was getting under way, both of the big railroad combinations raised their rates. Three days later the Panic of 1873 began.

Antimonopoly and antirailroad agitation in Wisconsin had first reached a peak in 1865–1866. In those two years a total of twenty-one railroad regulation bills was introduced in the legislature, and in every year thereafter to 1873 one or more regulatory measures were proposed. Only two were passed. An 1867 law prohibited forever the consolidation of the Chicago and North Western with the Milwaukee and St. Paul, but the law did nothing to prevent the interlocking directorate or the pooling arrangement that the two companies soon set up. An 1871 amendment to the state constitution restricted the legislature's power to pass special chartering acts, of the kind which previously had conferred excessive privileges on railroad companies. The amendment required the legislature to frame a new general incorporation law, and the legislature did so, but this left the existing companies with all the privileges they had obtained earlier in their special charters.

The antirailroad agitation that was to reach a new peak in 1873–1874 came from businessmen as well as farmers, from wheat dealers as well as wheat growers. Exorbitant charges for transportation and storage cut into the profits of commission merchants who bought the grain from farmers and shipped it to Milwaukee and stored it in elevators for later forwarding to Eastern markets. One of these merchants, Francis H. West, as president of the Milwaukee Chamber of Commerce from 1871 to 1873, made himself the outstanding critic of Alexander Mitchell, the railroads, and their monopolistic practices. Meanwhile the distressed farmers were joining the Patrons of Husbandry and discussing their common grievances at the meetings of their local Granges. In Wisconsin, where the first Grange was organized in 1871, the order grew very slowly until 1873. Then the number of Granges suddenly increased from less than three dozen to about 300.

Throughout the years of agitation, each of the major parties had occupied a rather equivocal position in regard to big business and its alleged abuses. From 1866 on, the Republican governors, Fairchild and then Washburn, had repeatedly warned of the dangers of monopoly and called for state regulation of railroads. In his 1873 message Governor Washburn told the lawmakers and the people once again that the "many vast and overshadowing corporations" were "justly a source of alarm." But Washburn himself was a very rich businessman, rapidly growing richer from flour milling and other enterprises. Some other prominent Republicans also were wealthy, among them the millionaire lumberman Philetus Sawyer. "In every instance, and at all times," the Oshkosh *City Times* contended in 1870, reviving the language of

Jacksonian Democracy, "the votes cast by Mr. Sawyer have been against the productive interests of the country, and in favor of the capital which is continually aggregating and combining to depress and control Labor, and establish a supremacy which will soon be seen in lines dividing the people into castes—making the poor dependent upon and subservient to the rich."

Yet the Democrats could hardly make convincing their boast of being the party of the common man when their leadership included the greatest plutocrat of all, Alexander Mitchell, who was elected to Congress in 1870. He and other so-called "Bourbons" ran the Wisconsin Democracy. "You are represented as being the favorite candidate of the monied monopolies and corporations," the Bourbon James R. Doolittle heard from a party strategist while running for governor in 1871. "I know there is a deeper & wider feeling on this subject in the state than you are aware of." The "anti-monopolist mob" had much greater voting strength than the monopolists. Could not the Democratic candidate be as much of a "people's" man as the Republican?

In addition to the stigma of Bourbonism, the taint of treason still handicapped the Democratic party. As late as 1871, one politician observed, many Wisconsinites continued to fear that, if the party should regain power in the state and nation, the Thirteenth, Fourteenth, and Fifteenth amendments would "be abrogated if possible, the rights of the Negro be ignored and the public debt be repudiated." At the beginning of 1872 the Madison *Democrat* asked, "Shall the Democratic party abandon its name" and form a new party? For the election of 1873, they were to do just that.

In 1873 the Grangers laid down a challenge to both of the major parties in Wisconsin. At a Watertown convention in August, they denounced corruption in government and demanded state regulation of the railroads. Some delegates urged the formation of a third party. This was not done; indeed, the rules of the Patrons of Husbandry forbade the Grange, as such, to take part in political activity. But there was nothing to prevent the members from throwing their support to one set of candidates or another.

When the Republicans met for their regular convention in August, they tried to identify their party with the farmers' cause. They renominated Washburn, the well-known advocate of railroad regulation. Keeping silent on temperance, they declared themselves in favor of honest government, the establishment of a state commission to regulate railroads, and the outlawing of the common railroad practice of awarding free passes to public officials.

Shrewdly the Democrats and the Liberal Republicans, who had maintained their coalition since the 1872 campaign, avoided giving any party name to their 1873 convention. They labeled it a "People's Reform Convention," and they invited the attendance of "all Democrats, Liberal Republicans, and other electors of Wisconsin friendly to genuine reform." Many Grangers responded. The emerging platform condemned temperance legislation and committed the new party to enacting laws "for the restriction of the power of chartered corporations, for the regulation of railway tariffs, and for the protection of the people against systematic plunder and legalized robbery." The candidate for governor was William R. Taylor, an organizer of the Grange in Wisconsin, president of the state agricultural society, and incidentally, a member of a temperance society, the Good Templars. The rest of the ticket included a German, an Irishman, and a Norwegian. Some of the candidates were Democrats and others Liberal Republicans, but only one, a former congressman now running for attorney general, was a prominent politician. Supposedly the candidates were men of the people, not professional office seekers. The new organization came to be known as the Reform party.

Urging on Republican campaigners, Boss Keyes cautioned them that their opponents had gotten up "a plausible programme and ticket"— even though in fact the "old Bourbon Democrats" were the "main spirit of the effort," the Reform convention had been "run and controlled in the interests of railroads," and the candidates were "wholly under the influence of these corporations."

True enough, the Reformers had the financial support not only of the beer and liquor interests but also of Mitchell's and other railroad companies. The railroad men feared manufacturer Washburn more than they did farmer Taylor, but many of the farmers apparently could see little choice between the two as antimonopolists. On election day a good many farmers, most of them probably Republicans, refrained from voting. Washburn, who had previously won by 10,000 votes, now lost by 15,000, as the Reformers elected their entire state ticket and fifty-nine assemblymen to forty-one for the Republicans, though only sixteen senators to seventeen. "You have been the victim of a situation

created by the follies or worse than follies of the party," a sympathizer
wrote to Washburn. "Moreover with a Granger who had the support
of the railways, & a Good Templar who had the confidence of the
whiskey & beer ring for an opponent, queer results might be looked
for."

The year 1873 marked a dividing line in the history of Wisconsin.
Not only did it complete the first quarter-century, roughly the first
generation, in the life of the state; it also brought cataclysmic changes—
the onset of economic depression for Wisconsin and the rest of the
country, the crescendo of a popular demand for reform in the relations between business and the state government, and the overthrow
of the party that had dominated state politics since before the Civil
War. The depression was to last for several years and was to prove the
worst that Wisconsinites and other Americans had yet experienced.
The reform effort was to bring forth only an ineffectual railroad-
regulation law, which was soon to be repealed. Within a few years the
Wisconsin Republicans were to be as securely in control of state politics as they had ever been, and not till 1890, with ethnic and economic
discontent again peaking simultaneously, were they to suffer another
overturn comparable to the one of 1873.

Even before the Panic of 1873, some Wisconsinites had begun to
take a pessimistic view of the state's future. One of these was Edward
G. Ryan, long a leader of Wisconsin Democrats, then somewhat dis-
credited as a wartime Copperhead, recently the Milwaukee City Attorney and recovering political influence as a crusader against railroad
abuses, and soon (1874) to become the state's Chief Justice. In June
1873, Ryan addressed the graduating class of the University at Madison, whose members gathered in the assembly chamber of the capitol
to hear him.

"There is looming up a new and dark power," he warned. This was
the power of "vast corporate combinations of unexampled capital."
Two of these combinations, the big railroad companies of Wisconsin,
were already threatening the very sovereignty of the state. "The question will arise and arise in your day, though perhaps not fully in mine,"
the aging lawyer told the youthful graduates, "which shall rule—wealth
or man; which shall lead—money or intellect; who shall fill public sta-
tions—educated and patriotic freemen, or the feudal serfs of corporate

capital." Among those listening to Ryan on that occasion was an eighteen-year-old who was yet to enter the University. This young man was never to forget the judge's "prophetic words," and he was to repeat them many a time in speeches of his own. His name was Robert M. La Follette.

Yet, as the state approached its twenty-fifth anniversary, the prevailing mood seemed to be one of optimism. Surviving pioneers, many of them members of recently formed old settlers' clubs, not only looked back with a feeling for history but also looked ahead with a sense of destiny. Milwaukeeans were reminded of the remarkable growth of their city—only a few decades ago a "small, unimportant village, situated on two bluffs and divided by a sluggish river and an almost impenetrable tamarack swamp"; now the "home of a hundred thousand busy people." What might they not expect in the next thirty years?

The people of towns still small and unimportant had grounds for similar self-congratulatory amazement. "I have lived in this country now twenty years," wrote Arnold Verstegen in 1870, "and the progress that I have seen in that short space of time is like a dream." When Verstegen had first appeared in Little Chute, in 1850, there was only one store in the forest-hidden hamlet. News of the outside world was weeks old when it got there, and traveling any distance was difficult, dangerous, and slow. "Now passengers arrive here in the afternoon, who in the morning were still in Chicago," he bragged to his Dutch relatives in the Old Country. "Daily papers gather news by telegraph from distant parts of the country, and it reaches the readers when it is still fresh." In addition to stores, office buildings, and factories, there were fine schools and churches, for there had been advancement in spiritual as well as material things. "The Catholic Church too has made great progress," and an imposing new brick edifice was under construction in Little Chute.

When the Reverend Alfred Brunson went from Prairie du Chien to New York City, to attend a Methodist conference in 1872, he could not help thinking how things had changed since he first made his way to Wisconsin, nearly forty years before. The trip then, by wagon, required six weeks. The same trip now, by train, took two days and two hours. But Brunson, too, was most impressed by the great strides that religion appeared to be making. At the Baraboo conference of the Methodists in 1873, one hundred years after the first Methodist conference in America, he preached the centennial sermon. Taking into account "all branches of the Christian Church, and their advancing Christian efforts," he said, "in another century the millennium must be near at hand."

Even after the financial panic had struck, faith in progress remained alive and comforting, as in the sermon that William H. Brisbane, a Baptist minister originally from South Carolina, delivered in the Congregational Church of Arena (Iowa County) on Thanksgiving Day, 1873. "Twenty years ago when I first came among you our neighborhood was comparatively a wilderness," the Reverend Mr. Brisbane recalled. "But see what a change"—nicely cultivated farms and beautiful farmhouses, all kinds of agricultural machinery, a railroad with passenger trains four times a day and freight trains at all hours of the day and night, a village with "comfortable if not elegant" residences, numerous stores and shops, "some devout Christians," and three meeting houses for the worship of God. "Surely for all these things we should 'offer unto God thanksgiving.' "